THE ULTIMATE GUIDE TO

2D GAMES DEVELOPMENT

WITH UNITY

Create 2D games with Unity and learn C# in the process

Patrick Felicia

THE ULTIMATE GUIDE TO
2D GAMES DEVELOPMENT WITH UNITY

First published: August 2020

Published by Patrick Felicia

CREDITS

- Author: Patrick Felicia

- Front cover: image based on the file "Boss Battle from Guacamelee" available from https://commons.wikimedia.org/wiki/File:Guacamelee!_screenshot_E.jpg and used under the Creative Commons Attribution-Share Alike 3.0 Unported license (https://creativecommons.org/licenses/by-sa/3.0/deed.en).

ABOUT THE AUTHOR

Patrick Felicia is a <u>lecturer and researcher</u> at Waterford Institute of Technology, where he teaches and supervises undergraduate and postgraduate students. He obtained his MSc in Multimedia Technology in 2003 and PhD in Computer Science in 2009 from University College Cork, Ireland. He has published several books and articles on the use of video games for educational purposes, including the Handbook of Research on Improving Learning and Motivation through Educational Games: Multidisciplinary Approaches (published by IGI), and Digital Games in Schools: a Handbook for Teachers, published by European Schoolnet. Patrick is also the Editor-in-chief of the <u>International Journal of Game-Based Learning (IJGBL),</u> and the Conference Director of the <u>Irish Conference on Game-Based Learning</u>, a popular conference on games and learning organized throughout Ireland.

Support and Resources for this Book

To complete the activities presented in this book you need to download the startup pack on the companion website; it consists of free resources that you will need to complete your projects, including bonus material that will help you along the way (e.g., cheat sheets, introductory videos, code samples, and much more).

To download these resources, please do the following:

- Open the following link: **http://learntocreategames.com/books/**

- Select this book "**The Ultimate Guide to 2D Games Development with Unity**".

- On the new page, click on the link labeled "**Book Files**", or scroll down to the bottom of the page.

- In the section called "**Download your Free Resource Pack**", enter your email address and your first name, and click on the button labeled "**Yes, I want to receive my bonus pack**".

- After a few seconds, you should receive a confirmation email to activate your account.

- If you are using Gmail and you don't see the email, please check your **Spam** and **Promotions** folders.

- Once you have clicked to confirm your account then a link to your free start-up pack should arrive shortly after.

- When you receive the link, you can download all the resources to your computer.

When you receive the email, and if you are using Gmail, please do the following to be able to receive subsequent updates:

- Add my address to your contact list.

- Drag the message to your **Primary** Tab.

- Frequently check the **Promotions** tab.

This book is dedicated to Mathis and Helena

TABLE OF CONTENTS

PREFACE

This book entitled "**The Ultimate Guide to 2D Games Development with Unity**" will show you all the techniques and tools that you need to create entertaining 2D games with Unity.

Too many people try to learn Unity the hard way, but with this book, you don't need to, as it will take you through the process of creating many 2D game genres easily without the frustration.

In this book you will learn to master Unity to create a wide range of 2D games including platformers, shooters, puzzles or word games. You will also learn to code in C# along the way and to use it with Unity with step-by-step instructions and plenty of guidance and screenshots.

If you ever wanted to create 2D games with Unity but did not know where or how to start, this book is for you.

CONTENT COVERED BY THIS BOOK

- Chapters 1, 2, 3, 4 and 5 will show you how to create a platformer game with most of the features that you usually find in this genre including a moving character, sound, a user interface, a mini-map, a timer, magic doors, a shaky bridge, and much more.

- Chapters 6, 7, 8, 9 and 10 will show you how to create a shooter game with most of the features that you usually find in this genre including a moving space ship controlled by the player, a scrolling background, missiles, moving asteroids, intelligent enemies that shoot missiles, power-ups, a shield for the player, and much more.

- Chapter 11 will show you how to create a word guessing game where the player needs to guess a word, picked at random, using a limited number of attempts; along the way you will learn to detect key strokes, select words from a file, track the score, and much more.

- Chapter 12 will show you how to create a memory game based on the famous "Simon Game" whereby the player has to remember and reproduce a pattern of colours and sounds.

- Chapter 13 will show you how to create a card guessing game where the player needs to memorise the location of cards on a board and to also match identical cards in order to remove them from the game. Along the way, you will learn how to display cards, shuffle them, process clicks on them and you will also add multiple cards to your game automatically.

- Chapter 14 will show you how to create a puzzle where the player has to move and combine puzzle pieces to complete the puzzle. Along the way you will learn how to slice images to create the pieces of a puzzle. You will also implement common features found in puzzles, including shuffling the pieces, moving the pieces, or snapping them to a specific location.

WHAT YOU NEED TO USE THIS BOOK

To complete the project presented in this book, you only need Unity 2019.2 (or a more recent version) and to also ensure that your computer and its operating system comply with Unity's requirements. Unity can be downloaded from the official website (http://www.unity3d.com/download), and before downloading it, you can check that your computer is up to scratch on the following page: http://www.unity3d.com/unity/system-requirements. At the time of writing this book, the following operating systems are supported by Unity for development: Windows 7 or Mac OS X 10.12+. In terms of graphics card, most cards produced after 2004 should be suitable.

In terms of computer skills, all knowledge introduced in this book will assume no prior programming experience from the reader. So for now, you only need to be able to perform common computer tasks, such as downloading items, opening and saving files, be comfortable with dragging and dropping items and typing, and be relatively comfortable with Unity's interface. This being said, because the focus of this book is on creating 2D games, and while all instructions are provided step-by-step, you may need to be relatively comfortable with Unity's interface and coding in C#, as well as creating and transforming objects (e.g., moving or rotating).

So, if you would prefer to become more comfortable with Unity and C# programming prior to starting this book, you can download the books in the series called Unity From Zero to Proficiency (Foundations, Beginner, Intermediate, or Advanced). These books cover most of the shortcuts and views available in Unity, as well as how to perform common tasks in Unity, such as creating objects, transforming objects, importing assets, using navigation controllers, creating scripts or exporting the game to the web. They also explain how to code your game using C# along with good coding practices.

WHO THIS BOOK IS FOR

If you can answer **yes** to all these questions, then this book is for you:

1. Would you like to learn how to create 2D games?

2. Would you like to know how to create reusable objects and save yourself some time?

3. Can you already code in C#?

4. Would you like to discover how to create a menu and levels?

5. Although you may have had some prior exposure to Unity and coding, would you like to delve more into 2D games?

WHO THIS BOOK IS NOT FOR

If you can answer yes to all these questions, then this book is **not** for you:

1. Can you already create 2D games?

2. Can you create menus and levels for 2D games?

3. Are you looking for a reference book on Unity programming?

4. Are you an experienced (or at least advanced) Unity user?

If you can answer yes to all four questions, you may instead look for the next book in the series on the official website.

HOW YOU WILL LEARN FROM THIS BOOK

Because all students learn differently and have different expectations of a course, this book is designed to ensure that all readers find a learning mode that suits them. Therefore, it includes the following:

- A list of the learning objectives at the start of each chapter so that readers have a snapshot of the skills that will be covered.

- Each section includes an overview of the activities covered.

- Many of the activities are step-by-step, and learners are also given the opportunity to engage in deeper learning and problem-solving skills through the challenges offered at the end of each chapter.

- Each chapter ends-up with a quiz and challenges through which you can put your skills (and knowledge acquired) into practice, and see how much you know. Challenges consist in coding, debugging, or creating new features based on the knowledge that you have acquired in the chapter.

- The book focuses on the core skills that you need; some sections also go into more detail; however, once concepts have been explained, links are provided to additional resources, where necessary.

- The code is introduced progressively and is explained in detail.

- You also gain access to several videos that help you along the way, especially for the most challenging topics.

FORMAT OF EACH CHAPTER AND WRITING CONVENTIONS

Throughout this book, and to make reading and learning easier, text formatting and icons will be used to highlight parts of the information provided and to make it more readable.

SPECIAL NOTES

Each chapter includes resource sections, so that you can further your understanding and mastery of Unity; these include:

- A quiz for each chapter: these quizzes usually include 10 questions that test your knowledge of the topics covered throughout the chapter. The solutions are provided on the companion website.

- A checklist: it consists of between 5 and 10 key concepts and skills that you need to be comfortable with before progressing to the next chapter.

- Challenges: each chapter includes a challenge section where you are asked to combine your skills to solve a particular problem.

Author's notes appear as described below:

> Author's suggestions appear in this box.

Code appears as described below:

```
public int score;
public string playersName = "Sam";
```

Checklists that include the important points covered in the chapter appear as described below:

- Item1 for check list

- Item2 for check list

- Item3 for check list

HOW CAN YOU LEARN BEST FROM THIS BOOK

- **Talk to your friends about what you are doing.**

We often think that we understand a topic until we have to explain it to friends and answer their questions. By explaining your different projects, what you just learned will become clearer to you.

- **Do the exercises.**

All chapters include exercises that will help you to learn by doing. In other words, by completing these exercises, you will be able to better understand the topic and gain practical skills (i.e., rather than just reading).

- **Don't be afraid of making mistakes.**

I usually tell my students that making mistakes is part of the learning process; the more mistakes you make and the more opportunities you have for learning. At the start, you may find the errors disconcerting, or that the engine does not work as expected until you understand what went wrong.

- **Export your games early.**

It is always great to build and export your first game. Even if it is rather simple, it is always good to see it in a browser and to be able to share it with you friends.

- **Learn in chunks.**

It may be disconcerting to go through five or six chapters straight, as it may lower your motivation. Instead, give yourself enough time to learn, go at your own pace, and learn in small units (e.g., between 15 and 20 minutes per day). This will do at least two things for you: it will give your brain the time to "digest" the information that you have just learned, so that you can start fresh the following day. It will also make sure that you don't "burn-out" and that you keep your motivation levels high.

FEEDBACK

While I have done everything possible to produce a book of high quality and value, I always appreciate feedback from readers so that the book can be improved accordingly. If you would like to give feedback, you can email me at learntocreategames@gmail.com.

DOWNLOADING THE CODE SOLUTIONS FOR THE BOOK

To download the code solutions for the activities presented in this book, you need to download the resource pack. To download these resources, please do the following:

- Open the following link: **http://learntocreategames.com/books/**

- Select this book "**The Ultimate Guide to 2D Games Development with Unity**".

- On the new page, click on the link labeled "**Book Files**", or scroll down to the bottom of the page.

- In the section called "**Download your Free Resource Pack**", enter your email address and your first name, and click on the button labeled "**Yes, I want to receive my bonus pack**".

- After a few seconds, you should receive a confirmation email to activate your account.

- If you are using Gmail and you don't see the email, please check your **Spam** and **Promotions** folders.

- Once you have clicked to confirm your account then a link to your free start-up pack should arrive shortly after.

- When you receive the link, you can download all the resources to your computer.

When you receive the email, and if you are using Gmail, please do the following to be able to receive subsequent updates:

- Add my address to your contact list.

- Drag the message to your **Primary** Tab.

- Frequently check the **Promotions** tab.

IMPROVING THE BOOK

Although great care was taken in checking the content of this book, I am human, and some errors could remain in the book. As a result, it would be great if you could let me know of any issue or error you may have come across in this book, so that it can be solved and the book updated accordingly. To report an error, you can email me (learntocreategames@gmail.com) with the following information:

- Name of the book.

- The page or section where the error was detected.

- Describe the error and also what you think the correction should be.

Once your email is received, the error will be checked, and, in the case of a valid error, it will be corrected and the book page will be updated to reflect the changes accordingly.

SUPPORTING THE AUTHOR

A lot of work has gone into this book and it is the fruit of long hours of preparation, brainstorming, and finally writing. As a result, I would ask that you do not distribute any illegal copies of this book.

This means that if a friend wants a copy of this book, s/he will have to buy it through the official channels (i.e., through Amazon, lulu.com, or the book's official website: http://www.learntocreategames.com/books).

If some of your friends are interested in the book, you can refer them to the book's official website (http://www.learntocreategames.com/books) where they can either buy the book, enter a monthly draw to be in for a chance of receiving a free copy of the book, or to be notified of future promotional offers.

CHAPTER 1: PLATFORM GAME (PART 1): CREATING A SIMPLE LEVEL

In this section, we will start by creating a simple level, including:

- A 2D character that will be able to jump and walk.

- Simple platforms.

- A camera that follows the player.

- A mini-map that displays the layout of the level.

- Objects that you can collect.

- Objects that bounce indefinitely.

So, after completing this chapter, you will be able to:

- Use a character that can jump and walk.

- Create 2D objects.

- Create a C# script.

- Detect collisions between objects.

- Destroy objects upon collision.

INTRODUCTION

In this chapter we will create a simple level with a 2D character that can walk and bounce off platforms; we will also create objects that the character has to collect or to avoid, and some of them will also have physics properties, which will make it possible for them to bounce.

ADDING THE MAIN CHARACTER

The very first thing that we will do is to create a simple 2D scene that includes a 2D character along with several platforms.

Luckily, Unity includes a set of 2D assets that we can use for this purpose. So we will proceed as follows:

- Import the 2D assets (including a 2D character).

- Create platforms from basic shapes (i.e., boxes).

- Create a camera that follows the main character.

- Create a mini-map.

So let's get started:

- Please launch Unity.

- Open the project called "**project_with_standard_assets**" located in the resource pack.

- Once the new project is open, please select the **2D** mode for the scene, by clicking on the 2D button located in the top left corner of the **Scene** view.

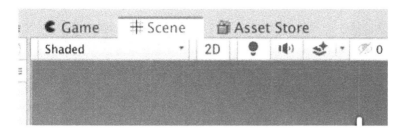

Figure 1: Using the 2D mode

- You can now create a new scene (**File | New Scene**).

As this blank project already includes Standard Assets, you will probably notice a folder called **Standard Assets** in the **Project** window, and within this folder, another folder called **2D** which includes several **2D** assets that we will use.

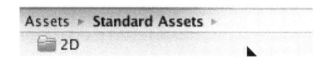

Figure 2: The new folder for 2D assets

Once this is done, it is time to add our 2D character:

- In the **Project** window, from the folder **Standard Assets | 2D | Prefabs**, drag and drop the prefab called **CharacterRobotBoy** to the **Scene** view.

Figure 3: Adding the character

As you will see, this will create a new object called **CharacterRobotBoy** in the **Hierarchy** view. It will also add a character to the scene, as illustrated on the next figure.

Figure 4: The game object CharacterRobotBoy

- You can set the position of this character to **(0, 2, 0)** using the **Inspector**.

Note that if your background does not look like the one illustrated on the previous figure, it is probably because a background image was not added automatically by Unity; you can change the background of your scene using the window: **Window | Rendering Lighting Settings**.

- If you click on this character in the **Scene** view, and then look at the **Inspector**, you should see that it includes several components, including a **Sprite Renderer** (to display the character), an **Animator** component (for the walking or jumping animations), two colliders (circle and box colliders), a **Rigidbody2D** component (so that it is subject to forces, including gravity) along with two scripts used to control the character. We don't need to know the content of the scripts for now; however, it is always good to have an idea of the different necessary component for this character.

Figure 5: Components for the RobotBoy character

Once this is done, you can play the scene, and you will see that the character will fall indefinitely; this is because of its **Rigidbody** component which exerts gravity on this character and also due to the fact that there is no ground or platform under the character; so the next thing we will do is to create a simple platform on which the player can walk.

Note that to play and stop the scene, you can press the shortcut CTRL + P, or use the black triangle located at the top of the window.

- Please create a new box: Click in the Assets folder in the **Project** window (so that the next asset is created in that folder), and then select **Create | Sprites | Square** from the same **Project** window.

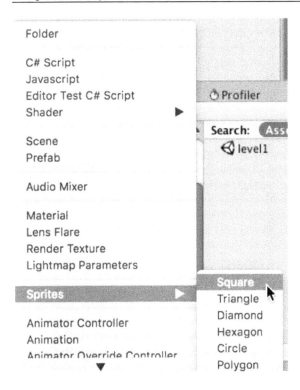

Figure 6: Creating a new sprite (square) – part 1

- This will create a **Sprite** asset;

- Please rename it **platform**.

Note that because this is an asset, it will be accessible throughout the project, irrespective of the scene that is open.

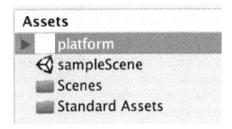

Figure 7: Creating a new sprite (square) – part 2

Once this is done, you can drag and drop this asset (i.e., the platform) to the **Scene** view.

- This will create a new object called **platform**.

- You can then resize this object, so that it looks like a platform, and place it just below the character; for example, you could set its scale property to **(18, 1, 1)** and its position to **(-6, -1.5, 0)**.

Figure 8: Adding a platform

Next, we need to add a collider to this object so that the player effectively collides with it (and stops falling).

- Please select the object called **platform** in the **Hierarchy** view (i.e., the object that you have just created).

- From the top menu, select **Component | Physics2D | BoxCollider2D**.

- This will add a **2DCollider** (shaped as a box) to our **platform** object.

- You can then duplicate this platform and move the duplicate to its right; you may also change the **scale** attribute of the duplicate to **(33, 1, 1)**, and its **position** to **(23, -1.5, 0)** so that your scene looks like the following figure.

Figure 9: The character and two platforms

Note that you can, if you wish, modify the color of each platform by selecting (and modifying) the attribute called **color** that is accessible within the component called **Sprite Renderer** for each platform.

You can now test the scene; you can move the character using the **arrow keys** (to go left and right), the **space bar** (to jump), or the **CTRL** key (to crouch).

FOLLOWING THE PLAYER WITH CAMERAS

Perfect. So we have a character that can move around the scene and jump on platforms; the only thing is that, whenever this character is outside the screen, we can't see it anymore; so we will need to make sure that it is onscreen all the time; and this can be achieved by setting the main camera to follow this character. Luckily, as part of the 2D assets, Unity provides a simple script, that can be applied to any camera, so that it follows a specific target. So we will use this script on the main camera so that it follows the character.

So let's do the following:

- In the **Hierarchy** window, please select the object called **MainCamera**.

- Then, after locating the folder **Standard Assets | 2D | Scripts** in the **Project** view, drag and drop the script called **Camera2DFollow** from this folder to the object called **MainCamera** in the **Hierarchy** window.

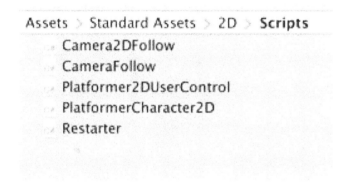

Figure 10: Adding the Camera2DFollow script

- Once this is done, please select the object called **MainCamera** in the **Hierarchy** window.

- As you do so, you will see, in the **Inspector** window, that it includes a new component, which is our script, and that this component also includes an empty field called **target**; this field will be used to specify the target for this camera (in our case, this will be the object **CharacterRobotBoy**).

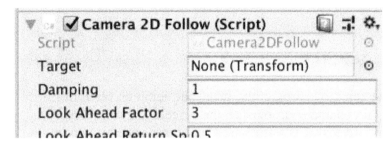

Figure 11: Setting the target for the camera (part 1)

- Please drag and drop the object called **CharacterRobotBoy** from the **Hierarchy** window to this field (to the right of the label **Target**).

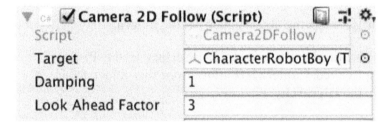

Figure 12: Setting the target for the camera (part 2)

- Once this is done, please test the scene, and check that the camera is now focusing on your character.

Figure 13: Following the character with the camera

CREATING A MINI-MAP

OK, so now our character is in focus and we can move it around the scene; however, wouldn't it be great to be able to see the overall scene (or what's ahead of the character) in the form of a mini-map; we could create a map displayed in the top right-corner of the window that shows a global view of the level; so let's do just that.

- Please create a new camera (**GameObject | Camera**) and rename it **mini-map**.

- Using the **Inspector**, change its **z** position value to **-20** (this is its depth and it indicates how close/far the camera will be from the player).

- Using the **Inspector,** change its **Viewport Rect** options to: **X = .75, Y= .75, W=.25, H=.25, and depth =1**.

The **ViewportRect** defines where the image captured by the camera is displayed; all these parameters are expressed as a proportion of the screen and range from 0 to 1. So in our case the top-left corner of this view port is located at 75% of the screen's height and 75% of the screen's width (i.e., **X = .75 and Y = .75**); its width is 25% of the screen's width and its height is 25% of the screen's height.

- Please add (i.e., drag and drop) the **Camera2DFollow** script (from the folder **Standard Assets | 2D | Scripts**) to the new camera (i.e., **mini-map**).

- Using the **Inspector**, set the target of the camera to the **CharacterRobotBoy** object, as we have done previously for the other camera: drag and drop the object called **CharacterRobotBoy** from the **Hierarchy** window to the field called **target** for this script.

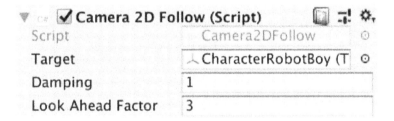

Figure 14: Setting the target for the second camera

- Please also deactivate the component called **AudioListener** for this camera, using the **Inspector**.

⊙ ☐ **Audio Listener**

- Please test the scene, and you should see an overview of the level in the top-right corner of the screen.

Figure 15: Displaying the mini-map

ADDING OBJECTS TO COLLECT

In this section, we will learn how to detect collisions; this will be used for our character to be able to collect objects, but to also detect when it collides with dangerous objects.

The process will be as follows, we will:

- Create new sprites that will be used as objects to collect or avoid.

- Create and apply tags to these objects (i.e., labels).

- Create a script, linked to the player, that will detect collisions and that will also detect the tag of the object we are colliding with.

- Depending on the tag of this object, we will trigger different actions (e.g., restart the current level or increase the score).

So let's get started.

- Please create a new circular sprite: from the **Project** window, click on the **Assets** folder, and then select: **Create | Sprites | Circle**.

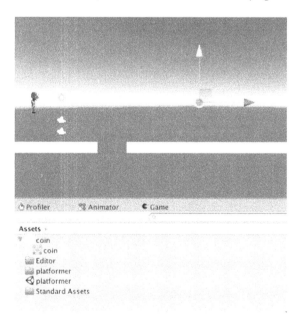

Figure 16: Creating a new sprite for coins

- In the **Project** window, rename this object **coin** (i.e., right-click + select the option **Rename**), and drag and drop it to the **Scene** view; this will create an object called **coin**.

- You can also change its position to **(15, 1, 0)**.

- Zoom-in on the coin: select **SHIFT + F**.

- Using the **Inspector**, we can change its color to yellow (i.e., using the color attribute for the component **Sprite Renderer**).

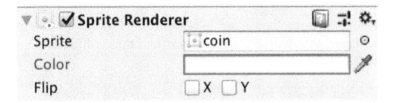

- You may also ensure that its **z** coordinate is **0**.

We will also need to add a collider to this object (i.e., the coin), so that the player can collide with (and eventually collect) this object:

- Please select the object called **coin** in the **Hierarchy** window; then, using the top menu, select **Component | Physics2D | Circle Collider 2D**. This will create a collider for our coin, so that collisions between the player and this object can be detected.

We can now create the mechanisms to collect the coin; it will consist of a script that will detect collisions between the player and the objects, and, in the case of a collision with a coin, remove or destroy the coin.

First, we will assign a tag to this object, at it will help to identify each object in the scene, and to see what object the player is colliding with; to do so, please select the coin, and then using the **Inspector** window, select the tag called "**pick_me**" from the drop-down menu.

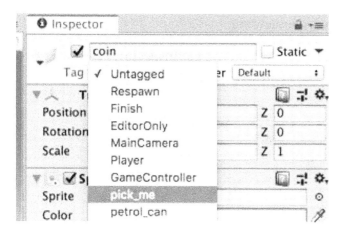

If this tag is not already available, then you can create as follows:

- Please select the object called **coin** in the Hierarchy.

- In the **Inspector** window, select the option **Add Tag...**

Figure 17: Adding a tag (part 1)

- In the new window, click on the + button and then specify a name for your tag (i.e., **pick_me**), using the field to the right of the label **Tag 0**.

Figure 18: Adding a tag (part 2)

- Press **Return** on your keyboard to save your new tag.

- Select the object **coin** in the **Hierarchy** again, and, using the **Inspector**, select the tag **pick_me**, that you have just created.

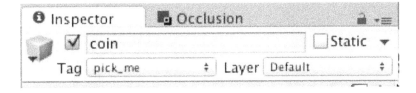

Figure 19: Adding a tag (part 3)

Once the tag has been created, we can now create our new script and detect whether we have collided with an object tagged as **pick_me**.

Creating the collision script

- Please create a new script called **DetectCollision** (i.e., select **Create | C#** from the **Project** window)

- Open this script by double-clicking on it in the **Project** view.

- Add the following code (new code in bold) to this script.

```
using UnityEngine;
public class DetectCollision : MonoBehaviour
{
    void Start () { }
    void Update () {}
    void OnCollisionEnter2D (Collision2D coll)
    {
        string tagName = coll.collider.gameObject.tag;
        if (tagName == "pick_me")
        {
            Destroy(coll.collider.gameObject);
        }
    }
}
```

In the previous code:

- We declare a function called **OnCollisionEnter2D**.

- This function is called by Unity whenever a collision occurs with the object linked to this script.

Please note that the name of this function is **case-sensitive** which means that when a collision occurs, Unity will call a function called **OnCollisionEnter2D**; however, if you name your function with a different spelling or case, let's say **onCollisionEnter2D**, this function will not be called upon collision; so it is important that you use this exact spelling. Interestingly, if you make a spelling mistake, it will still compile, as Unity will assume that you have created your own custom function.

- When a collision occurs and that this function has been defined properly, Unity provides an object of type **Collision2D** that includes information about the collision; we have named this object **coll** here, but any other name could have been used instead.

- We then check the tag of the object that we have collided with using the following code:

```
coll.collider.object.tag;
```

- If the tag is **pick_me**, we then destroy the other object using the following code:

```
Destroy(coll.collider.gameObject);
```

- Once this is done, please save your script, and check that it is error-free.

- Drag and drop this script (**DetectCollision**) on the object **CharacterRobotBoy**.

- Test the scene by moving the character so that it collides with the coin that should now disappear.

ADDING OBSTACLES

Ok, so now that we have created coins to collect, we could also create objects to avoid; in our case, we will code the game, for the time-being, so that colliding with these objects (i.e., the object to be avoided) will cause the player to restart the level.

- Using the **Hierarchy** window, please duplicate the object called **coin**, and rename the duplicate **boulder**. To duplicate this object, you can right-click on it, and select **Rename** from the contextual menu, or select the object and use the shortcut **CTRL + D**.

- Move this object (**boulder**) to the right of the **coin**.

- Change the label of the object called **boulder** to **avoid_me**, by creating (and applying) a new tag called **avoid_me** to it, as we have done in the previous section.

- We will also change its color to **red** using the **Inspector**.

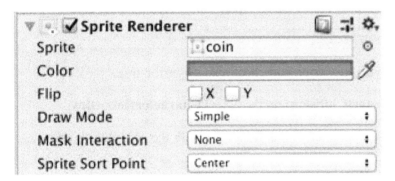

Figure 20: Changing the properties of the boulder

Next, we will add some physics properties to this object so that it bounces on the ground.

ADDING PHYSICS PROPERTIES

- Please select the object called **boulder** in the **Hierarchy**.

- Then, from the top menu, select **Component | Physics2D | Rigidbody2D**; this will create a **Rigidbody2D** component for the **boulder** object, which will now be subject to forces (e.g., gravity or push from the player).

- In the **Project** window, navigate to the folder **Assets | Standard Assets | 2D | Physics Material** and drag and drop the asset called **Bouncy Box** to the object called **boulder**.

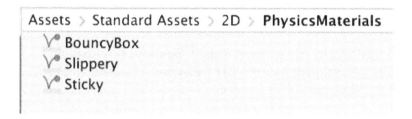

Figure 21: Adding a Physics Material component (part 1)

This will change the **Material** attribute of the **Circle Collider** for this object to **Bouncy Box**.

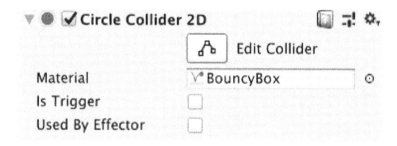

Figure 22: Adding a Physics Material component (part 2)

You can now test the scene, and you should see that the boulder is bouncing; however, it is not bouncing for long; this is because the **Physics** material that we have applied includes some frictions to the boulder; this means that the bouncing will eventually stop as the energy of the ball is progressively absorbed (or dissipated). You can see this by selecting the Physics Material **Bouncy Box** in the folder **Assets| Standard Assets|2D|Physics Material** and by looking at the **Inspector** window.

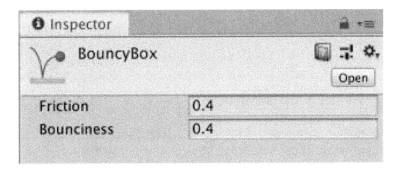

Figure 23: Checking the attributes of the BouncyBox material

As illustrated on the previous figure, we can see that frictions are applied to the boulder when we use this **Physics Material**; so what we will do is to create our own **Physics Material**, and set it up so that no frictions are applied.

- Using the **Project** window, duplicate the material called **Bouncy Box** that is currently in the folder **Assets | Standard Assets | 2D | Physics Material** (left-click on the material to select it, then press *CTRL + D*).

- Rename the duplicate: **MyBouncyBox**.

- Select this new Physics Material (i.e., **MyBouncyBox**) by clicking once on it.

- Using the **Inspector**, change both its **Friction** and **Bounciness** to **1**.

- Last but not least, please drag and drop this new material (i.e., **MyBouncyBox**) on the object **boulder** that is in the **Scene** view, so that this new material is applied instead of the previous one.

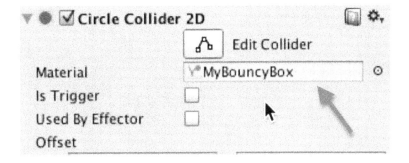

Figure 24: Applying our new Physics Material

- You can now test the game again and see that the boulder is bouncing indefinitely.

RESTARTING THE LEVEL

Once this is done, we just need to modify our collision script so that we restart the current level if we collide with the red boulder.

- Please open the script **DetectCollision** and modify the code as follows.

- Add the following code at the start of the script:

```
using UnityEngine.SceneManagement;
```

In the previous code, we add the path to the class called **SceneManagement**; this is because, in the next code, we will be using this class to reload the current scene.

- Add the next code within the method **OnCollisionEnter2D** (new code in bold).

```
if (tagName == "pick_me")
{
     Destroy(coll.collider.gameObject);
}
if (tagName == "avoid_me")
{

     Destroy(coll.collider.gameObject);
     SceneManager.LoadScene(SceneManager.GetActiveScene().name);

}
```

In the previous code:

- We check that the tag of the object that we are colliding with is **avoid_me**.
- We then destroy this object and reload the current scene.
- We use the class **SceneManager** to obtain the name of the current scene, and to load it.

Once this is done, please save your script, check that it is error-free, and run the game.

Please test the game and check that, upon collision with the boulder, the scene is restarted accordingly.

You can now save your scene (**Files | Save Scene**) and choose a name of your choice (for example **platform**).

LEVEL ROUNDUP

In this chapter, we have learnt how to create a simple level with platforms, a main character, and objects that need to be collected or avoided. We also managed to create a camera that follows the player, and a mini-map, along with a script that detects the tags applied to some of the objects in the scene. Finally, we also learned to apply physics materials so that some of the objects (the boulder), could bounce indefinitely. So, we have covered considerable ground to get you started with the first level of your platformer.

Checklist

You can consider moving to the next stage if you can do the following:

- Use the **2D Asset** package.

- Use the asset **CharacterRobotBoy**.

- Use built-in scripts so that a camera can follow a particular target.

- Apply a tag to an object.

- Detect collision from a script.

- Detect the name of a tag from a script.

Quiz

Now, let's check your knowledge! Please specify whetehr the following staretemnst are true or false or select the correct answer.

1. The method **OnCollisonEnter2D** is used when a collision has been detected between two sprites.

2. The script **Camera2DFollow**, can be used so that a camera follows a target.

3. Physics materials can be used to paint a sprite.

4. A **View Port** can be used to specify where a camera can be added to the scene.

5. The following code opens the scene called **level1**.

```
Scenemanager.OpenScene("level1");
```

6. Only one camera at a time can be used for a scene.

7. When specifying a viewport for a camera, the values usually range between 0 and 100.

8. It is possible to change the color of a sprite using the component **Sprite Render**.

9. A new sprite can be created using the **Create** menu available in the **Project** view.

10. Only square sprites can be created in Unity.

Answers to the Quiz

1. TRUE.

2. TRUE.

3. FALSE.

4. FALSE.

5. FALSE.

```
Scenemanager.OpenScene("level1");
```

6. FALSE.

7. FALSE.

8. FALSE.

9. FALSE.

10. FALSE.

Challenge 1

Now that you have managed to complete this chapter and that you have created your first level, you could improve the level by doing the following:

- Create additional platforms (e.g., using duplication).

- Change their colors.

- Create other objects to collect with other shapes (e.g., triangle or square) and apply the tag **pick_me** to them.

- Create additional physics materials and apply them to new objects that need to be avoided.

CHAPTER 2: PLATFORM GAME (PART 2): MANAGING SCORE, LIVES AND LEVELS

In this section, we will learn how to create and keep track of the score, and the player's number of lives. We will also get to use specific conditions to load a new level.

After completing this chapter, you will be able to:

- Understand the importance of (and use) prefabs.

- Create variables to track the score and the number of lives.

- Understand how to load a new level.

- Create buttons and manage events (i.e., users'clicks).

- Create a simple splash-screen.

INTRODUCTION

In this chapter we will learn how to maximize your time and avoid repeating yourself by using prefabs, which are extremely useful once you start adding them to your games. We will also get to keep track of the score and the number of lives, and complete the structure of our game by creating a **splash-screen** (displayed at the start of the game)**, a win** screen (displayed when the player has won) and an **end** screen (displayed when the player has lost).

ADDING AND MANAGING THE SCORE

At present, we can pick-up objects, and it would be great to be able to add a scoring feature, whereby our score is increased by **1** every time we collect a coin.

So let's just add this feature:

- Please open the script **DetectCollision**.

- Add a declaration for a variable **score** as follows (new code in bold):

```
public class DetectCollision : MonoBehaviour {
    int score;
```

- Modify the method **OnCollisionEnter2D** as follows:

```
if (tagName == "pick_me")
{
    Destroy(coll.collider.gameObject);
    score++;
    print ("score" + score);
}
```

In the previous code we increase the score by one every time we collide with a coin; we also print the value of the **score** in the **Console** window.

- Once this is done, please save your script, and check that it is error-free.

- You can also duplicate the object **coin** three times, so that the player can collect more than one object.

- Please run the game and look at the **Console** window to make sure that the score is increased by one every time you collect a coin.

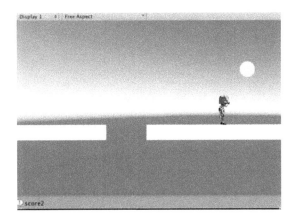

Figure 25: Collecting coins

USING PREFABS

At the moment, we have the basic skeleton for a game with platforms, objects to collect and also objects to avoid; in fact, we could just duplicate one of these two objects several times to complete our level; however, let's say that we want to have 100 coins in the level, and that at some stage we want to modify their attributes (e.g., color, or size); in this case, we would need to modify all these 100 objects, which would be time-consuming; one solution for this, is to create prefabs; prefabs are comparable to templates; you can create a prefab (i.e., a template), create objects based on this template, and modify all these objects at once by only modifying the template; in other words, any change applied to the template will also be applied to the objects based on this template. So let's see how this can be done.

- Please remove the duplicate coins that you have in your scene to keep only one object called **coin**.

- Select this object (i.e., **coin**).

- Select the folder called **Assets** in the **Project** window, and then drag and drop the object **coin** from the **Hierarchy** window to the **Project** window.

- This will create an asset called **coin**, but this time it is **symbolized** by a blue box; this is the usual symbol for a prefab in Unity. If you click on this prefab, you will see, in the **Inspector** window, that it has the exact same properties as the object called **coin** that is present in the **Hierarchy**.

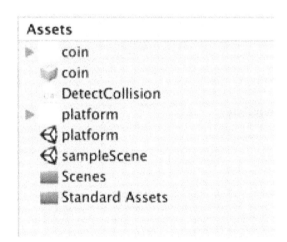

Figure 26: Creating a prefab for the coins

- We can now delete the object called **coin** in the **Hierarchy**.

- Please drag and drop the **coin** prefab from the **Project** window to the **Hierarchy** three times.
- This will create three coins.

Figure 27: Creating objects from a prefab

- Once this is done, please move these coins a few pixels apart in the **Scene** view, as described in the next figure.

Figure 28: Spacing out the new coins

We will now see how to modify their properties at once:

- Please click on the **coin** prefab in the **Project** window.
- Change its color to blue, as described in the next figure.

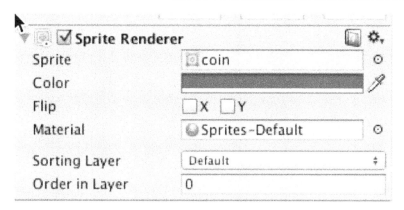

Figure 29: Changing the color of the coin prefab

- You should see that all three coins are now blue. This is because all three are based on the same prefab that we just modified.

Figure 30: Applying the changes to the coin objects

You can also change the prefab's properties from one of the individual coins, for example:

- Select the first coin (object called **coin**) in the **Hierarchy**.
- Change its color to green using the **Inspector** window.

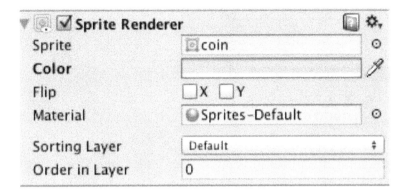

Figure 31: Changing the color of one of the coins

- At this stage only this coin will be green.

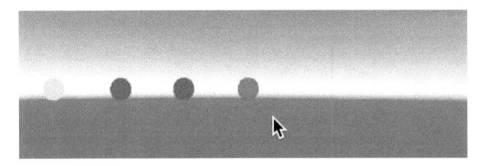

Figure 32: Changes applied to one the coins

- However, to apply this green color to all the other coins, you can select the option called **Overrides | Apply All** (top-right corner of the **Inspector**), as described in the next figure.

Figure 33: Applying changes to the prefab

- This will **apply** the properties of this particular object to all the other objects based on the same template (i.e., **prefab**).

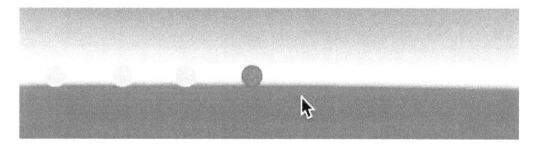

Figure 34: Generalizing the properties to other objects

So, prefabs are very important because they will save you a lot of time, and whenever you create a new feature (or object) that will probably be duplicated in your game, it is good practice to make it a prefab early in the development process.

So, let's apply this principle to the boulder:

- Please drag and drop the **boulder** object to the **Project** window to create a prefab named **boulder**.

- Delete the **boulder** object from the **Hierarchy**.

- Drag and drop the **boulder** prefab to the **Scene** to create a **boulder** object based on this prefab.

- Please duplicate this object **three times**, to roughly have the layout illustrated in the next figure.

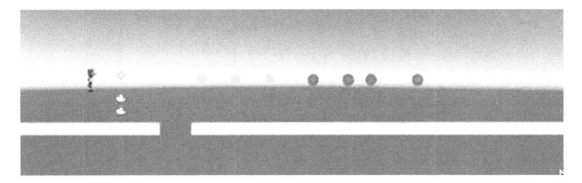

Figure 35: Including additional boulders

- Also add two new coins (either duplicates of an existing coin or by dragging and dropping the **coin** prefab to the scene twice) to the right of the boulders as described on the next figure.

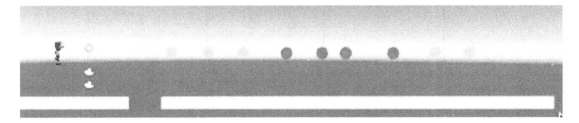

Figure 36: Including additional coins

- Please test the scene and check that all the boulders and the coins behave as expected (i.e., check that the score is increased by one after collecting a coin, or that the level is restarted after colliding with a boulder).

Last but not least, we will also create a prefab from our main character so that it can be reused in the next levels (yes, we will be creating several levels :-)).

- Please select the object **CharacterRobotBoy** in the **Hierarchy** window and drag and drop it to the **Project** window; this will create a prefab called **CharacterRobotBoy**.

- Please select the option "**Original Prefab**" in the new window.

Create Prefab

Would you like to create a new original Prefab or a variant of this Prefab?

Prefab Variant   Cancel   Original Prefab

- This will create a new prefab in the **Project** window.

Figure 37: Creating a prefab from the character

- Once this is done, rename this prefab **player** (i.e., select the prefab, left-click on the name of the prefab, and then modify its name or right-click on the prefab and select **Rename** from the contextual menu).

- You can now delete the object called "**CharacterRobotBoy**" from the **Hierarchy** window and then drag and drop the prefab "**player**" to the **Scene** view; this will create a new object called player in the **Hierarchy**.

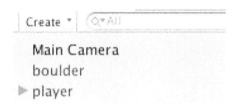

Figure 38: The character and its new name (player)

So that the main camera can follow the character and the score be updated, please drag and drop the object **player** to the variable **target** for the script **Camera2DFollow** located on the object "main Camera" and also for the script **Camera2DFollow** located on the object "**mini-map**".

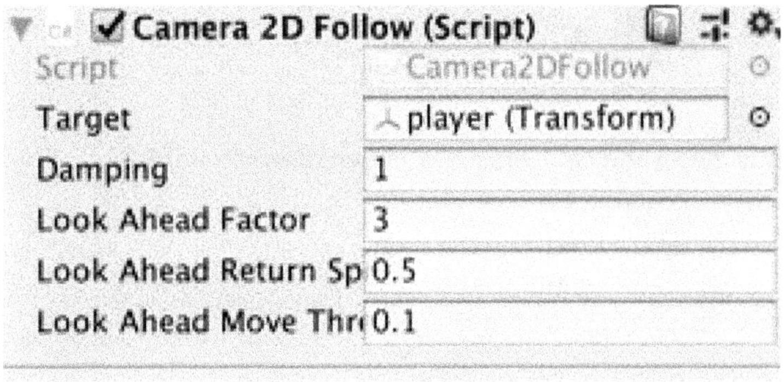
Camera 2D Follow (Script)
Script
Camera2DFollow
Target
player (Transform)
Damping
1
Look Ahead Factor
3
Look Ahead Return Sp
0.5
Look Ahead Move Thr
0.1

CREATING A NEW SCENE

Ok, so at this stage we have a level with objects to collect, and a score; what we will do next is to get the player to change level after collecting **five** coins or when the score is **5**.

- First let's save our current scene: select the folder **Assets** in the **Project** window, and then select **File | Save Scene as** from the top menu, and rename the scene **level1**.

> The new scene is saved in the active folder; so by selecting a particular folder in the **Project** window before saving a scene, this scene will be saved in this particular folder.

Then, we can create a new scene by duplicating the current scene.

- Please navigate to the folder **Assets** in the **Project** window.

- Select the scene that we have just saved (**level1**).

- Press **CTRL +D** or (**APPLE + D**); this will duplicate the current scene, and the duplicate will be automatically named **level2**.

- You can now open the second level by double-clicking on the scene called **level2** from the **Project** window.

- Unity may ask you if you want to save the current scene (since there were changes since the last time we saved the scene).

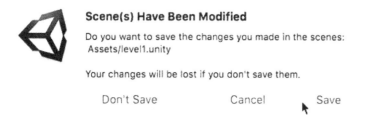

Scene(s) Have Been Modified

Do you want to save the changes you made in the scenes:
Assets/level1.unity

Your changes will be lost if you don't save them.

Don't Save   Cancel   Save

Figure 39: Saving changes made to the scene

- You can click on **Save**, to save your changes.

- You can now check that the current scene is **level2** by looking at the top of the window: the name **level2** should now appear.

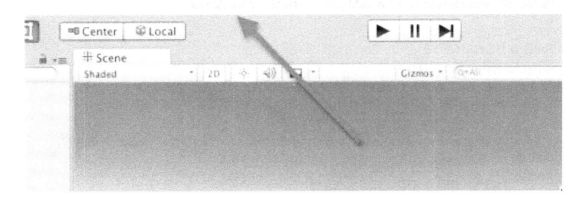

Figure 40: Checking the name of the current scene

Once this is done, we can just remove all coins and boulders from this scene, to only leave the player, the mini-map, and the platforms, for the time being.

- To select all the coins and boulders, you can drag and drop your mouse to select a rectangular area that encompasses all these objects; this will save you some time.

- You can then see that they are all selected either in the **Hierarchy** view, or in the **Scene** view.

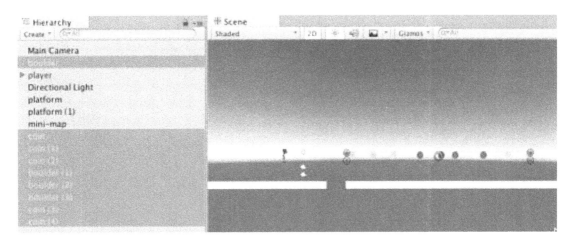

Figure 41: Selecting multiple objects

- Once this is done, you can select and delete these (e.g., **Edit | Delete**).

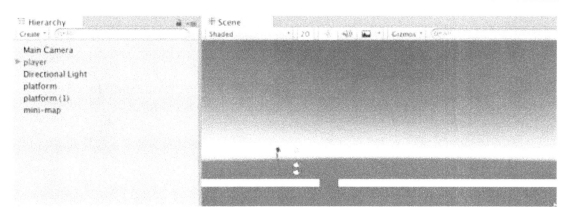

Figure 42: The scene without the coins or boulders

CHANGING LEVEL

Next, we will need to design a mechanism by which we can change level (from **level1** to **level2**) when we have collected **five** coins; this will be done using scripting.

- Please save the current scene (**CTRL + S**) and then open the scene **level1** (i.e., double click on it in the **Project** view).

- Open the script **DetectCollision**.

- Modify the first line of the class as follows:

```
int score, nbCoinsCollectedPerLevel;
```

- Add the following line to the **Start** function:

```
nbCoinsCollectedPerLevel = 0;
```

- Modify the function **OnCollisonEnter2D** as follows (new code in bold):

```
if (tagName == "pick_me")
{
     Destroy(coll.collider.gameObject);
     score++;
     nbCoinsCollectedPerLevel++;
     if (SceneManager.GetActiveScene ().name == "level1" &&
nbCoinsCollectedPerLevel >= 5)
     {
          SceneManager.LoadScene ("level2");
     }
     print ("score" + score);

}
```

- In the previous code, we increase the number of coins collected by one, and test whether we have collected five coins; in this case, if the current level is **level1**, we load the scene **level2**.

- Please save the code, and check that it is error-free.

Next, while the code is correct, there is a last thing we need to do; that is: we need to declare the scenes that will be used in our game, so that Unity can load them when we need them; so this will be done using what is called the **Build Settings**.

- In Unity, please select **File | Build Settings** from the top menu.

- This will open a new window with this same name.

- You can then drag and drop the scenes **level1** and **level2** from the **Project** window to the **Build Settings** window, as illustrated in the next figure.

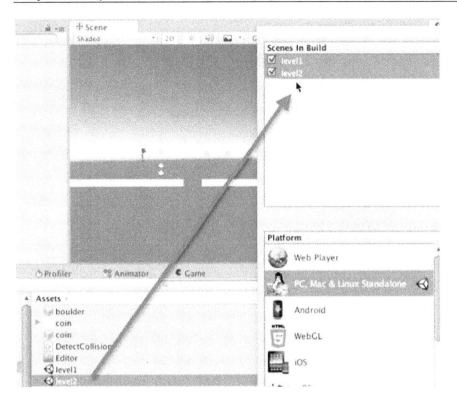

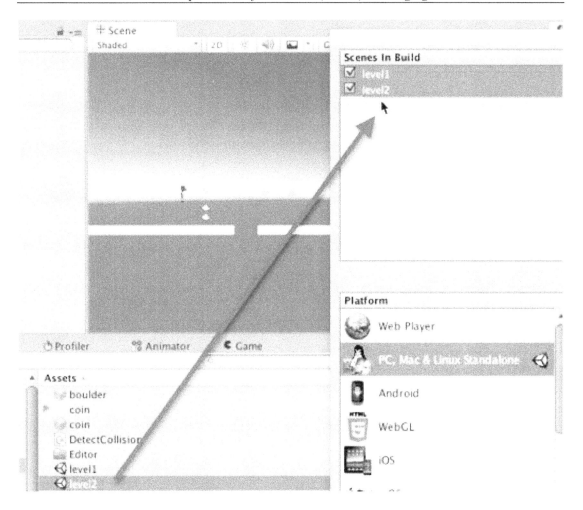

Figure 43: Modifying the build settings

Once this is done, you can close the **Build Settings** window, and test the scene; as you manage to collect five coins, you should transition to the next level (i.e., **level2**).

MANAGING THE NUMBER OF LIVES

At present, we have a score and we can also count the number of coins collected; it would also be nice to be able to use the number of lives, so that the player starts with, for example, three lives, and loses a life whenever s/he falls or hits a boulder.

First, we will create code to check when the player falls; we will then create a mechanism through which the lives are initialized to three, and then decreased after a wrong move was made.

- Please create a new sprite; from the **Project** view, select: **Create | Sprites | Square**.

- Rename this sprite **reStarter**, and drag and drop it to the **Scene** view; this will create a new object called **reStarter**.

- Select this new object (**resSarter**) and, using the **Inspector**, change its position to **(0, -50, 0)** and its scale to **(1000, 1, 1)**. You might need to lower the y-coordinate depending on the starting position of your character.

- You can also deactivate its **SpriteRenderer** component, as illustrated on the next figure.

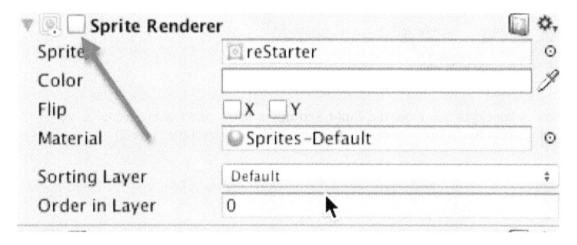

Figure 44: Deactivating the Sprite Renderer

- Please create a new tag (as we have done earlier) called **reStarter** and apply it to this object.

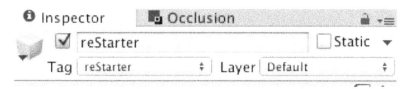

Figure 45: Adding a new tag reStarter

- The last thing will be to add a collider to this object: please select **Component | Physics2D | BoxCollider2D**.

So this object, although it won't be visible, will be collidable, and will be used to detect when the player is low enough that we can assume that it is falling.

The last thing we need to do is to modify our collision detection script to detect when the player collides with this object **reStarter**; in this case, we will restart the current level, as we have done for the collision with the boulders.

- Please open the script **DetectCollision**.

- Add the following code to it (new code in bold).

```
if (tagName == "avoid_me")
{
    Destroy(coll.collider.gameObject);
    SceneManager.LoadScene(SceneManager.GetActiveScene().name);
}
if (tagName == "reStarter")
{
    SceneManager.LoadScene(SceneManager.GetActiveScene().name);
}
```

- In the previous code, if we collide with an object with the tag **reStarter**, we then reload the current scene.

- Once this is done, check your code, and play the scene. Get the character to jump from a platform, and see as it is falling, that the level restarts automatically.

Once you have checked that this feature is working, you can create a prefab from the object **reStarter** by dragging and dropping this object to the **Project** window.

COMPLETING THE STRUCTURE OF OUR GAME

In the next sections, we will get to complete the skeleton of our game, by including, a **splash-screen**, **level1**, **level2** and a **game-over** or **win** screen. If the player manages to collect five coins, s/he will evolve to **level2**; then in **level2**, if s/he reaches the end of the level by jumping on platforms, s/he will win. The player will lose if s/he runs out of lives.

So let's complete the second scene, it will be a simple scene with platforms, a few pixels apart, that the player has to reach to complete the level.

- Please open the scene **level2**.

- Drag and drop the prefab **reStarter** from the **Project** window to the **Scene** view, this will create a new object called **reStarter**.

- Change its position to **(0, -50, 0)**.

We will now create a succession of small platforms that the player will need to jump on.

- Please select the platform to the right of the player (i.e., **platform1**).

- Change its scale to **(3.5, 1, 1)**.

- Rename it **small_platform**, and create a prefab with it, by dragging and dropping this object to the **Project** window.

Once this is done, you can duplicate this object (i.e., the small platform) seven times to create seven additional platforms that you can place side by side with some space in between, as illustrated on the next figure.

Figure 46: Adding small platforms

We can then do the following:

- Select the platform just below the player (i.e., the long platform) and rename it **long_platform**.

- Create a prefab from it (as we have done previously).

- Duplicate the object **long_platform** and move the duplicate to the right of the last small platform to obtain the layout that is illustrated in the next figure.

Figure 47: Completing the second level

To add some rewards, we can also include a few coins to the scene, above every small platform, by dragging and dropping the prefab called **coin** from the **Project** window to the **Scene** view several times.

Figure 48: Adding coins

The last thing is to create an object that symbolizes the end of **level2**; it will be used to transfer the user to the **win** screen (that we yet have to create).

Please do the following:

- Create a new triangle sprite: from the **Project** view, select **Create | Sprites | Triangle**.

- This will create a new sprite in the **Project** view.

- Rename it **endOfLevel2**.

- Once this is done, you can drag and drop it to the **Scene** view so that it appears to the right of the second long platform (as illustrated on the next figure).

- This will create a new object called **endOfLevel2**.

- You can then change the color of this object to green, using the **Inspector** window, by modifying its component called **Sprite Renderer**.

- We can also change its rotation to **(0, 0, -90)** and its scale to **(3, 3, 1)**.

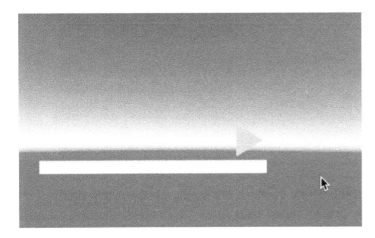

Figure 49: Creating the end of the level

- Finally, we will add a collider to this object by selecting **Component | Physics2D | BoxCollider2D**.
- You can now test your scene. As you reach the end of the level, you will collide with the object **endOfLevel2** (i.e., the green triangle); however, nothing will happen (i.e., no transition to the win screen) since we have not coded this feature yet.

To finish the basic structure of our game, we will be adding a splash-screen and an end screen.

CREATING A SPLASH SCREEN

Our splash screen will be the first screen displayed for our game; it will consist of a background image and a button.

- Please save the current scene (**File | Save Scene**).

- Create a new Scene (**File | New Scene**) and rename it **splashScreen** (**File | Save Scene As…**).

- By default, this new scene will include a camera and a light.

First we will create a button that will be used to load the first scene.

So let's create this button:

- Please select: **GameObject | UI | Button**. This will create a new button along with an object called **Canvas**.

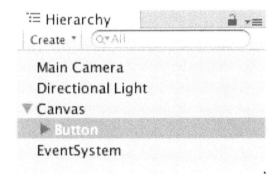

Figure 50: Creating a new button

- You can focus the view on this button by double-clicking on the button in the **Hierarchy** (or by selecting the button and then pressing *SHIFT + F*).

- This should display the button, along with a white rectangle that marks the boundary of the screen view.

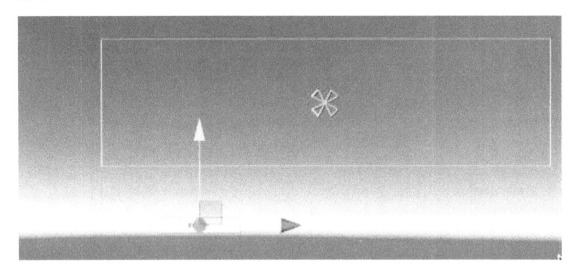

Figure 51: Focusing on the button

- Please move the button to the center of the white rectangle or, using the **Inspector**, change the **PosX**, **PosY** and **PosZ** properties of its **Rect Transform** component to **(0, 0, 0),** as illustrated on the next figure.

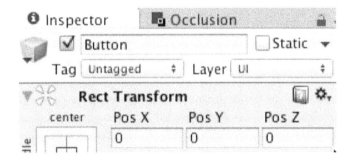

Figure 52: Changing the position of the button (part 1)

- The button should now be in the middle of the screen.

Figure 53: Changing the position of the button (part 2)

We can now change the text displayed on the button:

- Using the **Hierarchy**, select the object called **Text** that is a child of the object called **Button**.

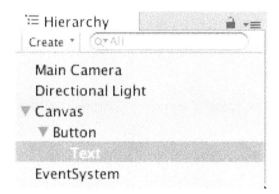

Figure 54: Selecting the text of the button

- Using the **Inspector**, you can change the **Text** property of the component called **Text** to **"Start"**.

Figure 55: Changing the label of the button

Once this is done, we will start to create a script that will be used to change levels.

- Please create a new C# script and name it **ControlButtons**.

- Open this script.

- Add this code at the start of the file.

```
using UnityEngine.SceneManagement;
```

- Add the following code within the class.

```
public void startLevel1()
{
        SceneManager.LoadScene("level1");
}
```

In the previous code, we create a new function called **startLevel1**; when this function is called, it will load the scene called **level1**.

Once this is done:

- Please save your code.

- Check that it is error-free.

- Create a new empty object (**GameObject | Create Empty**) and rename it **manageButtons**.

- Drag and drop the script **ControlButtons** to this empty object (i.e., the object **manageButtons**).

Last, we will select an action to be performed whenever the user clicks on the button.

- Click once on the button (called **Button**) in the **Hierarchy.**

- In the **Inspector** window, scroll down to the section called **Button** (i.e., at the bottom of the **Inspector** window).

- Click on the + sign below the text **"List is Empty"**.

Figure 56: Adding a new event handler

- This will reveal new attributes.

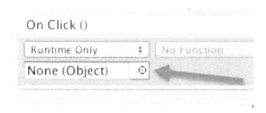

Figure 57: Displaying new attributes for the button

- You can now drag and drop the object called **manageButtons**, from the **Hierarchy** view, to the field labelled as **"None (Object)"**.

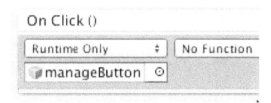

Figure 58: Adding the empty object to the button

For this to work, you need to drag the empty object to the field **None (Object)**, but NOT the script. In other words, if you drag and drop the script to this field, you will not be able to access it functions; instead, you need to drag and drop an empty object that includes the script **ControlButtons**. This will then give access to the functions within the script.

- Once this is done, click on the label **"No function"** and select **ControlButtons | StartLevel1** from the drop down menu.

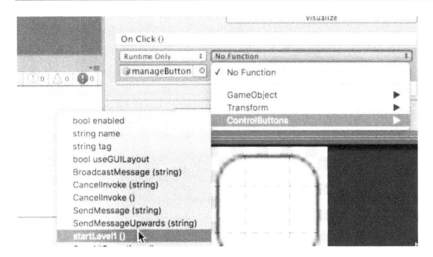

Figure 59: Selecting the function to be called (part 1)

- • By doing this, we effectively tell the system that in case the user clicks on the button, the function **startLevel1**, that is included in the script (or class) **ControlButtons**, should be called.

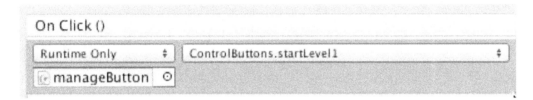

Figure 60: Selecting the function to be called (part 2)

Last, but not least, we just need to include this scene to the **Build Settings**, by opening the corresponding window (**File | Build Settings**) and clicking on the button **Add Open Scenes**.

Figure 61: Adding the current scene to the Build Settings

In the previous figure, you can see that all the scenes listed have an associated number (to the right) that indicates the order in which they will appear in the game; so we could also drag and drop the splash-screen scene in this view from the third to the first position in this list, as described in the next figure.

Figure 62: Moving the splash-screen to the first position

- We can now close the **Build Settings** window, and test our button. As you play the scene and click on the button, the first level (**level1**) should be loaded.

CREATING THE END SCREENS (WIN AND LOSE)

We will now create the last two screens for the skeleton of our game: a screen when the player wins (after reaching the end of the second level) and a screen for when the player loses after s/he has no more lives. Note that we have not dealt with the management of lives yet, and this will be done just after this section.

- Please save the current scene (**Files | Save Scene**).

- Create a new Scene (**File | New Scene**).

- Save this scene as **win** (**File | Save Scene As**).

- Add a new **UI Text** object (**GameObject | UI | Text**). This will create a new object called **Text**, as illustrated on the next figure.

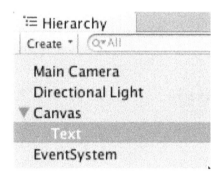

Figure 63: Adding a text UI object

Select this new object called **Text**, and, using the **Inspector**, change its attributes as follows:

- Component **Rect Transform**: **PosX = 0, PosY = 0**.

- Component **RectTransform**: **width = 500**; **height = 200**; **Anchor Preset** (the box just below the label **Rect Transform**) = **Middle - center**.

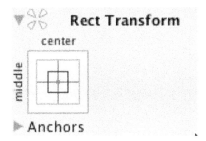

Figure 64: Modifying the RectTransform component

- Component **Text Script**: **Text** = "Well Done!"; **Font-Style = Bold; Font-Size = 91; Color=Green; paragraph alignment (middle-center)**.

Figure 65: Modifying the Paragraph component

Figure 66: Displaying the text after the changes

Once this is done, we will just create a button that will be used to restart the game.

- Please create a button as we have done previously (**GameObject | UI | Button**).

- Using the **Move** tool, move this button below the text that you have just created.

- Select the **Text** object that is a child of this button in the **Hierarchy**.

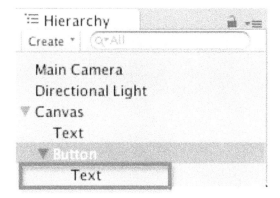

Figure 67: Selecting the label for the button

- Using the **Inspector**, change the text attribute of the **Text** component for this object to >> **Restart Game**<<.

Once this is done, we just need to modify our previous class **ControlButtons**, to include a function that loads the splash-screen, and we can then attach this script to an empty object.

- Please open the script **ControlButtons**.

- Add the following code to the class (at the end).

```
public void loadSplashScreen()
{
    SceneManager.LoadScene("splashScreen");
}
```

- In the previous code, we declare the function **loadSplashScreen** that will load the scene called **splashScreen** when it is called.

- Please save your code.

- Create an empty object called **manageButtons**.

- Drag and drop the script called **ControlButtons** to this empty object.

- Add this scene (i.e., **win**) to the **Build Settings**.

Figure 68: Adding the scene to the Build Settings

Next, we will define the function that is called when this button is pressed.

- Click once on the button in the **Hierarchy.**

- In the **Inspector** window, scroll down to the section called **Button** (i.e., bottom of the **Inspector** window).

- Click on the + sign below the text **"List is Empty"**.

Figure 69: Selecting an event handler (part 1)

- This will reveal new attributes.

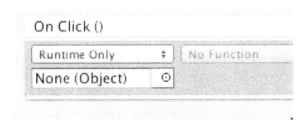

Figure 70: Selecting an event handler (part 2)

- You can now drag and drop the object called **manageButtons**, from the **Hierarchy** view, to the field labelled as "**None (Object)**".

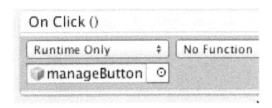

Figure 71: Selecting a function (part 1)

- Once this is done, click on the label "**No function**" and select **ControlButtons | LoadSplashScreen**.

By doing this, we effectively tell the system that in case the user clicks on the button, the function **loadSplahScreen**, that is included in the script (or class) **ControlButtons**, should be called.

Figure 72: Selecting a function (part 2)

- You can now test the scene and check that by clicking on the button, you are redirected to the splash-screen.

We can now create a prefab from the object **manageButtons**, as the scripts within will be used later on:

- Please drag and drop the object **manageButtons** to the **Project** view, this will create a prefab called **manageButtons**.

Figure 73: The new prefab manageButtons

Once this is done, we just need to create a new scene for when the player loses; this will be quite identical to the **win** scene, except from the message displayed onscreen.

- Please save the current scene (**File | Save Scene**).

- Duplicate this scene (i.e., the **win** scene): from the **Project** view, select the scene called **win** and duplicate it *(CTRL + D or APPLE + D)*; rename the duplicate **lose** (i.e., click once on it then change its name, or select it and press **Enter**), this will be the scene used when the player loses.

- In the **Project** view, double-click on the scene called **lose** to open it.

- Once the scene is open, using the **Hierarchy**, select the object called **Text**, that is a child of the object **canvas**.

Figure 74: Selecting the Text object

- Using the **Inspector**, change its text attribute to "**You lost!**"

- The button's label does not need to be changed since it will also ask the player to restart the game.

The only thing that we need to do now is to add this scene to the **Build Settings** by opening the **Build Settings** window (**File| Build Settings**), and by then selecting the option **Add Open Scenes**.

Figure 75: Adding a new scene to the Build Settings

That's it. We can now close the **Build Settings** window, and the last thing we can do is to make sure that the **win** scene is displayed when the player reaches the end of the second level.

So let's proceed:

- Please open the scene called **level2**.

- Select the object **endOfLevel2**.

- Create a new tag (as we have done previously) called **endOfLevelTwo** and apply it to this object.

- Open the script **DetectCollision**.

- Add this code at the end of the function **OnCollisionEnter2D**.

```
if (tagName == "endOfLevelTwo")
{
    SceneManager.LoadScene("win");
}
```

- Please save your code.

- Play the scene (**level2**) and make sure that the **win** screen is displayed once the player reaches the end of the level.

LEVEL ROUNDUP

Well, this is it!

In this chapter, we have learned about creating a simple splash-screen, adding buttons, processing clicks on buttons, and changing levels; in the process, we also learned how to use prefabs to optimize your time. We have, by now, a very simple, but almost complete, platform game with two levels, along with the out-of-game screens (i.e., win, lose, and splash-screen).

Checklist

You can consider moving to the next chapter if you can do the following:

- Duplicate a scene.

- Create a prefab.

- Create an object based on a prefab.

- Create a button and the corresponding code to detect a click on it.

- Know how to access and use the **Build Settings**.

Quiz

It's now time to check your knowledge with a quiz. Please specify whether the following statements are true or false!

1. You can duplicate a scene by selecting it in the **Project** view and by then pressing *CTRL + D.*

2. If a scene is called **level1**, its duplicate will automatically be renamed **level2** (unless **level2** exists already).

3. A prefab can be created by selecting an object in the **Hierarchy** and by then pressing *CTRL + P.*

4. You can create a new button, by selecting **GameObject | Button** from the top menu.

5. You can create a new button, by selecting **GameObject | Text** from the top menu.

6. In the **Build-Settings** window, the number to the right of each scene indicates the order in which it would usually appear in the game.

7. For a scene to be loaded from a script, this scene has to be included in the **Build Settings**.

8. So that something happens when a button is clicked, a function needs to be selected using the **Inspector**.

9. To modify the label of a button, you can change the text object that is a child of this button.

10. Whenever the first **UI** object of a scene is added to this scene, an object called **canvas** is also created.

Answers to the Quiz

1. TRUE.

2. TRUE.

3. FALSE.

4. FALSE.

5. FALSE.

6. TRUE.

7. TRUE.

8. TRUE.

9. TRUE.

10. TRUE.

Challenge 1

Now that you have managed to complete this chapter and that you have improved your skills, let's do the following.

- Add a **Text UI** object to the splash-screen, above the **Start** button, with the title of the game.

- Create a new scene called **Instructions** (e.g., duplicate the **splash-screen** scene).

- Add a button called <<**Back** to this scene. Upon clicking on this button the player should go back to the splash-screen.

- Add a button called **Instructions** to the splash-screen. Upon clicking on this button the player should go to the scene called **Instructions**.

Challenge 2

In this challenge, you will be adding a new background to the splash-screen

- Import the texture called **RobotBoy** from the resource pack (or use any texture of your choice).

- Create a new canvas: select **GameObject | UI | Canvas**.

- Select this canvas.

- Using the Inspector, change its **Sort Order** attribute (in the component called **Canvas**) to **-1**; this will ensure that any UI object within this canvas is displayed behind the button (the **Sort Order** of the canvas used for the button is 0 by default).

- Create a new **RawImage:** select **GameObject | UI | Raw Image** from the top menu, and make sure that this image is a child of the new canvas that you have created

- Modify the position and scale of this image, so that it fills the screen.

- Test your scene.

CHAPTER 3: PLATFORM GAME (PART 3): ADDING SOUND AND DISPLAYING VALUES ONSCREEN

In this section, we will discover how to display the score and the number of lives onscreen, as well as how to be able to access these variables throughout the game.

After completing this chapter, you will be able to:

- Display and update text onscreen.

- Store and access information saved in the player preferences.

- Keep objects across scenes.

- Display or hide text depending on the current scene.

- Create a background music and sound effects.

- Play one or multiple sounds.

INTRODUCTION

In this chapter we will improve the current game by adding a few tweaks that will make it more enjoyable and easy-to-play. We will start by keeping the score (and the number of lives) between scenes, so that the game does not reset these values at the start of every level; instead of displaying the score and the number of lives in the **Console** window, we will get to display them onscreen thanks to **UI Text** objects, so that the user can see this information at a glance. Finally, we will add some background music to our scenes

MANAGING LIVES AND SCORE THROUGHOUT THE GAME

Ok, so at this point we have several levels, and the skeleton of our platform game, including a **splash-screen**, a **win** screen and a **lose** screen; we also keep track of the score and the number of lives.

Now, about these two: although we have created variables to keep track of the number of lives and the score, the following issue remains: the score is usually reset at the start of each level because it is declared and initialised in the **Start** function which is called whenever the scene starts; so we need to keep track of these variables throughout the game.

The first way we could do this is to create an **nbLives** variable in the **DetectCollision** script, initialize it to three in the **Start** function, and then decrease its value every time we restart the level; however, there are two issues with this approach: whenever we go to the next scene, this number of lives will be reset to zero; in fact, this would be the same for the score; so we need to find a way to be able to store data that will be kept as we move from one scene to the next.

This can be done with what is called the **Player Preferences**. Using **Player Preferences**, you can store information in variables of types integer, boolean, or string, that will be accessible (and maintained) throughout the game.

So, using the **Player Preferences**, we will do the following:

- Set the score (in the player preferences) to 0 and the number of lives to 3 in the splash-screen.

- The score (in the player preferences) and the number of lives will be updated in every scene, by accessing the player preferences, reading the current number of lives or the score, and modifying this value.

So let's get started:

- Please open the **splashScreen** scene.

- Create an empty object called **initGame**.

- Then create a new C# script called **initGame**: from the **Project** window, please select **Create | C# Script** and rename this script **initGame**.

- Open this script and modify the **Start** function as follows:

```
void Start ()
{
    PlayerPrefs.SetInt("score",0);
    PlayerPrefs.SetInt("nbLives",3);
}
```

In the previous code:

- We create the variable **score** that is stored in the player preferences; it can be considered as a global variable as it is accessible throughout the game; it is set to **0**.

- The same is done with the variable **nbLives** that is set to **3**.

- Once you have saved your script and checked that it is error-free, you can drag and drop it to the object **initGame**.

Next, we need to use these variables throughout the game, especially when the player collects items or loses a life by falling or colliding with dangerous objects.

- Please save your scene, and then open the scene called **level1**.

- Open the script called **DetectCollision**.

- Replace this line…

```
int score, nbCoinsCollectedPerLevel;
```

with this line…

```
int score, nbLives, nbCoinsCollectedPerLevel;
```

- Then, in the **Start** function, you can comment the line that sets the score to 0, as follows:

```
//score = 0;
```

- We can then modify the code that deals with the **score** as follows (new code in bold):

```
if (tagName == "pick_me")
{
      Destroy(coll.collider.gameObject);
      //score++;
      score = PlayerPrefs.GetInt("score");
      score++;
      PlayerPrefs.SetInt("score", score);
```

In the previous code:

- We comment the line that used to increase the local score by 1.

- We then fetch the value of the **score** that is stored in the player preferences.

- We increase this value by one, and save the new value in the player preferences.

We now need to modify the code that deals with the number of lives; please add the following code to the script **DetectCollision** (new code in bold):

```
if (tagName == "avoid_me" || tag == "reStarter")
{
     Destroy(coll.collider.gameObject);
     nbLives = PlayerPrefs.GetInt("nbLives");
     nbLives--;
     PlayerPrefs.SetInt("nbLives", nbLives);
     if                     (nbLives                >=              0)
SceneManager.LoadScene(SceneManager.GetActiveScene().name);
     else SceneManager.LoadScene("lose");
     print ("lives" + nbLives);
}
/*if (tagName == "reStarter")
{
     SceneManager.LoadScene(SceneManager.GetActiveScene().name);

}*/
```

In the previous code:

- We have grouped the two conditional statements that checked for collision with a **reStarter** object or a boulder (i.e., tag = **avoid_me**).

- In this case, we decrease the current number of lives by accessing its value from the player preferences, decreasing the value, and updating the player preferences accordingly.

- We also commented the code that used to be employed to detect the tag **reStarter**, since this is now done in the code just above (i.e., in the combined conditional statement).

Once this has been done, please save your code, check that it is error-free, and test the game as follows:

- Save the current scene.

- Open the scene called **splashScreen**.

- Play the game and proceed to the first level.

- Test that if you fall, the number of lives displayed in the **Console** window is correct and that after 3 falls, you are redirected to the scene called **lose**.

- Check that your score is kept when you go from the first scene to the second scene.

REMOVING ERRONEOUS MESSAGES

As it is, you may have noticed that every time you play the scene, there is a message in the **Console** window saying "**There are two audio listeners in the scene...**"; this is because we use two cameras, each using one **Audio Listener**; however, we only need to have one audio listener in each scene; so we just need to deactivate one of these audio listeners as follows:

- Please open the scene called **level1**.

- Please select the camera called **mini-map** in the **Hierarchy**.

- Using the **Inspector** window, deactivate its **Audio Listener** component.

Figure 76: Deactivating the Audio Listener component

- Please do the same in the scene called **level2**.

- If you play the game again, this error message should have disappeared.

ADDING A USER INTERFACE

Ok; so far so good; we can keep our score and number of lives between scenes. The next step will be to display the number of lives and the score onscreen for the player. For this, we will create what are called **UI elements** and update them accordingly when the score or number of lives have been changed; and since these (the UI for the score and the number of lives) will be used across all scenes, we will also learn how to create them once and then keep them for all the out-of-game scenes (i.e., the scenes where there is no game play and that consist of menu and buttons).

So let's get started:

- Please open the scene **level1**.

- Select: **GameObject | UI | Text**; this will create a text object, that we can use for the score, named **Text**.

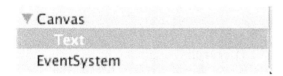

Figure 77: Adding a Text UI

You can rename it **scoreUI** and move it in the top-left corner of the white rectangle that defines the game window.

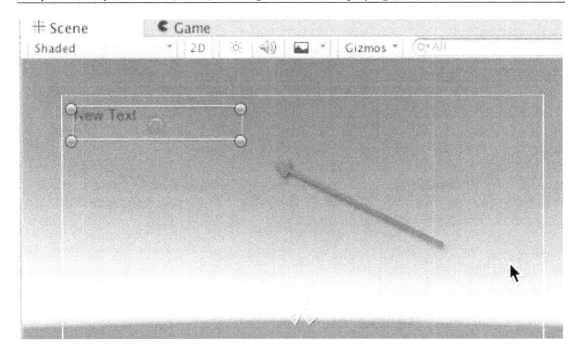

Figure 78: Adding a UI for the score

- Once this is done, you can select this object in the **Hierarchy**, duplicate it, rename the duplicate **livesUI**, and move the duplicate (i.e., **livesUI**) just below the previous **Text** object, as illustrated in the next figure.

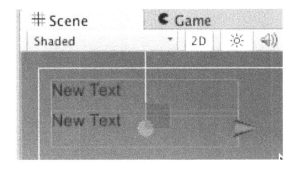

Figure 79: Adding a UI for the number of lives

- You should now have two **TextUI** elements in your **Hierarchy**: **scoreUI** and **livesUI**.

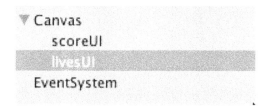

Figure 80: The two UI elements

Once this is done, using the **Inspector**, you can change the font color of each of these **Text** objects, for more visibility, using their **Text Component**.

Figure 81: Changing the color of the text

Next, we need to update these text objects from our scripts, at the start of the game, and also whenever the score or the number of lives change.

- Please open the script **DetectCollision**.

- Add the following code at the beginning of the script.

```
using UnityEngine.UI;
```

- Add the following code just before the end of the script.

```
void updateUI()
{
      score = PlayerPrefs.GetInt("score");
      nbLives = PlayerPrefs.GetInt("nbLives");
      GameObject.Find("scoreUI").GetComponent<Text>().text        =
"Score: "+score;
      GameObject.Find("livesUI").GetComponent<Text>().text        =
"Lives: " +nbLives;
}
```

In the previous code:

- We create a new function called **updateUI**.

- We access the score and the number of lives from the player preferences.

- We then update the two UI objects **scoreUI** and **livesUI** with these values.

Now, we just need to initialise these **Text** fields:

- Please modify the function **Start**, in the script **DetectCollision**, as follows (new code in bold):

```
void Start ()
{
      updateUI ();
      nbCoinsCollectedPerLevel = 0;
}
```

In the previous code we call the function **updateUI** and also set the value of the variable **nbCoinsCollectedPerLevel** to **0**.

- Please add the following code at the end of the function **OnCollisionEnter2D**, so that the UI elements (i.e., **scoreUI** and **livesUI**) are updated after colliding with boulders or after falling.

```
updateUI();
```

- Save your script and play the scene (i.e., **level1**); you should see that the score and the number of lives are displayed at the start, and updated as you fall or when you collect items.

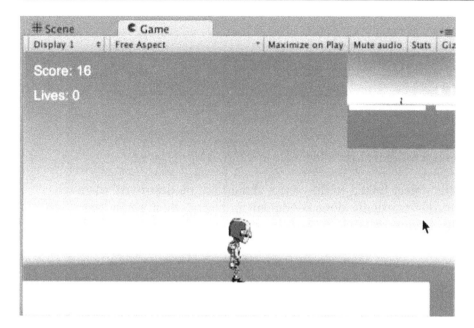

Figure 82: The UI with the score and number of lives

As you test the scene, and if you complete this level (i.e., **level1**) and proceed to the next level, you will also see that the score is not displayed in **level2**; this is because, at present, there are no UI elements added to this scene that can display this information; so we could do two things:

- Create new UI elements with the exact same name as in the first scene.

  OR

- Keep the UI elements created in the first scene.

We will opt for the second option; although the first one is also viable, the second solution decreases the workload (on the long run) as we don't have to recreate UI elements for the subsequent scenes.

So let's implement this solution.

- Create a new C# script called **KeepUI**.

- Add the following function to it.

```
void Awake()
{
        DontDestroyOnLoad(transform.gameObject);
}
```

In the previous code:

- We use the function **Awake** that is called once at the start of the game.

- We specify that the object linked to this script should not be destroyed when we load a new scene (this is usually done by default in Unity when a new scene is loaded); since this script will be linked to the canvas that includes both UI elements (**scoreUI** and **livesUI**), we make sure that these will be kept for the next scene(s).

- Please save this script, and drag and drop it on the object called **Canvas**.

- Test the scene, you should see that after completing the first scene, the second scene includes the UI elements and displays the score and the number of lives.

The only thing is that:

- When you reload the first scene (after falling) the UI is displayed twice.

- These UI elements (i.e., **scoreUI** and **livesUI**) should not be displayed in the out-of-game scenes such as the **splashScreen** or the **lose** or **win** screen; so we just need to change our code to be able to specify when these UI elements should be displayed.

So let's solve these issues one by one; first, by removing duplicate UI elements.

- Please open the scene **level1**.

- Select the object **Canvas**.

- Using the **Inspector**, create a new label called **player_ui** as we have done before.

- Apply this label to the object called **Canvas**.

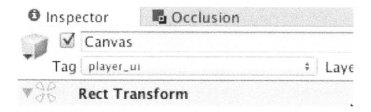

Figure 83: Setting a label for the canvas

- Once this is done, open the script called **KeepUI**.

- Add this line at the beginning of the script.

```
using UnityEngine.UI;
```

- Add this code to the function **Start**.

```
int        nbUIs        =              GameObject.FindGameObjectsWithTag
("player_ui").Length;
if  (FindObjectsOfType  (GetType  ()).Length  >  1)  Destroy
(gameObject);
```

In the previous code:

- We count the number of objects with the tag **player_ui**; we effectively check whether there is more than one object called **canvas** (i.e., the object that includes the UI elements for the score and the number of lives).

- Since the function **GameObject.FindGameObjectsWithTag ("player_ui")** returns an array, **GameObject.FindGameObjectsWithTag ("player_ui").Length** will return the number of objects in this array.

- If we find a duplicate and if we are in the scene **level1** (which is bound to happen) we destroy the duplicate.

Note that the function **GameObject.FindGameObjectsWithTag** returns an array that includes all objects with a specific tag; so using the code **GameObject.FindGameObjectsWithTag[0]** will return the first object in the array.

Last but not least, we will hide the text that is in the UI text fields whenever we are in a scene that includes a button (e.g., win, lose, or splash-screen). Now, ideally, we could use the **Start** function in the **KeepUI** script to do that; however, because this script is linked to an object that is persistent (thanks to the method **DontDesroyOnLoad**), the **Start** method will only be called in the scene **level1**; this is because it is called only when the script is loaded; however, because of the function **DontDestroyOnLoad**, the script is loaded only once (in the scene level1) and then kept throughout the game; so the **Start** function for the script **KeepUI** is loaded once; hence its **Start** function is only called once (throughout the game); so, for this purpose, we will use the **Start** method of an object that is loaded in the menu scenes, that is, the script called **ControlButtons**; this script is loaded every time an out-of-game scene is loaded; this means that we will be able to check whether the UI elements should be displayed every time a new scene is loaded; we will therefore be using the **Start** function of the script **ControlButtons** as follows.

- Please open the script **ControlButtons**.

- Add this code at the beginning of the script.

```
using UnityEngine.UI;
```

- Add this code in the **Start** function.

```
if     (SceneManager.GetActiveScene     ().name     ==     "win"     ||
SceneManager.GetActiveScene ().name == "lose")
{
     GameObject.Find ("scoreUI").GetComponent<Text>().text = "";
     GameObject.Find ("livesUI").GetComponent<Text>().text = "";
}
```

In the previous code:

- We test whether we are in the **win** or **lose** scene.

- If this is the case, we then set the text of both UI elements to an empty string

Once this is done, we can save and use this script.

- Please save the script **ControlButtons**.

- Open the **splashScreen** scene (so that the game starts with this scene).

- Test the scene, and check that the UI elements for the score and number of lives are displayed only in the in-game scenes (i.e., **level1** and **level2**).

Finally, you can also modify the **DetectCollision** script to update the UI whenever objects are collected:

- Open the script **DetectCollison**.

- Replace the code ...

```
print ("score" + score);
```

with...

```
//print ("score" + score);
updateUI();
```

You may also notice the text "**New Text**" in both UI fields at the start of each scene, as you play them; to remove this text, you can do the following:

- Open the scene **level1**.

- Select each UI elements (i.e., **uiScore** and **uiLives**).

- Using the **Inspector**, please delete the text in the **Text** Component of these objects.

Figure 84: Deleting the text in each UI Text object

- Please test the scene and check that the text "**New Text**" has disappeared.

ADDING SOUND

Ok, so far, the game runs as expected and it could be used as it is; however, we will, in this and the next sections, add some features that will make it more enjoyable and challenging. This will consist of audio clips and additional game mechanics.

We will add **Audio** components to the game in two forms: a background music that will be played in every scene, along with sound effects played when objects are collected or when the player falls.

So first let's add a background sound:

- Please import the audio tracks **Rainbows, On-My_Way,** and **collect_coin** from the resource pack by dragging and dropping them from their folder to the **Project** folder in Unity.

> The first two audio file were created by *Kevin McLeod* and are available on the site: http://incompetech.com/music/royalty-free/music.html; the other audio file called **collect_coin**, present in the resource folder, was created using the site http://www.bfxr.net/, which is a free tool to create your own sound effects for your game.

- You can, for the time being, create a folder called **Audio** in the **Project** window, and then add the audio files to this folder; this will make it easier to find them later.

The two first files will be used for the background music, while the last file will be used when coins have been collected.

- Please open the **splashScreen** scene.

- Create an empty object called **bg_sound** (select **GameObject | Create Empty**).

- Drag and drop the audio file **On_My_Way** on this empty object; this will create an **Audio Source** component for this object with the option **playOnAwake** set to **true** by default.

- Please select the empty object **bg_sound**, and, using the **Inspector** view, set the attribute **Loop** for the component **Audio Source**, to **true**.

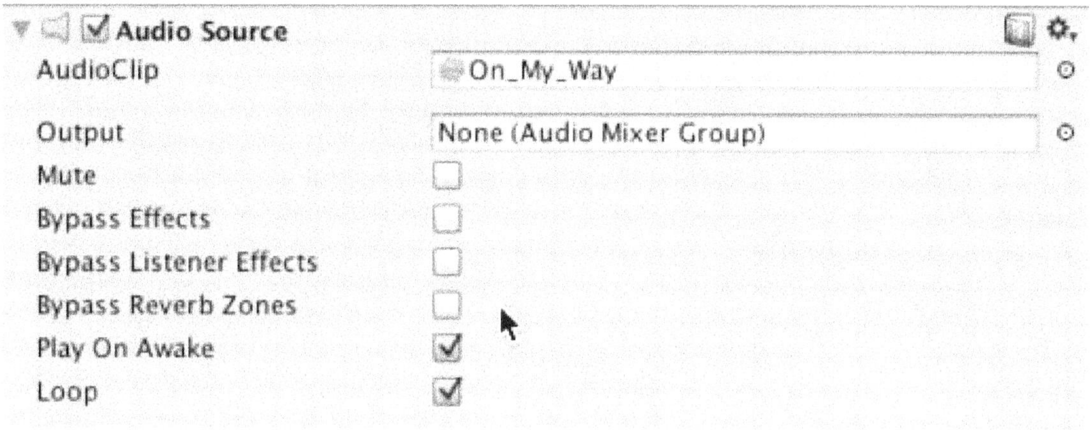

Figure 85: Setting the attributes of the background sound

- Once this is done, you can play the scene and check that the background sound is played.

When you have checked that it is working, you can repeat the last steps to add the same background sound to the scenes **win**, and **lose**, and the background sound called **Rainbows** to the scenes **level1** and **level2**.

Once this is done, please check that the background music plays as expected; you can, of course, use other types of background sounds of your choice if you wish, using **wav** or **mp3** files, for example.

Next, we will add sound effects when objects are collected.

- Please open the scene **level1**.

- Select the object **player** in the **Hierarchy**.

- From the top menu, select **Component | Audio | Audio Source**; this will add an **Audio Source** component to your object;

Whenever you need to play a sound, an **Audio Source** is needed, and it is comparable to an mp3 player in the sense that it plays audio clips that you need to select, the same way you would select a particular track on your mp3 player (hoping mp3 player are still popular when this book comes out :-)).

- Please, drag and drop the audio file called **collect_coin** from the **Project** window to the **Audio Clip** attribute of the **Audio Source** and set the attribute **Play on Awake** to **false** (i.e., unchecked) so that this sound is not played automatically at the start of the scene, as illustrated on the next figure.

Figure 86: Setting the attributes of the sound effect

Next, we will write code that will access this **Audio Source** and play the clip, whenever we collect an object.

- Please open the script called **DetectCollision**.

- Add the following code to the function **OnCollisionEnter2D** (new cold in bold).

```
if (tagName == "pick_me")
{
        GetComponent<AudioSource> ().Play ();
```

In the previous code, we access the **AudioSource** component that is linked to the object **player** (i.e., the object linked to this script), and we play the clip that is included in this **AudioSource** (i.e., **collect_coins**).

- Please save your code, test the scene, and check that the audio clip is played whenever you collect an object.

PLAYING MULTIPLE SOUNDS

As you know, feedback is very important in video games, as it provides additional information to the users on their progress; using audio is one of the many ways to provide feedback and to make sure that the experience is entertaining and interactive.

Since we are adding audio for collecting coins, we could also add audio when the user has made a wrong move; this is, again, for feedback.

Now, because the **Audio Source** will need to play several sounds (a different sound depending on whether the player collects a coin or hits a boulder), we will need to specify which track needs to be played, so we will modify our script accordingly.

- Please import the audio file called **hurt.wav** from the resource pack (i.e., drag and drop this file to the **Project** window).

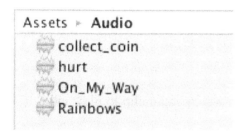

Figure 87: Importing the hurt.wav audio file

- Please open the script **DetectCollision**.

- Add the following lines at the beginning of the script:

```
public AudioClip collect, hurt;
```

- This code declares two audio clips; because they are public, they will be accessible from the **Inspector**, and as a result, we will be able to set (or initialize) these variables by dragging and dropping objects to their placeholders in the Inspector window.

- Please save your script, switch to Unity, select the **player** object and display the **Inspector** window.

[107]

- You should see that two variables, that act as placeholders, are now available.

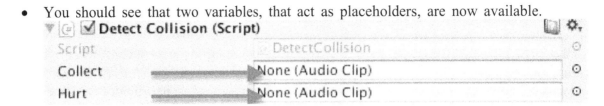

Figure 88: Initializing the audio clips (part1)

- Please drag and drop the sound **hurt.wav** from the **Project** view, to the variable **hurt** in the **Inspector**, and the sound **collect_coin** from the **Project** view to the variable **collect** in the **Inspector** view, as illustrated in the next figure.

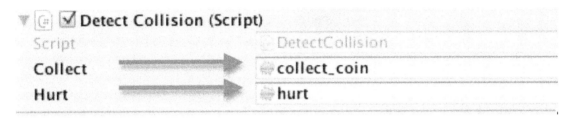

Figure 89: Initializing the audio clips (part 2)

Now, it's time to modify the script further to tell the system which audio clip to play and when.

- Please open the script **DetectCollision**.

- Add the following code (new code in bold):

```
if (tagName == "pick_me)
{
      GetComponent<AudioSource> ().clip = collect;
      GetComponent<AudioSource> ().Play ();
```

In the previous code:

- We specify that the new clip to be played is the clip called **collect** (which contains the audio **collect-coin.wav**); this track is now the default track for the **Audio Source**.

- We then play the track that we have selected.

We will also use similar code to play a different sound when the player is hurt.

- Please add the following code in the function **OnCollisionEnter2D** (new code in bold).

```
if (tagName == "avoid_me" || tag == "reStarter")
{
        GetComponent<AudioSource> ().clip = hurt;
        GetComponent<AudioSource> ().Play ();
```

In the previous code, following the same principle, we select the clip that contains the audio file **hurt.wav** and we then play this clip.

- You can now save your script and test the scene **level1**;

- You should hear a different sound every time you collect an object or collide with a boulder.

Now, this code works well in the first level; however, we may obtain an error message after progressing to the second level whenever you collide with a coin; the message may read "**There is no Audio Source attached to the player**"; this is because the player that we are using in **level2** is different to the one used in **level1** as it has no **AudioSource** component yet; to avoid this issue, we will update our **player** prefab in the scene **level1** (so that the prefab for the **player** object includes an **Audio Source**) and then use the same prefab in the scene **level2** (or any other subsequent in-game scene).

- Please open the scene **level1**.

- Select the object called **player**.

- Using the **Inspector**, click on the button called **Overrides | Apply All**, as illustrated on the next figure.

Figure 90: Applying changes to the player prefab

- This will apply the changes to the **player** prefab; and since **level2** includes a player based on the same prefab, the error mentioned earlier should now disappear if we play the game again.

- Please play the second scene and check that the error has disappeared.

Note that if you see the following error message, this is totally normal; this is due to the fact that the script tries to access the UI elements for the score and number of lives; however, since these are created in the splash screen and kept onwards, they won't be present if we test **level2** in isolation.

 NullReferenceException: Object reference not set to an instance of an object
DetectCollision.updateUI () (at Assets/DetectCollision.cs:84)

LEVEL ROUNDUP

Summary

In this chapter, we have managed to use the player preferences to store information that is now accessible throughout the level; we also created a mechanism by which the UI for the score and the number of lives is created only once but displayed in every in-game scene. Finally, we also learned to import and to play sounds either as a background music or as a sound effect.

Checklist

You can consider moving to the next stage if you can do the following:

- Understand when the function **Awake** is called.

- Understand how to create and access variables stored in the player preferences.

- Understand the difference between the components **Audio Clip** and **Audio Source**.

Quiz

Now, let's check your knowledge! Please specify whether the following statements are true or false.

1. It is possible to store integers, Booleans or strings in the player preferences.

2. The following code will create a new variable called **score** in the player preferences.

```
PlayerPrefs.SetInt("score",10);
```

3. The following code will read a variable called **score** from the player preferences.

```
int s = PlayerPrefs.ReadInt("score");
```

4. Provided that this code is attached to an object with an **Audio Source** component, it will play its default clip.

```
GetCOmponent<AudioSource>().Play();
```

5. In Unity, it is possible to play several **Audio Clips** using just one **Audio Source**.

6. By default, the attribute **Play on Awake** for an **Audio Clip** is set to true.

7. By default, the attribute **Loop** for an **Audio Clip** is set to true.

8. The following code, when attached to an object, will ensure that it is not destroyed when the next scene loads.

```
void Awake()
{
     DontDestroyOnLoad(transform.gameObject);
}
```

9. For a particular script, the function **Start** is called when the script is loaded.

10. For a particular script, the function **Start** is called <u>only</u> when the game is loaded.

Answers to the Quiz

1. TRUE.

2. TRUE.

3. TRUE.

4. FALSE.

5. TRUE.

6. TRUE.

7. FALSE.

8. TRUE.

9. TRUE.

10. FALSE.

Challenge 1

For this chapter, your challenge will be to mute the sound when the player presses the key **M**, and you could do as follows:

- Detect when the key **M** has been pressed; you can use the following code in the **Update** function:

```
If (Input.GetKeyDown(KeyCode.M)) {}
```

- Whenever this happens, access the **Audio Source** attached to this object.
- Then, access the **mute** option of the audio source using the following code, and set it to **true** or **false,** or to the opposite of the current value using the operator **!**:

```
GetComponent<AudioSource>.mute
```

For more information about the mute attribute, you can look at the official documentation using the following link:

https://docs.unity3d.com/ScriptReference/AudioSource-mute.html

CHAPTER 4: PLATFORM GAME (PART 4): ADDING CHALLENGING GAMEPLAY

In this section, we will start to include game mechanics that improve the gameplay for the platform game that we have been creating so far; after completing this chapter, you will be able to:

- Create moving platforms.

- Create a shaky bridge for which the steps fall down as you walk on them.

- Create a timer.

- Teleport the character.

Some of the skills you will learn in the process include:

- Using **Time.deltaTime**.

- Enabling or disabling gravity for **Rigidbody2D** components.

- Animate objects.

INTRODUCTION

At present, the scenes that we have created include some simple game mechanics that may challenge the player; however, as you will expand your game, it is always a good idea to change and vary the types of challenges that the player has to overcome; so, in the next sections, we will create a series of game mechanics or challenges, that you will be able to save as prefabs and to reuse in any level of your choice; these will consist of:

- **A time challenge**: the player has to complete the level before the time is up.

- **Moving platforms**: these include platforms moving horizontally or vertically.

- **A shaky Bridge**: a bridge for which the steps progressively fall as the player walks on them, forcing the player to keep moving forward, and fast.

- **Magic doors (i.e., teleportation)**: this consists of a door that teleports the player to a different part of the game when reached by the player.

THE TIME CHALLENGE

So, let's start with the time challenge, it will consist of a timer that counts down from 30 seconds; whenever the timer reaches 0, the player loses a life and the level needs to be restarted; the time is displayed onscreen.

So let's get started:

- Please open the first scene (**level1**).

- Create an empty object, and rename it **timer**.

- Create a new C# script (from the **Project** window, select **Create | C# Script**).

- Rename this script **Timer**.

- Add the following code at the beginning of the script.

```
using UnityEngine.SceneManagement;
```

- Add the following code at the beginning of the class.

```
float timer;
int seconds;
```

In the previous code

- We declare a variable called **timer** that will be used to calculate the time; it is declared as a **float**.
- We also declare an **integer** variable called **seconds** (used to store the number of seconds remaining).

- Please modify the **Start** function as follows:

```
void Start ()
{
    timer = 30;
    seconds = 0;
}
```

- In the previous, code we initialize the variable **timer** to **30** and the number of seconds elapsed to **0**.

- Please modify the function **Update** as follows:

```
void Update ()
{
      timer -= Time.deltaTime;
      seconds = (int) (timer);
      print ("Seconds"+seconds);
      if (seconds <= 0)
      {
            int nbLives = PlayerPrefs.GetInt("nbLives");
            nbLives--;
            PlayerPrefs.SetInt("nbLives", nbLives);
            if               (nbLives             >=              0)
SceneManager.LoadScene(SceneManager.GetActiveScene().name);
            else SceneManager.LoadScene("lose");
      }
}
```

In the previous code:

- We use the variable **Time.deltaTime** to update the variable **timer**; **Time.deltaTime** is the number of seconds elapsed since the last frame; so it effectively returns the number of seconds, regardless of the computer where the game is played; this solves any possible issue (or differences) linked to frame rate, so that the time is consistent across players.

- We decrease the value of the variable **timer**.

- We then convert the **timer** from a **float** type to an **integer**; this is because we don't need the decimals values; this will also be useful if we want to display the time onscreen without the decimals.

- We then check for the value of the variable **seconds**.

- If it is **0** or less (i.e., if the time is up) we update the number of lives and restart the current level or load the scene called **lose**.

That's it!

You can now drag and drop the script **Timer** to the object **timer** and play the scene; please check that you can see the time displayed in the **Console** window and that the scene restarts if the time is up.

You may notice that the last part of the code is identical to the code included in the script **DetectCollision**; in fact, it is an exact copy/paste from it:

```
int nbLives = PlayerPrefs.GetInt("nbLives");
nbLives--;
PlayerPrefs.SetInt("nbLives", nbLives);
if                    (nbLives                >=                0)
SceneManager.LoadScene(SceneManager.GetActiveScene().name);
else SceneManager.LoadScene("lose");
```

So what we could do, instead of repeating this code, and also to have it in only one place (i.e., this is neater and more practical), is the following:

- Create a function in the script **DetectCollsion**, that executes this code.

- Call this function from the script **Timer** when needed.

So let's do just that:

- Please open the script called **DetectCollision**.

- Locate the following code.

```
nbLives = PlayerPrefs.GetInt("nbLives");
nbLives--;
PlayerPrefs.SetInt("nbLives", nbLives);
if                    (nbLives                >=                0)
SceneManager.LoadScene(SceneManager.GetActiveScene().name);
else SceneManager.LoadScene("lose");
```

- Cut (*CTRL + X*) this code.

- Type the following code exactly where you removed the previous code (new code in bold).

```
if (tag == "avoid_me" || tag == "reStarter")
{
    DecreaseLives ();
    GetComponent<AudioSource> ().clip = hurt;
    GetComponent<AudioSource> ().Play ();
```

- Then create a new function in the same script, and called **DecreaseLives**.

- Paste the code that you have just copied inside this function.

```
public void DecreaseLives()
{
      int nbLives = PlayerPrefs.GetInt ("nbLives");
      nbLives--;
      PlayerPrefs.SetInt ("nbLives", nbLives);
      if (nbLives >= 0)
            SceneManager.LoadScene      (SceneManager.GetActiveScene
().name);
      else
            SceneManager.LoadScene ("lose");
}
```

Note that this function is public, so it is accessible from outside the class **DetectCollision**; this is important as we will need to access it from the script called **Timer**.

Finally, we can now call this function from the script **Timer**.

- Please open the script called **Timer**.

- Replace this code....

```
if (seconds <= 0)
{
      int nbLives = PlayerPrefs.GetInt("nbLives");
      nbLives--;
      PlayerPrefs.SetInt("nbLives", nbLives);
      if                 (nbLives                >=              0)
SceneManager.LoadScene(SceneManager.GetActiveScene().name);
      else SceneManager.LoadScene("lose");


}
```

with this code...

```
if (seconds <= 0)
{
    GameObject.Find        ("player").GetComponent<DetectCollision>
().DecreaseLives ();
}
```

In the previous code, we access the function called **DecreaseLives**, from the script called **DetectCollosion**, that is attached to the object **player**.

That's it.

- Please save both scripts (**DetectCollision** and **Timer**) and test the game.

- Check the time in the **Console** window, and that when it has elapsed the player restarts the level or the scene called **lose** is played.

The last thing we need for this game mechanic is to display the time onscreen; so we will use **UI** elements.

- Please open the scene **level1**, and duplicate the object **livesUI** (that is a child of the object called **canvas**).

- Rename it **timerUI** and move it slightly down so that it does not overlap with the object livesUI.

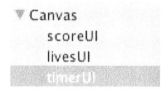

Figure 91: Creating a UI object for the timer

Once this is done, it is time to update the content of the **timerUI** object from our **Timer** script.

- Please open the script called **Timer**.

- Add the following code to the beginning of the script.

```
using UnityEngine.UI;
```

- In the **Udpate** function, replace the code

```
print ("Seconds"+seconds);
```

with…

```
GameObject.Find ("timerUI").GetComponent<Text> ().text = "time: "
+ seconds;
```

- In the previous code, we set the text of the UI Text component to include the message "**time:** " followed by the time in seconds.

- Please save your script.

Last but not least, so that the timer does not appear on the menu scenes, we just need to modify the script called **ControlButtons**.

- Please open the script **ControlButtons**.

- Add the following line to the **Start** function (new code in bold).

```
GameObject.Find ("scoreUI").GetComponent<Text>().text = "";
GameObject.Find ("livesUI").GetComponent<Text>().text = "";
GameObject.Find ("timerUI").GetComponent<Text>().text = "";
```

- Please save your script and test the scene.

That's it; so our time is working fairly well; we just need to make a prefab from it so that it can be reused in other scenes:

- Please drag and drop the object called **timer** from the **Hierarchy** to the **Project** window.

- This will create a prefab called **timer**.

Figure 92: Creating a timer prefab

You can now keep the object called **timer** in the **Hierarchy** or deleted it to use it only in other levels.

CREATING MOVING PLATFORMS.

Moving platforms are also great gameplay elements; they are challenging as the player needs to adjust the timing of the jump to the changing position of the platform. So, in this section:

- We will create both horizontal and vertical platforms.

- Each of these platforms will move forth and back or up and down from their initial position; we will also ensure that the player, once s/he has reached the platform, sticks to it, until s/he jumps again.

- We will then create prefabs from these platforms so that they can be reused in different scenes.

So let's create these platforms.

- Please open the scene **level2**.

As you can see on the next figure, it consists of simple static platforms; so we will modify some of these so that they start moving indefinitely.

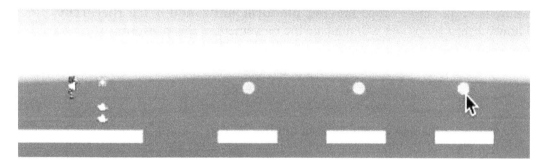

Figure 93: An overview of level2

- Please select the first small platform (the closest to the character), as indicated in the next figure.

Figure 94: An overview of level2

- Drag and drop it (the small platform) to the **Project** view, to create a new prefab.

- Call this prefab **moving_platform_horizontal**.

- Delete the first small platform in the **Scene** view (i.e., the platform that was used to create the prefab).

- Drag and drop the prefab **moving_platform_horizontal** at the same location in the **Scene** view.

You should now have an object called **moving_platform_horizontal** in the **Hierarchy**, and we will now create a script that will manage the movement of this platform.

- Please create a new C# script named **MovingPlatformHorizontal**.

- Open this script.

- Add the following code to it (new code in bold).

```
float timer, direction;
void Start ()
{
        direction = 0.1f;
}
```

In the previous code:

- We declare a variable **timer**, used to time the movement of the platform, as well as a variable called **direction** that will be used to set the direction of the platform (i.e., left or right).

- We then initialize the direction; **1** will be for **right** and **-1** will be for **left**; so initially, the platform will be moving to the right.

- Please add the following code (new code in bold):

```
void Update ()
{
    timer += Time.deltaTime;
    transform.Translate (Vector3.right * direction);
    if (timer >= 1)
    {
        direction *= -1;
        timer = 0;
    }
}
```

In the previous code:

- We use a timer, as we have done in the past; this timer will tick and once it reaches 1 (i.e., one second), we will then change the direction of the platform (to the opposite direction using **-1**).

- We set the direction of the platform to the right (**Vector3.right** multiplied by one).

- If the timer reaches **1** then we change the variable direction to **-1**; this will result in changing the overall direction to its opposite (i.e., **left**), and we then initialize the timer again.

- Please save the script and check that it is error-free.

Once this is done, we can attach this script to the object **moving_platform_horizontal**:

- Please drag and drop the script called **moving_platform_horizontal** from the **Project** window to the object called **moving_platform_horizontal** in the **Hierarchy**.

- Select the object **moving_platform_horizontal** and click on the button **Overrides | Apply All**, to apply the changes to the corresponding prefab.

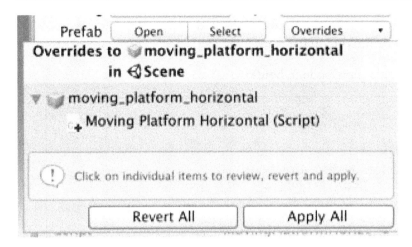

Figure 95: Applying changes to the prefab

- Please play the scene and check that the platform is moving.

As you play the scene, you may also notice that when you are moving on the platform, the character slides on it; so, while this could be an extra challenge, we could, for the time being improve this behaviour so that the player, just after landing on the platform, does not slide (i.e., so that it sticks to it).

- Please select the object called **moving_platform_horizontal** in the **Hierarchy**.

- Create a new tag called **moving_platform** and apply it to this object.

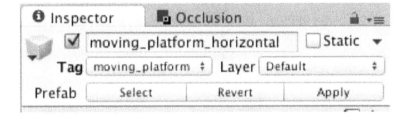

Figure 96: Applying a new tag

- Once this is done, please open the script **DetectCollision**.

- Add this code at the beginning of the class.

```
bool isOnMovingPlatform = false;
```

- This variable will be used to check whether we are on the moving platform.

- Please add the following code to the function **OnCollsionEnter2D**.

```
if (tagName == "moving_platform")
{
    transform.parent = coll.gameObject.transform;
    isOnMovingPlatform = true;
}
```

- In the previous code, if we collide with the moving platform (i.e., the object with the tag **moving_platform**), then the player becomes a child of this object; this means that any movement applied to the platform (e.g., translating to the right or left) will also be applied to the player.

- We also set the variable **isOnMovingPlatform** to **true**.

- You can save your script and test the scene; you will see that when the player jumps on the platforms, it will, without any further action from the payer, move with the platform.

Figure 97: The player moving with the platform

This being said, if you try to jump again from the platform, the movement will not be smooth and it will be difficult to reach the other edge; this is because your movement is then calculated based on the platform which is now the parent of the player; so to remove this issue, we can, specify that the platform is no longer a parent of the **player** object when the player jumps from (or off) the platform;

- Please open the script **DetectCollision**.

- Add the following function.

```
void OnCollisionExit2D (Collision2D coll)
{
    if (isOnMovingPlatform)
    {
        transform.parent = null;
        isOnMovingPlatform = false;
    }
}
```

In the previous code:

- We use the function **OnCollisionExit2D** which is called when the player is exiting a collision with an object; in our case, whenever s/he jumps off the platform.

- In this case we specify that the platform is no longer its parent, using the **null** object.

- We also set the variable **isOnMovingPlatform** to **false**.

That's it!

- Please save your code and test the scene again.

Note: you may notice errors in the **Console** window saying "**Object reference not set..**"; this is because the script **DetectCollision** is looking for one of the **UI** elements that is not present in the scene yet; these elements would usually be created in **level1** and then kept (remember, the score and live UI objects are created in the first scene and then kept); so you may ignore these messages for the time being, as you are testing this scene independently.

So that is working well; we can now update and save our moving platform prefab.

- Select the object **moving_platform_horizontal** and, using the **Inspector**, click on the button **Overrides | Apply All**, located in the top-right corner of the **Inspector** window, to apply the changes to the corresponding prefab.

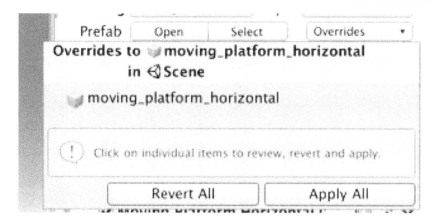

Figure 98: Applying changes to the prefab

Last but not least, we could create moving platforms that move, this time, vertically, just like an escalator. The principle will be the exact same as what we have done so far, except that the movement will be using the up and down directions. For this we will duplicate both the prefab and the script used for the horizontal moving platform and modify these slightly.

- Using the **Project** window, please duplicate the prefab called **moving_platform_horizontal**, and rename it **moving_platform_vertical**.

Figure 99: Duplicating the platform prefab

- Duplicate the script **MovingPlatformHorizontal** and rename it **MovingPlatformVertical**.

- As you do so, Unity may let you know of an error; this is because the name of the new script (**MovingPlatformVertical**) does not match the name of the class inside this script (**MovingPlatformHorizontal**).

- Please open the script **MovingPlatformVertical** and modify the first line as follows.

- Change this code...

```
public class MovingPlatformHorizontal: MonoBehaviour {
```

to…

```
public class MovingPlatformVertical : MonoBehaviour {
```

This will remove the error due to the clash between the name of the class and the name of the script.

We can now change the movement of the platform:

- Please change the line…

```
transform.Translate (Vector3.right * direction);
```

to …

```
transform.Translate (Vector3.up * direction);
```

- You can now save the script.

We just need to link this new script to the corresponding prefab.

- Please select the prefab **moving_platform_vertical** from the **Project** window.

- Using the **Inspector** window, remove the script component **MovingPlatformHorizontal** from this prefab: right-click on the component **MovingPlatformHorizontal**, and select **Remove Component**.

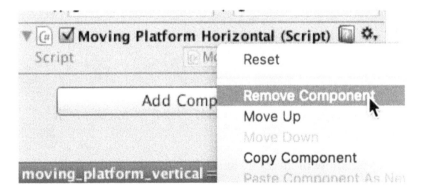

Figure 100: Removing the previous script component

- Now that the previous script has been removed, please drag and drop the script **MovingPlatformVertical** to this object from the **Project** window; this will create a new script component called **MovingPlatformVertical**, as illustrated on the next figure.

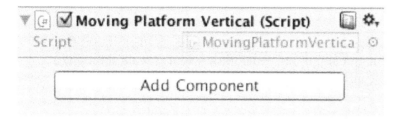

Figure 101: Adding a new script

- Once this is done, we can drag and drop the prefab **moving_platform_vertical** to the **Scene** view; this will create a new object called **moving_platform_vertical** in the **Hierarchy**.

- Please save your scene and test it; you should see both the horizontal and vertical platforms moving at the same time.

Note that you can use and modify this game mechanic to create a moving character from left to right. In this case, every time you change the direction of this character, you can also flip the image horizontally, so that the image matches the direction where this character is going. This can be achieved using **GetComponent<SpriteRenderer>().flipX.** For more information on this function, you can check the official documentation on the following page:

https://docs.unity3d.com/ScriptReference/SpriteRenderer-flipX.html

Using this same game mechanic, you could also create two spikes moving vertically, one moving up and one moving down at the same time; these could be made of triangles, for example.

CREATING MAGIC DOORS

So our platforms are working well, and it would be great to add another interesting gameplay element called **magic door**; put simply, if you collide with (or walk through) a special object, your player will be teleported to a different part of the level.

Let's create this feature:

- Please open the first level (**level1**).

- Create a new sprite (i.e., square), using the **Project** window (**Create | Sprites | Square**), and rename it **door**.

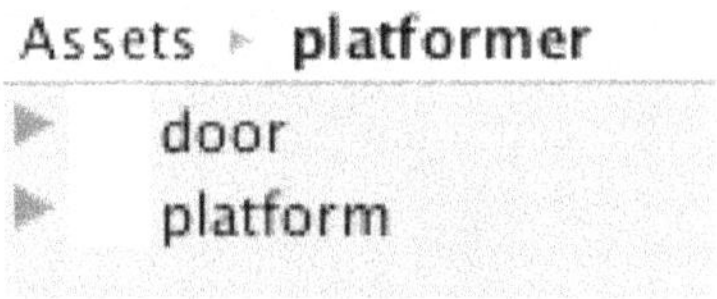

Assets ▸ **platformer**

▸   door
▸   platform

Figure 102: Creating a new sprite

- Once this is done, you can drag and drop this asset to the scene, it will create an object called **door**.

- Please rename this new object **magic_door_entrance**.

- Duplicate this object and rename the duplicate **magic_door_exit**.

- Move the first one (i.e., the object **magic_door_entrance**) just before the boulders and the second one just after the boulders; the idea will be that the player will be able to avoid going through the boulders by just entering the magic door, as described on the next figure.

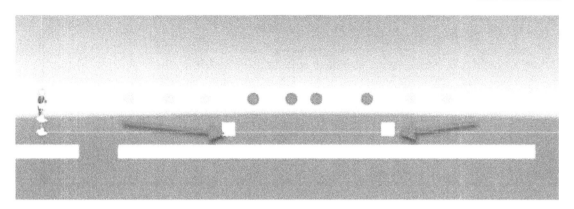

Figure 103: Adding the magic entrance

Once this is done, we will modify the properties of these objects:

- Please select the object **magic_door_entrance** in the **Hierarchy**.

- Add a **Box Collider2D** to it: select **Component | Physics2D | Box Collider2D**.

- Using the **Inspector**, modify the attribute **Is Triger** to true for the component **Box Collider2D** for this object.

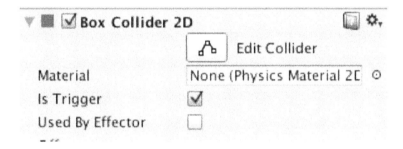

Figure 104: Setting the collider as a trigger

So, what is the difference between a trigger and a collider?

Well, when a collider is added to an object, it will collide with the other objects; in this case, the function **OnCollisionEnter2D** will be called; however, when the attribute called **Is Trigger** is set to true, this object becomes a trigger; this means that the object no longer has the ability to collide with other objects; however, its shape is used to define a space that is used as a trigger; in other words, by entering this space the trigger is set (i.e., we detect that an object has entered this area); in this case, the function **OnTriggerEnter2D** is called instead.

Next, we will make sure that the exit is not visible, as we just want the player to be teleported to the location defined by the object **magic_door_exit**.

- Please select the object called **magic_door_exit**.

- Using the **Inspector** window, please deactivate its **Sprite Renderer** component (i.e., for the object **magic_door_entrance**).

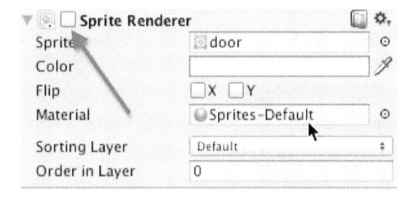

Figure 105: Deactivating the Sprite Renderer

Once this is done, we can then modify the code in the script called **DetectCollision**, so that our player is **teleported** to the second door upon entering the trigger defined by the first one.

- Please open the script **DetectCollision**, and add the following function:

```
void OnTriggerEnter2D(Collider2D coll)
{
     if (coll.gameObject.name == "magic_door_entrance")
     {
          transform.position            =            GameObject.Find
("magic_door_exit").transform.position;
     }
}
```

In the previous code:

- We use the function **OnTriggerEnter2D**.

- We check for the name of the trigger that we are entering.

- If it is the **entrance**, we then move our player to the position of the **exit**.

Please save this script and test the scene. As the character walks through the entrance, it will then appear directly at the exit.

Once you have checked that the magic doors are working, we can create a prefab accordingly by doing the following:

- Create an empty object called **magic_doors**.

- Using the **Hierarchy** window, drag and drop the objects **magic_door_entrance** and **magic_door_exit** on the empty object **magic_doors**, so that they become children of this object, as illustrated on the next figure.

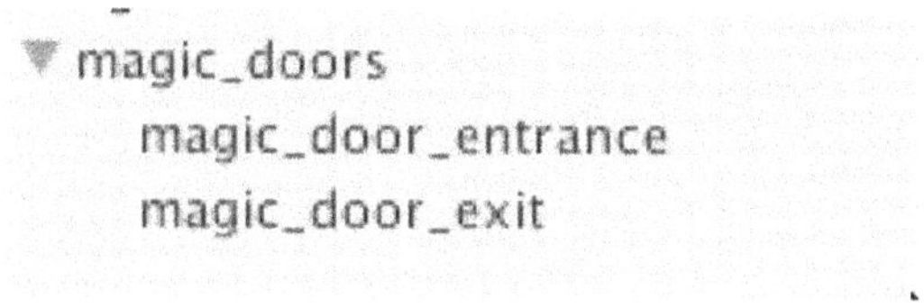

▼ magic_doors
     magic_door_entrance
     magic_door_exit

Figure 106: Grouping the two doors

- We can then drag and drop the object called **magic_doors** to the **Project** window, to create a corresponding prefab that can be used in other scenes.

Figure 107: Creating a prefab for the doors

Note that, when reusing this prefab, you can move each door separately to different locations to match your level and design.

CREATING A SHAKY BRIDGE

In this section, we will create a shaky bridge, a bridge that collapses as the player walks on it. For this, we will reuse the **small_platform** prefab and modify it by adding a **Rigidbody2D** component to it. We will then either activate or deactivate the gravity on this object so that it starts to fall only when the player collides with it.

So let's get started:

- Please duplicate the scene **level2**: in the **Project** window, select the scene **level2** and then press *CTRL + D (or APPLE + D)*.

- This will create a new scene called **level3**.

- Remove all the objects present in the scene except from the player, the mini-camera, and the platform that is underneath the player.

- In the **Project** window, locate the prefab called **small_platform** (to make things easier, you can use the search window located in the **Project** view).

- Duplicate the prefab **small_platform** and rename the duplicate **shaky_step**.

> If you can't find the **small_platform** prefab, you can still open **level2** and create a prefab from one of the **small_platform** object present in the scene.

- Drag and drop this new prefab (**shaky_step**) to the **Scene** view three times to create three steps as per the next figure.

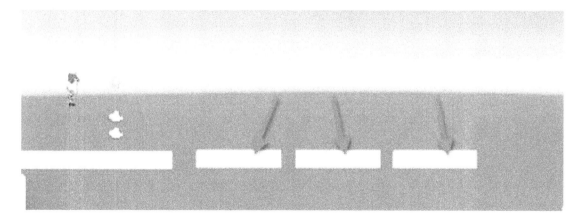

Figure 108: Creating more steps

Once this is done, we will modify these objects:

- Please select thee three steps in the **Hierarchy**.

Note that you can select several objects by pressing the *CTRL* key, as you click on these items individually in the **Hierarchy**.

- From the top menu, select **Component | Physics2D | RigidBody2D**; this will add a **Rigidbody** component to these objects so that they can fall (i.e., subject to gravity).

Once this is done, we just need to make sure that these start to fall only when the player collides with them.

- Please create a new C# script called **ShakyStep**.

- Add the following code to it (new code in bold).

```
void Start () {
    GetComponent<Rigidbody2D> ().isKinematic = true;
}
void Update () {

}
void OnCollisionEnter2D (Collision2D coll)
{
    GetComponent<Rigidbody2D> ().isKinematic = false;
    Destroy (gameObject, 3.0f);
}
```

In the previous code:

- In the **Start** function, we access the **Rigidbody2D** component of the object linked to the script (this will be the shaky step), and we set the variable **isKinematic** to true; this will have the effects of keeping the object in place (i.e., removing gravity) for the time-being.

- Then, whenever a collision is detected (we assume that only the player will collide with these steps, but we could also have checked for the name of the object colliding with the step), we set the variable **isKinematic** to false, so that the step can start to fall; we also destroy the step after 3 seconds.

We can now save our script and prefab:

- Please save this script and drag and drop it on all the three steps.

- You can also update the corresponding prefab by selecting one of these steps and by then clicking on the button called **Overrides | Apply All** located in the top right corner of the **Inspector**.

- After this, you can test the scene and check that the steps fall when the player jumps on them.

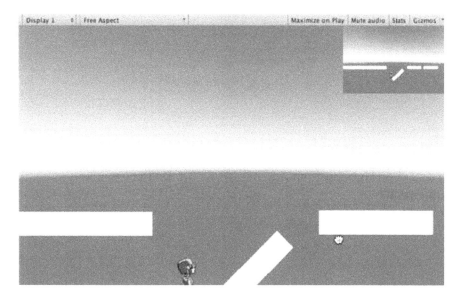

Figure 109: Falling step from the bridge

Once we know that this is working, we could also create a prefab called **shaky_bridge** that includes a series of 10 shaky steps; again, this will make future levels creation much easier.

- Please duplicate one of the shaky steps seven times and arrange all the steps so that the 10 steps form a bridge, with some small gaps between the steps.

Figure 110: Creating a bridge

- Create an empty object called **shaky_bridge**.

- In the **Hierarchy**, drag and drop all the shaky steps to this empty object so that they become children of this object.

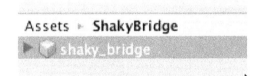

```
▼ shaky_bridge
    shaky_step
    shaky_step (1)
    shaky_step (2)
    shaky_step (3)
    shaky_step (4)
    shaky_step (5)
    shaky_step (6)
    shaky_step (7)
    shaky_step (8)
    shaky_step (9)
```

- You can then drag and drop the object **shaky_bridge** to the **Project** window to create a corresponding prefab.

```
Assets ► ShakyBridge
  ► 🔷 shaky_bridge
```

Last but not least, we will complete this level:

- Please duplicate the long platform and place the duplicate just after the last step (to the right of the scene).

- This will be useful so that you can reuse this level later on if you wish, as part of your game, or simply re-use the prefabs **shaky_step** and **shaky_bridge** to add more challenge to your game.

Please note that, if the steps are very close, they might start to fall, even if the player is not walking on them; this is because of the **Rigidbody2D** component on each of the steps; to avoid this issue, you could, for example, modify the script **ShakyStep**, so that we test first if the collision is with the player (and not with other steps) as follows:

```
void OnCollisionEnter2D (Collision2D coll)
{
        if (coll.gameObject.tag == "Player")
        {
                GetComponent<Rigidbody2D> ().isKinematic = false;
                Destroy (gameObject, 3.0f);
        }
}
```

In this case, you would also need to ensure that the player object has been assigned a tag called **Player**.

INCLUDING LEVEL3 IN THE GAME

As it is, you may notice that **level3** is in isolation, as it is not linked to any of the other levels; so if you'd like it to be accessed through the other levels, you could do the following:

- Add the scene **level3** to the **Build Settings**, as illustrated in the next figure.

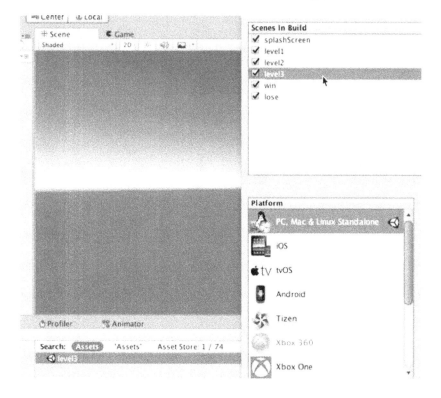

Once this is done, we will need to change the script **DetectCollision**, so that upon completing the second level, the player goes to the **level3** scene;

- Please open the script **DetectCollision**.

- Modify the line that detects the end of level2 as follows (new code in bold).

```
if (tag == "endOfLevel2")
{
    //SceneManager.LoadScene ("win");
    SceneManager.LoadScene ("level3");
}
```

Once this is done, you can save the script **DetectCollision**. The next step will be to create an object that will symbolize the end of level3 and upon collision with this object, the player will be redirected to the win screen.

- Open the scene **level3**.

- In the project window, look for the object called **endOfLevel2** (i.e., the white square).

- Duplicate this object and call it **endOfLevel3**.

- Drag and drop the asset **endOfLevel3** (i.e., the white square) from the **Project** window to the **Scene** view, towards the end of the level.

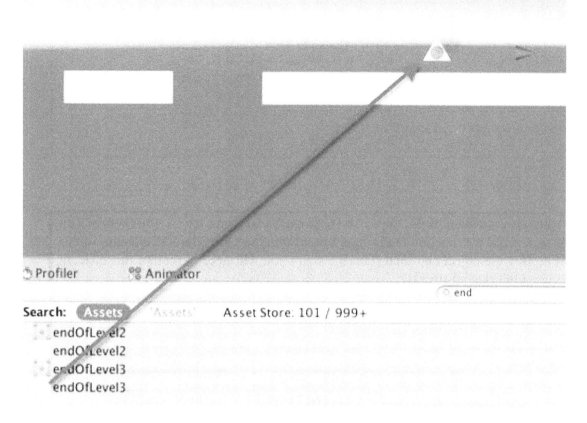

- This will create a new object called **enOfLevel3** in the **Hierarchy** window.

- Add a **Polygon Collider2D** component to this object (**Component | Physics2D | PolygonCollider2D**).

- Create a new tag called **endOfLevel3** and apply this tag to the object **endOflevel3**.

Last but not least, we just need to modify the script **DetectCollision**, so that we can detect when we have reached the end of the third level:

- Please open the script **DetectCollision**.

- Add the following code (new cold in bold).

```
if (tagName == "endOfLevel2")
{
     SceneManager.LoadScene ("level3");
}
if (tagName == "endOfLevel3")
{
     SceneManager.LoadScene ("win");
}
```

If you want the collection of the coins to be smoother, you could set the objects to collect to triggers, and use the function **OnTriggerEnter2D** in the script **DetectCollision**. In this case, to destroy the object collected from the script you will need to replace this code, in the function **OnTriggerEnter2D**:

```
Destroy (coll.collider.gameObject);
```

With this code:

```
Destroy (coll.GetComponent<CircleCollider2D>().gameObject);
```

If you would like the coins to rotate, you could create a new script attached to each coin (or the prefab called **coin**), with the following code:

```
void Update ()
{
     transform.Rotate (new Vector3(0,1,0));

}
```

In the previous code, we rotate the object around the y-axis every frame.

LEVEL ROUNDUP

In this chapter, we have learned how to improve the game by adding some challenging gameplay components, all stored as prefabs, so that they can be reused in other levels.

Checklist

You can consider moving to the next stage if you can do the following:

- Understand how the option **isKinetic** can be used for **Rigidbody** components.

- Understand how **Time.deltaTime** can be used.

- Understand how to modify the position of an object from a script.

Quiz

Now, let's check your knowledge! Please specify whether the following statements are true or false.

1. An object can be moved from a script using its transform component.

2. **Time.deltaTime** can be used to calculate the delta (difference), in minutes, between two different times.

3. By default, an object with a **Rigidbody2D** component will fall.

4. Using the attribute **isKinematic**, it is possible to ensure that gravity is (temporarily) not applied to an object that includes a **Rigidbody2D** component.

5. To be used as a trigger, an object needs a collider.

6. When an object is used as a trigger, entering its collider will cause the function **OnTriggerEnter2D** to be called.

7. Triggers only apply to square sprites.

8. A scene can be duplicated using the shortcut *CRTL + D*.

9. To copy and paste an object, you can use the shortcut CTRL + D.

10. To update a prefab, you can select an object based on this prefab, select the **Inspector** window, and click the **Overrides | Apply All** button.

Answers to the Quiz

1. TRUE.

2. FALSE.

3. TRUE.

4. TRUE.

5. TRUE.

6. TRUE.

7. FALSE.

8. TRUE.

9. TRUE.

10. TRUE.

Challenge 1

For this chapter, you can improve and expand your existing scenes by adding some of the game mechanics that we have just created; these include:

- Horizontal moving platforms.
- Elevators made of vertical moving platforms.
- Magic doors.
- Shaky bridges.

Challenge 2

You can also try to export your game for the web or as a standalone application:

- Open the **Build Settings**.

- Select the type of export (e.g., Mac/PC/WebGL).

- Click **Build and Run**.

CHAPTER 5: PLATFORM GAME: FREQUENTLY ASKED QUESTIONS

This chapter provides answers to the most frequently asked questions about the features that we have covered in the previous sections. Please also note that some videos are also available on the companion site to help you with some of the concepts covered in this book.

SCENES

How can I create a scene?

You can create a scene by selecting: **File | New Scene** or by duplicating an existing scene *(CTRL + D)*.

How can I load a new scene from a script?

This scene will need to be added to the **Build Settings** first; then, you can use a code similar to the following to load this scene.

```
Using UnityEngine.UI;
...
...
SceneManager.LoadScene("nameofTheScene");
```

How can I know the name of the current scene from a script?

This can be done by using the following code.

```
SceneManager.GetActiveScene().name;
```

COLLISIONS

What do I need to detect collision?

All objects involved in a collision need to have a **Collider2D** component. Then, you can implement a script that includes the function **OnCollisionEnter2D**.

How do I detect (check the name or the tag of) the object I collided with?

When a collision occurs, the function **OnCollisionEnter2D** will return an object that includes information about the collision; you can use it to access information about the object that you have just collided with, as illustrated in the next code snippet.

```
void OnCollisionEnter2D (Collision2D coll)
{
       string tag = coll.collider.gameObject.tag;
       ...
}
```

What is the difference between a trigger and a collider?

When a collider has been added to a sprite, it can also be set as a trigger; as a collider, it will ensure that the object collides with other objects; in this case, the collision will be detected and processed through the script **OnCollisionEnter2D**; however, in the case of a trigger, this sprite will not collide with other sprites; instead its shape will determine an area that acts as a trigger when entered by another object; in this particular case the function **OntriggerEnter2D** will be called.

How can I make the collection of the coins smoother?

If you want the collection of the coins to be smoother, you could set the objects to collect to triggers, and use the function **OnTriggerEnter2D** in the script **DetectCollision**. This will ensure that the player does not bounce off the objects to be collected, and that they disappear as the player is very close to them (thanks to the trigger).

SAVING DATA OR OBJECTS ACROSS SCENES

What are player preferences?

Player preferences are data that can be stored and access throughout the game as integers, booleans or strings. They can be compared to global variables because their scope (i.e., where they can be used and accessed) is the entire game; so using this concept, data can be saved between scenes.

How do I store or access player preferences?

Player preferences can be accessed and stored easily using a code similar to the following snippet.

```
int score = PlayerPrefs.GetInt("score");//we write information to
the player preferences
PlayerPrefs.SetInt("score", 10); //we read information from the
player preferences
```

How can I keep objects from being destroyed every-time a new scene is loaded?

You can specify, using the function **Awake**, that the object linked to a particular script should not be destroyed in the next scene; this can be done as follows:

```
void Awake()
{
     DontDestroyOnLoad(transform.gameObject);
}
```

What is the difference between the functions Awake and Start?

The function **Start** is called whenever the script is loaded; so this is usually done at the start of the scene; the function **Awake**, on the other hand, is loaded only once, when the game starts.

SPRITES

Can I create my own sprites in Unity?

Yes, while the 2D assets provided by Unity includes built-in sprites, you can create (and subsequently modify) your own sprites by using the menu **Create | Sprites** from the **Project** window. This makes it possible to create sprites of different shapes including: triangles, circles, or squares. You can also add color to these sprites.

Can I create animated sprites?

Yes, although this is not covered in this book, you can create animated sprites; for this you will need to import several sprites, and then drag and drop the sprites that make-up the animation to the scene view, this will create an animated sprite.

Can I create invisible sprites?

Yes, this can be done by deactivating the **Sprite Renderer** component for a particular sprite.

CHAPTER 6: SPACE SHOOTER (PART 1): CREATING A SIMPLE LEVEL

In this section, we will start by creating a simple level, including:

- A spaceship symbolized by a triangle that you will be able to move in four directions.

- The ability for the spaceship to fire missiles.

- The ability for the player to destroy targets with the missiles.

- A camera that displays the scene.

- Meteorites (or moving targets) generated randomly.

So, after completing this chapter, you will be able to:

- Detect keystrokes.

- Generate random events.

- Instantiate objects.

- Add velocity to objects (i.e., to the moving targets).

- Modify sprites' properties such as their color.

- Move objects from a script.

ADDING THE SPACESHIP

So, in this section, we will start to create the spaceship that will be used by the player; it will consist of a simple sprite (for the time-being) that we will be able to move in four directions using the arrow keys on the keyboard: left, right, up and down.

So, let's get started:

- Please launch Unity and create a new Project (**File | New Project**).

Figure 111: Creating a new project

- In the new window, you can specify the name of your project, its location, as well as the **2D** mode (as this game will be **2D**).

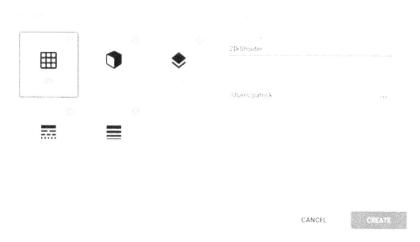

Figure 112: Specifying the name and location for your project

- Once this is done, you can click on the button called **Create** (at the bottom of the window) and Unity should open.

- Once this is done, you can check that the 2D mode is activated, based on the 2D logo located in the top right-corner of the **Scene** view.

Figure 113: Activating the 2D mode

We will now create a new sprite for our spaceship; it will be made of a simple triangle.

- From the **Project** view, please select **Create | Sprites | Triangle**, as illustrated on the next figure.

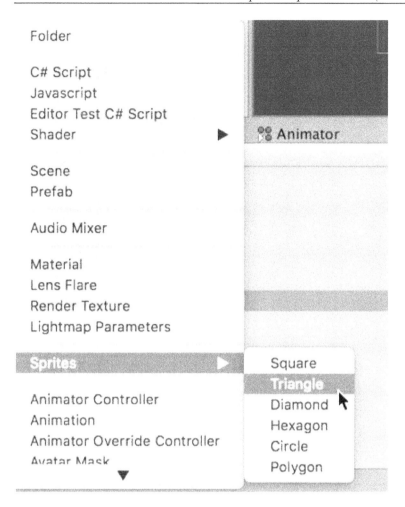

Figure 114: Creating a new sprite

- This will create a new asset called **Triangle** in the **Project** window.

Figure 115: Creating a new triangle asset

- Once this is done, you can drag and drop this sprite (i.e., the white object with the label **Triangle**) from the **Project** window to the **Scene** view; this will create a new object called **Triangle** in the **Hierarchy** view.

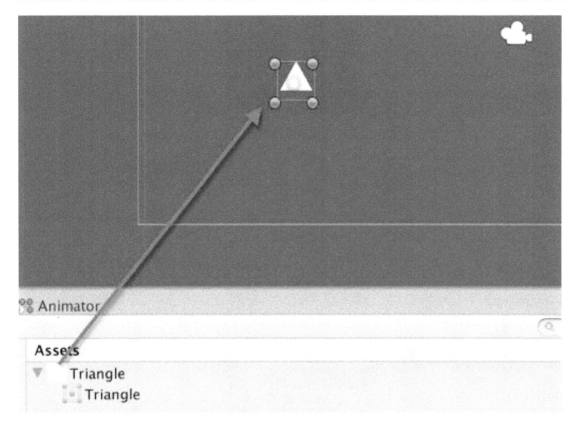

Figure 116: adding the player character

In the previous window, you may notice the white lines at the bottom and to the left of the screen; these are the boundaries that define what will be visible onscreen; so by dropping your object within these lines, you ensure that the player will be seen (or captured) by the camera.

- Please rename this object **player** for now, using the **Hierarchy** window: to rename this object, you can right-click on it in the **Hierarchy** window, and then select the option **Rename** from the contextual menu.

So at this stage, we have a new player character (i.e., the spaceship) and we will need to move it according to the keys pressed on the keyboard; so let's do just this:

- Please create a new C# script (i.e., select **Create | C# Script** from the **Project** window) and rename this script **MovePlayer**.

- Once this is done, please open this script and add the following code to it (new code in bold):

```
void Update ()
{
    if (Input.GetKey (KeyCode.LeftArrow))
    {
        gameObject.transform.Translate (Vector3.left * 0.1f);
    }
    if (Input.GetKey (KeyCode.RightArrow))
    {
        gameObject.transform.Translate (Vector3.right * 0.1f);
    }
    if (Input.GetKey (KeyCode.UpArrow))
    {
        gameObject.transform.Translate (Vector3.up * 0.1f);
    }
    if (Input.GetKey (KeyCode.DownArrow))
    {
        gameObject.transform.Translate (Vector3.down * 0.1f);
    }

}
```

In the previous code:

- We use the function **Update** to check for keyboard inputs.

- If the **left** arrow is pressed, we move the object linked to this script (i.e., the spaceship) to the **left** (i.e., 0.1 meter to the left).

- If the **right** arrow is pressed, we move the object linked to this script (i.e., the spaceship) to the **right** (i.e., 0.1 meter to the right).

Note that we use the function **GetKey** that checks whether a key has been pressed; however, if you wanted to check whether a key has been released then you could use the function **GetKeyDown** instead.

You can now save the script, check for any error in the **Console** window, and link the script (i.e., drag and drop it) to the object called **player** that is in the **Hierarchy** view. Once this is done, you can play the scene and check that you can move the player left or right. After pressing the arrow keys on your keyboard, you should see that the spaceship moves in four directions.

Note that to play and stop the scene, you can press the shortcut **CTRL + P**, or use the black triangle located at the top of the window.

SHOOTING MISSILES

In this section, we will get the player to shoot missiles whenever s/he presses the space bar; this will involve the following steps:

- Creating an object for the missile.

- Saving this object as a prefab (i.e., a template).

- Detecting when the space bar has been pressed (and then released) by the player.

- Instantiating the missile prefab and adding velocity to it so that it moves up when fired.

First, let's create a new object for the missile:

- You can now stop the scene (e.g., CTRL + P).

- Using the **Project** window, please create a new circular sprite (**Create | Sprites | Circle**), and rename it **bullet**.

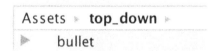

Figure 117: Creating a bullet

- Once this is done, please drag and drop this **bullet** asset from the **Project** window to the **Scene** (or **Hierarchy**) window, this will create a new object called **bullet**.

- Using the **Inspector**, rescale this object to **(0.1, 0.1, 0.1)**. The position of this object does not matter for now.

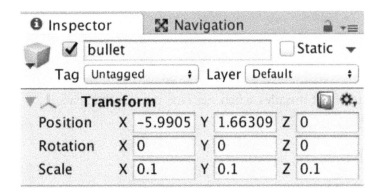

Figure 118: Scaling-down the bullet

- Add a **Rigidbody2D** component to this object (i.e., select **Components | Physics2D | Rigidbody2D** from the top menu) and set the **Gravity Scale** attribute of this component (i.e., **Rigidbody2D**) to **0,** as illustrated in the next figure.

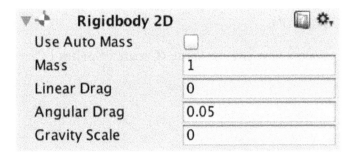

Figure 119: Setting the gravity scale

By adding a **Rigidbody2D** component to this object, we ensure that we can apply forces to it, or modify its velocity; this being said, because we have a top-down view, we do not want this object to be influenced by gravity (otherwise it would fall down), and this is why we set the **Gravity Scale** attribute to **0** for this object.

- We can now convert this **bullet** to a prefab by dragging and dropping this object (i.e., **bullet**) to the **Project** view.

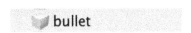

Figure 120: Creating a prefab for the bullet

- You can now delete the object called **bullet** from the **Hierarchy**.

Last but not least, we need to add some code that will be used to instantiate and propel this bullet if the player presses the space bar.

- Please open the script called **MovePlayer**.

- Add the following code at the beginning of the script (new code in bold).

```
public class MovePlayer : MonoBehaviour
{
    public GameObject bullet;
```

- Please add the following code to the **Update** function:

```
if (Input.GetKeyDown (KeyCode.Space))
{
    GameObject    b    =    (GameObject)(Instantiate    (bullet,
transform.position + transform.up*1.5f, Quaternion.identity));
    b.GetComponent<Rigidbody2D>   ().AddForce   (transform.up   *
1000);
}
```

In the previous code:

- We create a new **GameObject**.

- This **GameObject** will be based on the template called **bullet**.

- If the player hits the space bar, the new bullet is instantiated just above the spaceship.

- We then add an upward force to the bullet so that it starts to move.

You can now save your script, and check that it is error-free in the **Console** window.

- If you click on the object called **player** that is present in the **Hierarchy**, and if you look at the **Inspector**, you should see that a new field called **bullet** has appeared for the component **MovePlayer**.

- Please drag and drop the prefab called **bullet** to this field (as illustrated on the next figure).

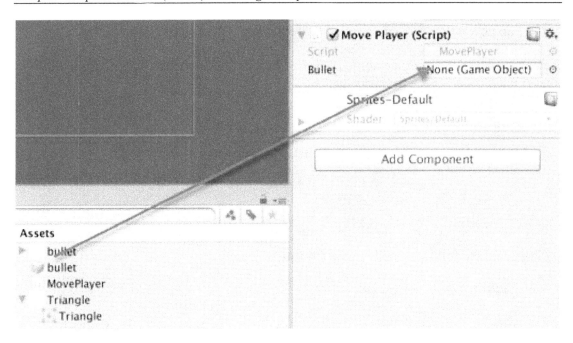

Figure 121:Adding the bullet prefab

Once this done, you can play the scene, and check that after pressing the space bar, you are able to fire a bullet.

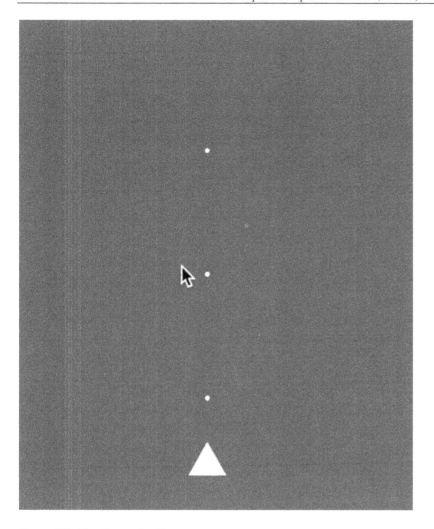

Figure 122: Shooting projectiles

DESTROYING THE TARGET

Now that we can shoot missiles (or bullets), we just need to be able to destroy the objects colliding with the missiles; so we will create new objects that will be used as targets for the time being.

- Please create a new **Square** sprite (from the **Project** window, select: **Create Sprites | Square**).

- Rename this new sprite **target**.

- Drag and drop this sprite to the **Scene** view.

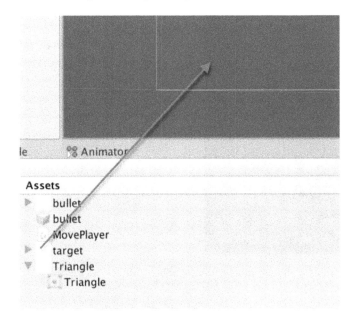

Figure 123: Adding a target to the scene

- This will create a new object; rename this new object **target**.

- Please select this object.

Add a **BoxCollider2D** to this object (i.e., select **Components | Physics2D | BoxCollider2D** from the top menu). This is so that collisions can be detected.

We will now create a new tag for this object. A **tag** will help to identify each object in the scene, and to see the objects that the bullets (or the player) are colliding with.

- Please select the object called **target** in the **Hierarchy**.

- In the **Inspector** window, click on the drop-down menu called **Untagged** (to the right of the attribute called tag), as described on the next figure.

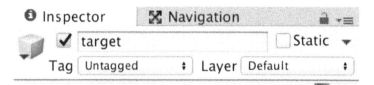

Figure 124: Creating a tag (part1)

- From the drop-down menu, please select the option **Add Tag...**

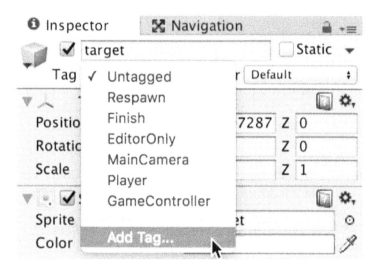

Figure 125: Creating a tag (part 2)

- In the new window, click on the + button that is located below the label "**Tags/List is Empty**".

Figure 126: Creating a tag (part 3)

- Please specify a name for your tag (i.e., **target**), using the field to the right of the label **Tag 0**.

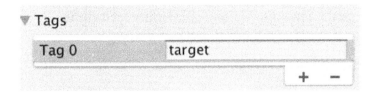

Figure 127: Adding a tag (part 2)

- Press the **Enter/Return** key on your keyboard to save your new tag.

- Select the object **target** in the **Hierarchy** again, and, using the **Inspector**, select the tag **target**, that you have just created.

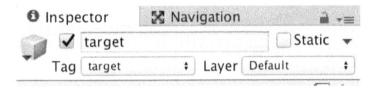

Figure 128: Adding a tag (part 3)

- Last but not least, we will create a prefab from this target by dragging and dropping the object **target** to the **Project** window.

Next, we will create a new script that will be linked to the bullet (or missile), so that, upon collision with a target, this target should be destroyed (based on its tag).

- Please create a new script called **Bullet**: from the **Project** window, select **Create | C# Script**.

- Open this script.

- Add the following code to it (just **after** the function **Update**).

```
void OnCollisionEnter2D(Collision2D coll)
{
      if (coll.gameObject.tag == "target")
      {
            Destroy (coll.gameObject);
            Destroy (gameObject);
      }
}
```

In the previous code:

- We detect the objects colliding with the bullet.

- When this occurs, we check if this object is a target; if this is the case, this target is then destroyed.

- The bullet is also destroyed in this case.

Once this is done, we can save our script and link it to the **bullet** prefab.

- Please save the script called **Bullet** and check that it is error-free.

- Once this is done, please drag and drop it on the prefab called **Bullet**, in the **Project** window.

- You can then click once on the prefab called **bullet**, and check, using the **Inspector** window, that it includes the script **Bullet**.

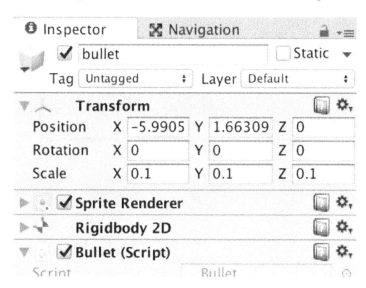

Figure 129: Checking the components of the Bullet prefab

Last but not least, we will need to add a collider to our **Bullet** prefab, so that it actually collides with other objects:

- Please select the prefab called **bullet**.

- From the top menu, select **Components | Physics2D | BoxCollider2D**.

You can now test your game:

- Move the target object just above the **player**, as illustrated in the next figure.

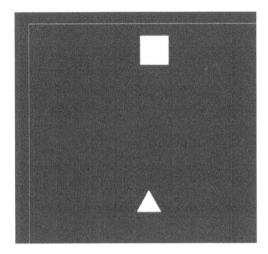

Figure 130: Checking the bullet prefab

- Please play the scene, fire a missile (i.e., press the space bar), and check that, upon collision between the bullet and the target, both objects are destroyed.

Note that since you will be firing several bullets, we could choose to destroy a bullet after 10 seconds (by this time it should have hit a target), by modifying the script **Bullet** as follows (new code in bold):

```
void Start ()
{
      Destroy (gameObject, 10);
}
```

You can test your scene and see that after 10 seconds the bullet is destroyed.

Before we go ahead, it may be a good idea to save our scene:

- Please select **File | Save Scene As** from the top menu, and save your scene as **level1**.

- You can also save your project (**File | Save Project**).

Next, we will just create a slightly different type of target; that is: a moving target that will move downwards and that the player will have to avoid or to destroy; so let's implement this feature:

- Using the **Project** window, please duplicate the prefab called **target**, that we have just created (i.e., select the **target** prefab, and the press *CTRL + D*).

- Rename the duplicate **moving_target** (i.e., right-click + **Rename**).

- Select the prefab **moving_target** in the **Project** window and add a RigidBody2D component to it (i.e., select **Component | Physics2D | RigidBody2D**).

- Using the Inspector window, set its attribute called **Gravity Scale** (for the component **Rigidbody2D**) to 0, as illustrated on the next figure. This is so that the object does not fall indefinitely (since it is a top-down view).

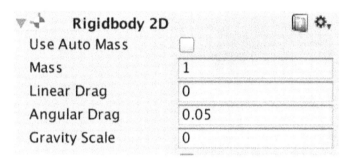

Figure 131: Adjusting the gravity scale

Next, we will create a script that will be linked to this object and that will set its initial velocity downwards.

- Please create a new C# script called **MovingTarget**.

- Modify the **Start** function as follows (new code in bold).

```
void Start ()
{
        GetComponent<Rigidbody2D> ().velocity = Vector2.down * 10;
}
```

In the previous code, we access the **Rigidbody2D** component of the object linked to this script (this will be the moving target), and then set the velocity downwards.

- You can now save your script, check that it is error-free, and drag and drop it to the prefab called **moving_target**.

Figure 132: Linking the script to the target

- So that we can test the scene, please drag and drop the prefab **moving_target** to the **Scene** view and play the scene, you should see that this target moves downwards.

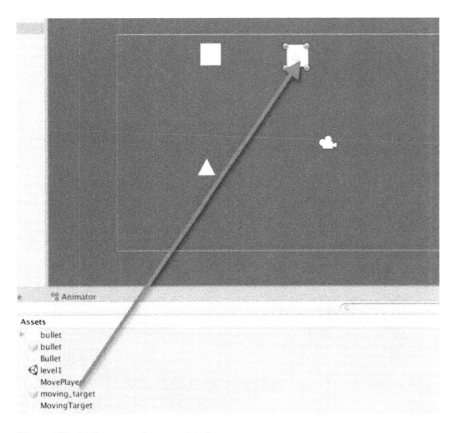

Figure 133: Adding a moving target to the scene

SPAWNING MOVING TARGETS RANDOMLY

Last but not least, we will create a mechanism through which the moving targets are created randomly, a bit like meteorites, so that flying "meteorites" appear randomly onscreen and move downwards. For this, we will be doing the following:

- We will create an empty object that will spawn these moving targets.

- These will be instantiated at regular intervals and at random positions.

- We will also ensure that the moving targets are spawned in the current view (i.e., relatively close to the player so that they can be captured and displayed by the camera).

So let's get to it:

- Please create a new empty object called **targetSpawner** in the **Hierarchy** window (i.e., select **GameObject | Create Empty**).

- Create a new C# script called **SpawnMovingTargets**.

- Open the script.

- Add the following code at the beginning of the class (new code in bold):

```
public class SpawnMovingTargets : MonoBehaviour {
float timer = 0;
public GameObject newObject;
```

- Add the following code to the **Update** function (new code in bold):

```
void Update ()
{
      timer += Time.deltaTime;
      float range = Random.Range (-10, 10);
      Vector3        newPosition        =        new        Vector3
(GameObject.Find("player").transform.position.x        +        range,
transform.position.y, 0);
      if (timer >= 1)
      {
            GameObject t = (GameObject)(Instantiate (newObject,
newPosition, Quaternion.identity));
            timer = 0;
      }
}
```

In the previous code:

- We increase the value of our timer every seconds.

- We then define a variable called **range**; it will be a random number between **-10** and **10**; this variable will be used to define a random position that is to the left (i.e., **-10 to 0**) or to the right (i.e., **0 to +10**) of the player; this is so that the target instantiated is close enough to the player and within the field of the view of the camera.

- We then create a new vector called **newPosition** that uses the variable **range** defined earlier for the **x coordinate;** the **y-coordinate** of the object linked to this script (this will be the empty object **targetSpawner**) is then used for the **y-coordinate** of the object that is being instantiated.

- A new object is then instantiated every second: every time the value of the variable **timer** is greater than 1, **timer** is reset to 0 and a new prefab (i.e., moving target) is instantiated

There are of course many other ways to create this feature, but this version is relatively simple, to start with.

Next, we just need to set-up the **targetSpawner** object:

- Please check that the script that you have just created is error-free.

- Drag and drop this script (i.e., **SpawnMovingTargets**) to the object called **targetSpawner** in the **Hierarchy**. Alternatively, you can add the script to the object **targetSpawner** by selecting this object in the **Hierarchy**, and by then dragging and dropping the script (i.e., **SpawnMovingTargets**) to the **Inspector** window, as illustrated on the next figure.

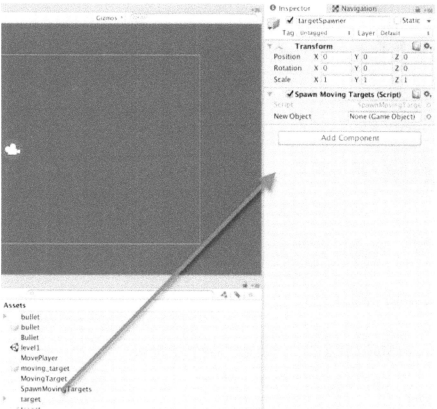

Figure 134: Adding a script to the object targetSpawner

- Please select the object **targetSpawner** in the **Hierarchy** window.

- Drag the prefab called **moving_target** from the **Project** window to the field called **newObject** in the **Inspector**, as described in the next figure.

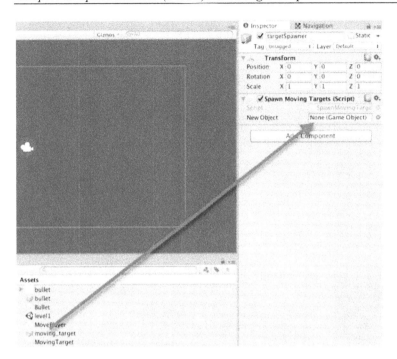

Figure 135: Setting the prefab to be spawn (part 1)

- The component **SpawnMovingTarget** should then look as follows.

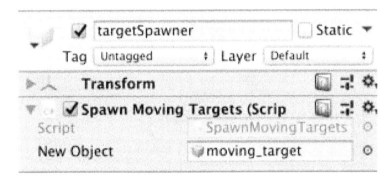

Figure 136: Setting the prefab to be spawn (part 2)

Last, using the **Scene** view, we just need to move the object called **targetSpawner** at the upper boundary of the screen; this is so that the moving targets are instantiated at the very top of the screen, just above the player.

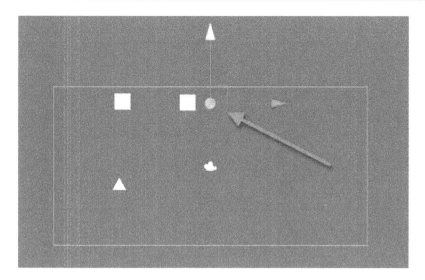

Figure 137: Moving the targetSpawner object

Once this is done, you can delete or deactivate the objects called **moving_target** and **target** that are already in the scene (i.e., the two squares that you could see in the previous figure), and test the scene. To deactivate these objects, you can select them and, using the **Inspector** window, uncheck the box to the left of their name.

Figure 138: Deactivating the moving target

Figure 139: Deactivating the target

As you play the scene, you should see that a new moving target is instantiated every second at random, as described on the next figure.

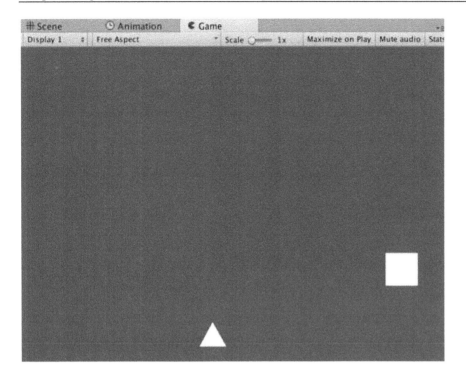

Figure 140: Spawning moving targets

MANAGING DAMAGE

Now that we have created a moving target that the player can shoot, we will create a script that manages the damage taken by the target so that it is destroyed only after being hit several times by the player's bullets.

- Please create a new script called **ManageTargetHealth** (i.e., select **Create | C# Script** from the **Project** window)

- Add the following code at the beginning of the class (new code in bold).

```
public class ManageTargetHealth : MonoBehaviour {
    public int health, type;
    public static int TARGET_BOULDER = 0;
```

- In the previous code, we create three variables: **health**, **type**, and **TARGET_BOULDER**.

- **health** will be used to determine the health (or strength) of each target so that we know how much damage it can sustain before being destroyed.

- **type** is used to set different types of targets; each of these will have different levels of health (or strength).

- **TARGET_BOULDER** will be used as a type for our moving targets (i.e., boulders). Note that this variable is both **static** and **public**; this means that it can be accessed from outside its class; also, because it is **static**, this variable can be accessed without the need to instantiate a new object of type **ManageTargetHealth**.

We will come back to this principle later, but in a nutshell, static variables and functions can be used by other classes with no instantiation required; you can consider these static variables and functions as utility classes and variables that can be used without the need to be part of a particular class, a bit like a friend granting your access to his or her car without the need for you to be the owner. For example, the function **Debug.Log** can be used from anywhere in your game, although, you don't need to instantiate an object of type **Debug** for this purpose; the same holds true for the function **GameObject.Find**; again, you can use this function to find a particular object; however, you don't need to instantiate an object of class **GameOBject** to be able to use this function **Find**.

Now, we just need to specify the health (or strength) of the target, based on its type, in the **Start** function.

- Please add the following code to the **Start** function (new code in bold).

```
void Start ()
{
    if (type == TARGET_BOULDER) health = 20;
}
```

- Add a new function called **gotHit**, at the end of the class (i.e., before the last closing curly bracket) as follows:

```
public void gotHit(int dammage)
{
    health-= dammage;
    if (health <= 0)
    destroyTarget ();
}
```

In the previous code:

- We declare a function called **gotHit**; its return type is **void** because it does not return any value; it takes a parameter of type **int** that will be referred to as **damage** within this function.

- We then set the value of the variable **health** by subtracting the value of the variable **damage** from the previous value of the variable **health**; this is equivalent to the following code:

```
health = health - damage;
```

- If the **health** is **0** or less, we then call the function called **destroyTarget**.

We now just need to create the function called **destroyTarget**.

- Please add a new function called **destroyTarget** at the end of the class (i.e., before the last closing curly bracket) as follows:

```
public void destroyTarget()
{
    Destroy (gameObject);
}
```

In the previous code:

- We create a new function called **destroyTarget** of type **void** (since it does not return any value).

- This function destroys the object linked to this script (i.e., the target).

Once this is done, we can save and use this script:

- Please save your code and check that it is error-free.

- Using the **Project** view, drag and drop this script (i.e., **ManageTargetHealth)** on both the **target** and the **moving_target** prefabs.

Next, we just need to modify the script **SpawnMovingTarget** so that we specify the type of the target that is to be created.

- Please modify the spawning script (i.e., **SpawnMovingTargets**) as follows (new code in bold).

```
if (timer >= 1)
{
    GameObject    t   =   (GameObject)(Instantiate   (newObject,
newPosition, Quaternion.identity));
    t.GetComponent<ManageTargetHealth>          ().type     =
ManageTargetHealth.TARGET_BOULDER;
    timer = 0;
}
```

In the previous code: we specify that the value of the variable called **type**, for the script called **ManageTargetHealth**, that is a component of the object **t** is **TARGET_BOULDER**.

Note that we have accessed the static variable **TARGET_BOULDER** from the class **ManageTargetHealth** without instantiating an object of type **ManageTargetHealth**; this is because the variable **TARGET_BOULDER** is static.

Last but not least, we can add the following code to the script **Bullet**.

```
if (coll.gameObject.tag == "target")
{
      //Destroy (coll.gameObject);
      coll.gameObject.GetComponent<ManageTargetHealth>().gotHit(10
);
      Destroy (gameObject);

}
```

You can now play the scene and test that the moving targets disappear after being hit twice.

For testing purposes, you can also drag and drop the script **ManageTargetHealth** on the prefab called **target**, reactivate the object **target** in the **Scene** view, and then fire bullets at this target. It should disappear after two bullets have been fired.

LEVEL ROUNDUP

In this chapter, we have learned how to create a simple level with a spaceship, for the player, that can fire missiles and destroy static or moving targets. We also managed to create moving targets spawn at regular intervals but at random locations. Finally, we also learned to create **Rigidbody2D** and **BoxCollider2D** components and detect collision between the player's bullets and the targets. So, we have covered considerable ground to get you started with the first level of your 2D shooter.

Checklist

You can consider moving to the next stage if you can do the following:

- Apply **Rigidbody2D** and **BoxCollider2D** components.

- Detect the keys pressed on the keyboard.

- Know the difference between **Input.GetKey** and **Input.GetKeyDown**.

- Apply a tag to an object.

- Understand how to generate random numbers.

- Detect collision from a script.

- Detect a tag from a script.

Quiz

Now, let's check your knowledge! Please answer the following questions (the answers are included in the resource pack) or specify if these statements are either correct or incorrect.

11. The method **Random.GenerateRandomNumber** is used to generate random numbers.

12. Sprites can be created using the menu **Create | Sprite**.

13. The function **Input.GetKeyDown** is called to detect when a key has been pressed and subsequently released.

14. The function **Input.GetKey** is called whenever a key is being pressed.

15. Static variables cannot be accessed outside their class.

16. The following code will add force to the **Rigidbody2D** component of the object linked to the script .

```
GetComponent<Rigidbody2D> ().AddForce (transform.up * 1000);
```

17. The following code will destroy 10 instances of the current object:

```
Destroy (gameObject, 10);
```

18. When a collision between two objects (each with a 2DCollider) occurs, the function **OnCollisionEnter2D** is called.

19. A function of type **void** does not return any value.

20. Only square sprites can be created in Unity.

Challenge 1

Now that you have managed to complete this chapter and that you have created your first level, you could improve the level by doing the following:

- Modify the color of each target.

- Modify the speed (or frequency) at which the moving targets are created.

Challenge 2

Now that you have managed to complete this chapter and that you have created your first level, you could improve it by doing the following:

- In the script **ManageTargetHealth**, create different types of targets; for example:

```
public static int TARGET_BOULDER_2 = 1;
```

- In the same script, modify the **Start** function so that the health of this particular target is set accordingly (i.e., different strength for different targets). For example:

```
If (type == ) health =;
```

- Modify the script **SpawnMovingTarget**, so that the boulder created is created at random; for example, you could generate a number between 1 and 2; based on this number, you will generate a boulder of type 0, or a boulder of type 1.

CHAPTER 7: SPACE SHOOTER (PART 2): ADDING SPECIAL EFFECTS

In this section, we will learn how to create special effects for our initial game to provide more visual feedback to the player when targets have been hit, and to also provide the illusion of movement by adding a scrolling background.

After completing this chapter, you will be able to:

- Access and modify the color of objects at run-time to make them blink temporary.

- Create a simple scrolling background.

- Know how to use the **Sprite Editor**.

- Create animated images that will be used for explosions.

- Understand how to import and slice sprite sheets to create animations.

INTRODUCTION

In this chapter, we will learn how to create visual effects when the target has been hit (a blinking color) and destroyed (i.e., explosion). We will also create a scrolling background from a texture to give the impression of continuous movement.

ADDING SPECIAL EFFECTS TO THE TARGETS

In this section we will add some special effects when the targets are being hit.

When they are hit, they should blink blue. For this we will proceed as follows:

- When the object is hit, we will change its color to red.
- We will then start a timer that will count for 0.2 seconds.
- Once the .2 seconds have elapsed, we will then switch this object back to its original color.

So let's proceed:

- Please open the script called **ManageTargethealth**.

- Add this code at the beginning of the class.

```
public bool isBlinking = false;
public float timer;
public Color previousColor;
```

In the previous code:

- We declare three variables.

- The variable **isBlinking** will be used to determine if the object is blinking (i.e., if it is being hit).

- The variable **timer** will be used so that a new color is applied to this object for a few milliseconds; this will create a blinking effect.

- The variable **previousColor** will be used to save the color of the target before it starts to blink, so that this color can be applied again after the color change.

Please add this code in the **gotHit** function (new code in bold).

```
public void gotHit(int dammage)
{
     health-= dammage;
     if (health <= 0) destroyTarget ();
     previousColor = GetComponent<SpriteRenderer> ().color;
     GetComponent<SpriteRenderer> ().color = Color.blue;
     isBlinking = true;
```

In the previous code:

- The initial (i.e., the previous) color of the target is saved in the variable **previousColor**.

- The current color of the target is changed to **blue**.

- The variable **isBlinking** is set to **true**; it will be used to start a timer that will define when the blinking should stop (i.e., to determine how long the blue color should be applied for).

Finally, we just need to restore the previous color, after the delay has elapsed.

- Please add the following code to the **Update** function:

```
if (isBlinking)
{
     timer += Time.deltaTime;
     if (timer >= .2)
     {
          isBlinking = false;
          GetComponent<SpriteRenderer> ().color = previousColor;
          timer = 0;
     }
}
```

In the previous code:

- We check whether the sprite is in the blinking mode (i.e., if it is being hit).
- We then update the variable **timer** every frame.
- Once the time has reached .2 seconds, we then switch back to the original color for our sprite.

Please save the script, play the scene and check that upon firing at a target, its color turns to blue very briefly. For testing purposes, you can activate the object called target and fire at this target and see if it blinks upon being hit), as illustrated on the next figure.

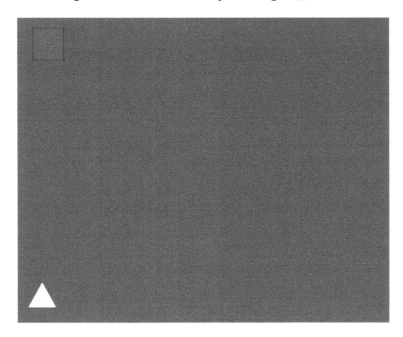

Figure 141: The target blinks after being hit

ADDING AN EXPLOSION

Now that the blinking effect is working, we will create an explosion when the target is destroyed; for this purpose, we will use existing sprites, and then sequence them to create an animation (or an animated sprite); when the target is destroyed, this animated sprite will be spawn at the target's position and subsequently removed once the explosion animation is complete.

- Please open the resource pack provided with this book.

- Import the texture called **explosion.png** from the resource pack folder to the **Project** window in Unity (e.g., drag and drop).

- After importing the texture, Unity will create a new asset called **explosion** in the **Project** window.

Figure 142: Importing the explosion sprite sheet

- Using the **Inspector**, change its **Sprite Mode** properties to **Multiple**, as illustrated on the next figure:

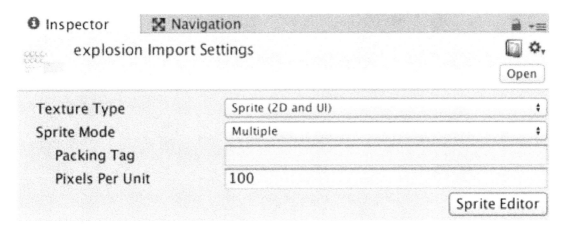

Figure 143: Importing the explosion sprite sheet

- By modifying this property, we indicate that this image includes possible sub-images to be generated for our animation.

- Please click on the button called **Apply** located in the bottom-right corner of the **Inspector** window, as described in the next figure.

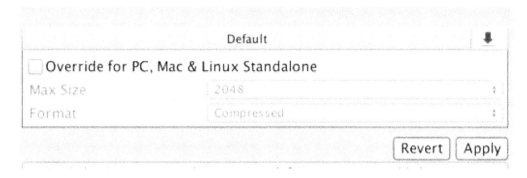

Figure 144: Applying changes

- Then click on the button called **Sprite Editor** (as illustrated on the next figure).

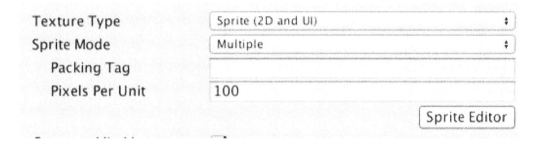

Figure 145: Opening the Sprite Editor (part 1)

- This should open the **Sprite Editor** window.

However, if the following message appears.

Please install the 2D Sprite packacge as follows:

- Select: Window : Package Manager.

- Select the package 2D Sprite.

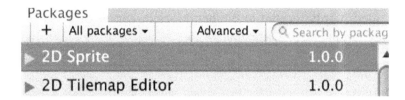

- Select the option to "**Install**".

- Once this is done, please close the **Package Manager** window, and click again on the **Sprite Editor** button; this should open the following window.

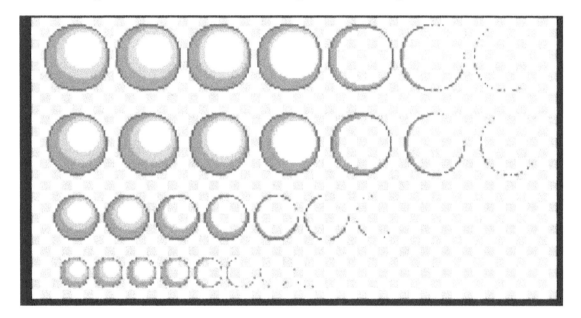

Figure 146: Opening the Sprite Editor (part 2)

The **Sprite Editor** makes it possible to edit sprites; in our case, we have imported a sprite sheet: an image made-up of other sub-images; what we want is to extract some of these images in order to create our animation. The idea is to "slice" this image (e.g., the sprite sheet) into sub-images and then to create an animation based on these "slices".

- When the **Sprite Editor** window opens, please click on the button called **Slice** located in the top-left corner of the **Sprite Editor** window.

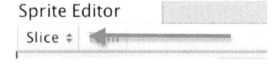

Figure 147: Clicking the Slice button

- A new window will appear.

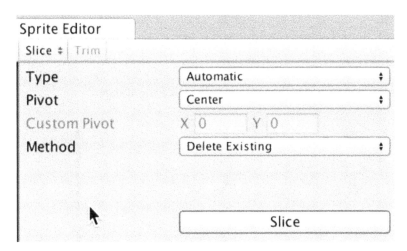

Figure 148: Slicing the sprite sheet (part 1)

- Please modify its settings as per the next figure.

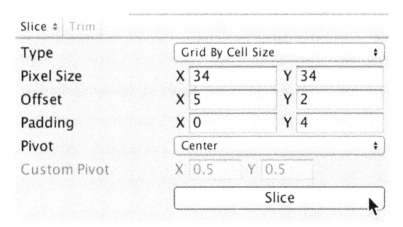

Figure 149: Slicing the sprite sheet (part 2)

The idea of this window is to specify how to capture the sub-images within.

- **Type**: By specifying "**Grid By Cell Size**" we mention that these are laid out as a grid.

- **Pixel Size**: Each sub-image (or sprite) is **34** by **34** pixels.

- **Offset**: For each row, there is a horizontal offset of 5 pixels and a vertical offset of 2 pixels from the start of the image (i.e., from the top-left corner).

- **Padding**: There is also padding between each cells, 0 horizontally and 4 pixels vertically.

- **Pivot**: If an image is rotated, the pivot used for this rotation will be its **center**, by default.

Once this is done, you can press the button called **Slice**, to actually slice the image.

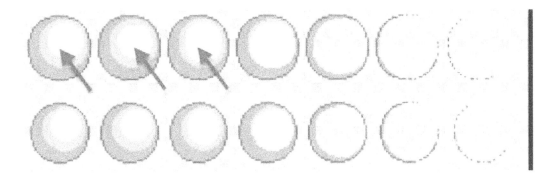

Figure 150: Slicing the sprite sheet (part 3)

- As you can see, we now have managed to define the sub-images from the original file. Each of these is defined by a grey square.

- Once this is done, you can, click on the button called **Apply** at the top of the **Sprite Editor** window.

Figure 151: Applying the slicing settings

- If you look in the **Project** window, you should now see that the original image for the explosion has now turned into a folder with several sprites.

Figure 152: The slices (sprites) from the original image

- If you click on the individual sprites in the list (e.g., **explosion_0**) and look at the **Inspector** window, you will be able to see what they look like; for example, **explosion_0**, may look like the next figure:

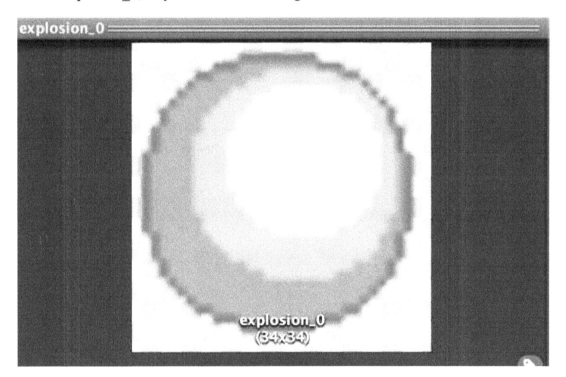

Figure 153: Visualizing the sprite explosion_0

Next, we will create an animation from the first seven sprites; if you remember well, the first row of the original image (i.e., the sprite sheet) included seven sprites that made up the animation that we needed; so now we will create an animation from these images.

Remember, an animation is a succession of sprites that, put together, give the illusion of movement.

- From the **Project** window, please select the seven first sprites (**explosion0**, **eplosion2**, ..., **explosion 6**) that we have created. To select all of these sprites, you can **left-click** on the first sprite (i.e., **explosion_0**), then press **CTRL** and then left-click on the six other sprites individually, as illustrated on the next figure. Alternatively, you can also **left-click** on the first sprite, and then press **SHIFT,** and left-click on the last sprite (i.e., **explosion_6**).

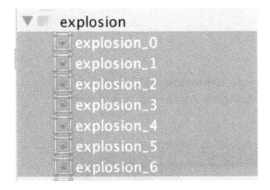

Figure 154: Selecting the seven sprites for the animation

- Once the seven sprites have been selected, please drag and drop these sprites to the **Scene** view, so that Unity can recognise this sequence of sprites (and save them) as an animation.

- As you drag these sprites to the **Scene** view, the mouse cursor will change to display the message <**Multiple**>, as illustrated on the next figure.

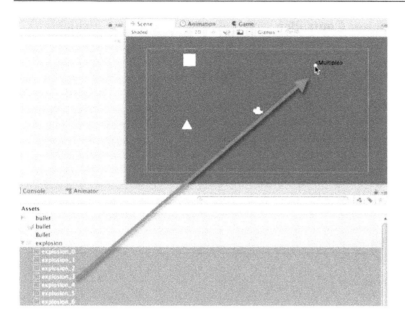

- Once you have dropped the sprites in the **Scene** view, a new window will appear, asking you to save the resulting animation.

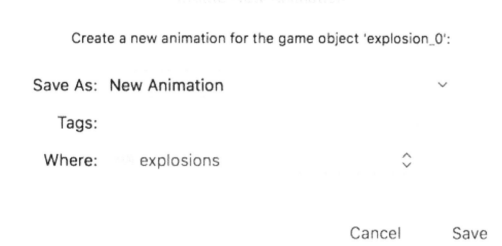

Create a new animation for the game object 'explosion_0':

Save As: New Animation   ⌄

Tags:

Where: explosions   ⌃⌄

                                              Cancel   Save

Figure 155: Saving the animation

- You can call this animation **explosion_animated_1** (or any other name of your choice) and then click on the button **Save**, in the same window.

- This will create three different assets: (1) a new object called **explosion_0** in the **Hierarchy**, (2) an animation called **explosion_animated_1** in the **Project**

[199]

window, and (3) an **Animator Controller** called **explosion_0** in the **Project** window.

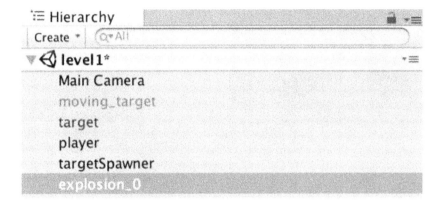

Figure 156: A new object created from the animation

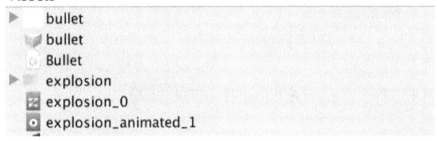

Figure 157: New assets created in the Project window

- In the **Hierarchy** window, please rename the object that you have just created (i.e., **explosion_0**) **explosion**.

If you play the scene, you should see the animated explosion, where you have dragged and dropped the animation in the scene.

You may also notice that the explosion is actually smaller than the target object; so we will rescale the explosion (so that it matches the size of the target) and also create a prefab from it.

- Please select the object called **explosion** in the **Hierarchy**, and, using the **Inspector**, change its scale to **(3.5, 3.5, 1)**;

You may also have noticed that this animation (i.e., the explosion) is looping continuously; however, for our game, we just want it to be played once; so we will modify the animation for the explosion.

- Using the **Project** window, locate the file called **explosion_animated_1**.

Note that you can use the search window located at the top of the **Project** to look for specific assets, and to find them quickly, as described in the next figure.

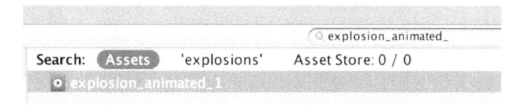

Figure 158: Looking for the explosion animation

- As you left-click on this asset in the **Project** window (i.e., **explosion_animated_1**), you can see its properties in the **Inspector** window.

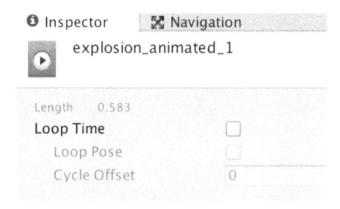

Figure 159: Modifying the explosion animation

- Please, set its attribute **Loop Time** to **false** (i.e., unticked); this means that the animation should not loop.

- Play the scene again, and you should see that the animation is played only once this time.

Once this is done, we just need to create a prefab from this explosion, as we will then instantiate this **explosion** prefab whenever a target is destroyed.

- Please clear the search field in the **Project** view, if you have used it earlier.

Figure 160: Clearing the search field for the Project view

- Please drag and drop the object called **explosion** from the **Hierarchy** to the **Project** window. This will create a new prefab called **explosion**.

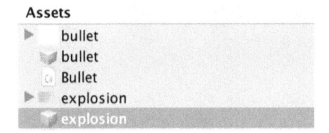

Figure 161: Creating the prefab called explosion

- You can then remove (i.e. delete or deactivate) the object called **explosion** form the **Hierarchy** now (since we have a corresponding prefab now). To do so, you can use the **SUP** or **DEL** keys on your keyboard.

We will then modify the script **ManageTargetHealth**, so that this prefab (i.e., **explosion**) is created at the point of impact between a bullet and a target.

- Please open the script **ManageTargetHealth**.

- Add the following code at the beginning of the script (new code in bold).

```
public float timer;
public Color previousColor;
public GameObject explosion;
```

- Add the following code to the function **destroyTarget** (new code in bold).

```
GameObject    exp    =    (GameObject)(Instantiate    (explosion,
transform.position, Quaternion.identity));
Destroy (exp, .5f);
Destroy (gameObject);
```

In the previous code:

- We instantiate an explosion.
- This explosion is then destroyed after .5 seconds.

Once this is done:

- Please save your script.

- In the **Project** window, select the prefab called **target**.

- Using the **Inspector**, scroll down to the component **ManageTargetHealth**.

- Click to the right of the attribute **Explosion**, as illustrated in the next figure

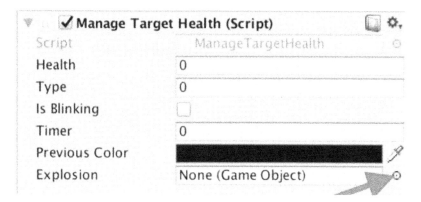

- Using the new window, search for and select the prefab called **explosion**.

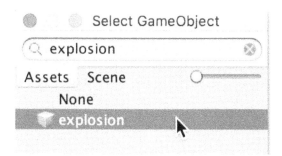

Figure 162: Selecting the explosion

Please repeat these steps for the prefab **moving_target**:

- In Unity, select the prefab **moving_target**.

- Using the **Inspector**, scroll down to the component **ManageTargetHealth**.

- Click to the right of the attribute **Explosion**.

- Using the new window, search and select the prefab called **explosion**.

Before we can play our scene, please makes sure that you have deleted (or deactivated) the explosion that is already present in the scene.

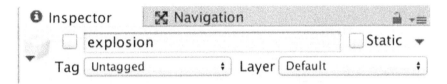

Figure 163: Deactivating the explosion present in the scene

Once this is done, you can play the scene. As you shoot at the static target, you should see an explosion after it has been hit twice; this explosion should then disappear after a few milliseconds.

CREATING A SCROLLING BACKGROUND

Ok, so now that we have created a moving object, we will start to create a moving background to give the illusion of movement; for this, we will do the following:

- Import a texture for our background.

- Modify its properties, so that it can be made scrollable.

- Apply this texture to a **Quad** object.

- Create a script that will make this texture scroll atop the **Quad** object.

So let's get started:

- Please locate the resource pack in your file system.

- Import the texture called **moving_bg_tile** to Unity's **Project** window.

Figure 164: Importing the scrolling background

Once this is done, please select this asset (i.e., **moving_bg_tile**) from the **Project** window and use the **Inspector** window to set its attributes as follows:

- **Texture Type: Default** (we use a texture here, as textures can be made scrollable).

- **Wrap Mode: Repeat** (this is also so that the texture can be made scrollable).

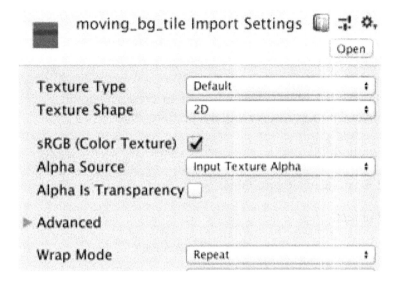

Figure 165: Setting the attributes of the scrolling background

- Once this is done, please click on the button **Apply** located at the bottom of the **Inspector** window, to apply these changes.

Next we will create a new object for our background and apply the texture to it:

- Please create a new **Quad** object (**GameObject | 3D Object | Quad**).

- Using the **Hierarchy**, rename this object **moving_background**.

- Drag and drop the texture **moving_bg_tile** from the **Project** window to this object in the **Hierarchy**.

- Rescale this object (i.e., **moving_background**) by changing its scale properties to **(40, 20, 1)**.

- Change its position to **(0, 0, 0)** so that its centre is close to the centre of the screen, as illustrated in the next figure.

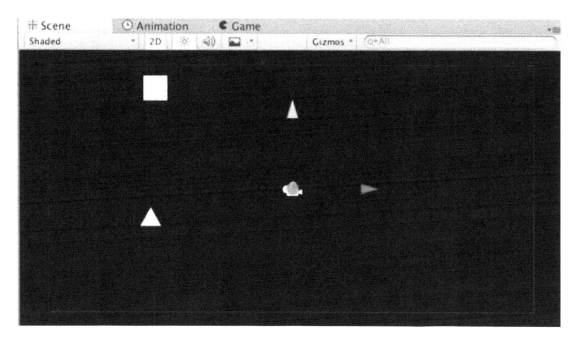

Figure 166: Aligning the moving background with the spaceship

- To check that the backround can be seen properly, please open the light settings (**Window | Rendering | Light Settings**) and make sure that the ambient color is white.

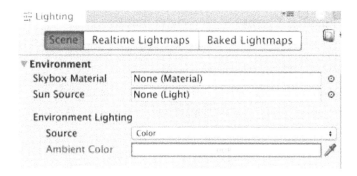

- You can look at the game view, and check that the background fills-up the screen (if not, you can scale-up the background a bit more).

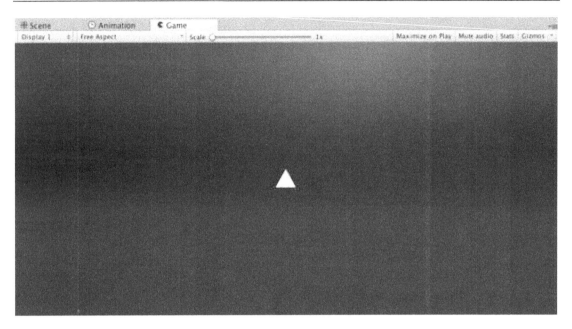

Figure 167: Checking the position of the moving background

Next, we will create a script that will perform the scrolling for us:

- Please create a new C# script and call it **ScrollingBackground**.

- Add the following code to it, in the function **Update** (new code in bold).

```
void Update ()
{
    GetComponent<Renderer>().material.mainTextureOffset  =  new
Vector2 (0,0.5f*Time.time);
}
```

In the previous code,

- We access the **Renderer** component of the object linked to the script. This component can be used to modify the way a texture is displayed; in our case, we will manage its vertical offset.

- We then access the main texture (the texture that we have just added to the Quad).

- We finally modify the vertical offset for this texture; in other words, we move it along the y-axis at .5 units per seconds (this would be 50 pixels per seconds, since our import settings for the background specified 100 pixels per units).

Once this is done; please save your code, check that it is error-free, and drag and drop this scrip on the object called **moving_background**.

- If you select the object **moving_background** in the **Hierarchy** and then look at the **Inspector** window, you should see that it includes the component **ScrollingBackground**.

Please play the scene and you should see that the background is actually scrolling vertically. However, you may also notice that the scene is quite dark, preventing you from seeing the background clearly.

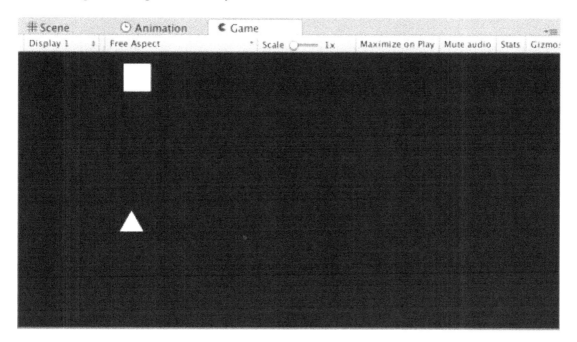

Figure 168: The scene before adding light

So in that case, we could add some light to the scene to solve this issue, as follows:

- Please select **GameObject | Light | Directional Light** from the top menu.

- This will create a new object called **Directional Light**.

- Rename this object **light**.

- Then, select it, and, using the **Inspector** window, change its rotation to **(0,0,0)** and its position to **(0,0,0)**. You can also change its intensity if you wish.

You can test the scene again and the scene should be much brighter.

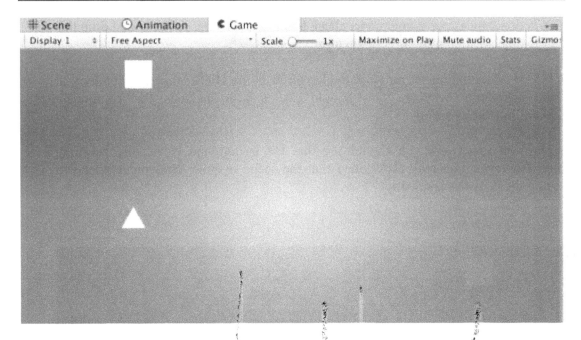

Figure 169: The scene after adding light

LEVEL ROUNDUP

Well, this is it!

In this chapter, we have learned about creating simple but powerful visual effects, including a blinking object, explosions made from sprites, along with a scrolling. So, we have, by now, a very simple but almost complete 2D shooter game.

Checklist

You can consider moving to the next chapter if you can do the following:

- Slice a sprite sheet.

- Create an animation from a sprite.

- Create a scrolling background.

Quiz

It's now time to check your knowledge with a quiz. Please specify whether the following statements are true of false.

1. You can select multiple assets by using CTRL + left-click.

2. You can select multiple assets by using SHIFT + left-click.

3. You can modify (i.e., change the color of pixels of) a sprite using the **Sprite Editor**.

4. For an image to be sliced, its **Sprite Mode** attribute should be set to **Single**.

5. You can create a new button, by selecting **GameObject | Text** from the top menu.

6. The following code will change the color of a sprite to red.

```
GetComponent<SpriteRenderer> ().color = Color.red;
```

7. The following code will scroll a texture vertically.

```
GetComponent<Renderer>().material.mainTextureOffset = new Vector2
(0.5f*Time.time,0);
```

8. The following code will scroll a texture horizontally.

```
GetComponent<Renderer>().material.mainTextureOffset = new Vector2
(0,0.5f*Time.time);
```

9. To create an animation from existing sprites, you need to select these sprites, and then select: **GameObject | New Animation**.

10. To create a directional light, you can select: **GameObject | Light | Directional Light**.

Answers to the Quiz

1. TRUE.

2. TRUE.

3. TRUE.

4. FALSE.

5. FALSE.

6. TRUE.

7. TRUE.

8. TRUE.

9. FALSE.

10. TRUE.

Challenge 1

Now that you have managed to complete this chapter and that you have improved your skills, let's do the following:

- Create your own background with the image editor of your choice, and use it as a scrolling background for the game.

- Modify the blinking color and the blinking speed used when a target has been hit.

CHAPTER 8: SPACE SHOOTER (PART 3): IMPROVING OUR GAME

In this section, we will improve our game by including additional features that will help to keep the spaceship onscreen, to manage its health levels, and to also make the game more challenging with some AI-driven NPCs.

After completing this chapter, you will be able to:

- Check if the player is in the field of view of the camera.

- Apply damage to the spaceship and manage the player's health.

- Include some artificial intelligence to the NPCs.

- Trigger attacks from the NPCs when the player is detected.

INTRODUCTION

In this chapter we will improve the current game by including a few add-ons:

- We will detect if the player is outside the camera's field of view and ensure that it is always visible.

- We will create NPCs, each with artificial intelligence, that will be moving horizontally and shoot at the player.

- We will also manage the player's health and detect when the spaceship has been hit or when it has collided with targets.

KEEPING THE PLAYER IN THE FIELD OF VIEW

So, all works well so far; the only thing is that, as you may have noticed, the player might be going off-screen, at times, and become invisible; so we will build a mechanism that will solve this issue; we will proceed as follows:

- We will need to detect when the player is no longer in the camera's field of view.

- For this purpose, we will need to translate the **world position** of the player into its position in relation to the camera view.

- So, we will convert the position of the player to the actual camera view port.

- We will then ensure that this position, in the camera view, is within the field of view of the camera; the position of the player, if the player is outside the view, may be modified if need be, so that it is no less that 0, but no more than 1. This is because, the position of objects, in the camera view, is using x and y coordinates that range from 0 to 1; for example, along the x-axis, 0 means the left side of the screen, and 1, means the right side of the screen.

- Once we have made sure that the player is in the field of view, we can then convert this position from the referential defined by the camera view (between 0 and 1) to a world position (from 0 to infinity).

Ok, so let's get started:

- Please open the script called **MovePlayer**.

- Add the following code to the function **Update** (at the end of the function).

```
Vector3                    viewPortPosition           =
Camera.main.WorldToViewportPoint(transform.position);
viewPortPosition.x = Mathf.Clamp01(viewPortPosition.x);
viewPortPosition.y = Mathf.Clamp01(viewPortPosition.y);
transform.position                                    =
Camera.main.ViewportToWorldPoint(viewPortPosition);
```

In the previous code:

- We define a new vector called **viewPortPosition**; this vector will be used to define the position of the object in relation to the camera view.

Note that, in the camera view (or **viewport**), objects' positions are expressed using x and y coordinates that range between 0 and 1; for the x coordinate 0 means the left side of the screen and 1 means the right side of the screen. For the y coordinate 1 means the top of the screen and 0 means the bottom of the screen.

- We then clamp the value of both x and y coordinates; in other words, we ensure that their values are within 0 and 1 (i.e., onscreen); this is done using the built-in function **Clamp01**.

- We then translate this position from the camera view (or viewport) to world coordinates using the function **ViewportToWorldView**.

In the previous code, what we have effectively done is a change of referential from the world view, to the camera view, and then back to the world view.

Please check your code and test the scene, you will notice that the player is now always onscreen; however, only half of the player is displayed when you try to move beyond the camera view, as illustrated in the next figure.

Figure 170: Improving position clamping

We could fix this as follows:

- Determine the size of our sprite on the x- and y–axis.

- Calculate how this size can be translated in the view port settings (i.e., what proportion of the screen the sprite would occupy).

- Clamp the player to the size of the screen (height or width) minus the size of the sprite.

- Translate this clamping to world view coordinates.

Please add (or comment) the following code to the script **MovePlayer** (new code in bold):

```
//Vector3                    viewPortPosition            =
Camera.main.WorldToViewportPoint(transform.position);
//viewPortPosition.x = Mathf.Clamp01(viewPortPosition.x);
//viewPortPosition.y = Mathf.Clamp01(viewPortPosition.y);
//transform.position                                     =
Camera.main.ViewportToWorldPoint(viewPortPosition);


Vector3                    viewPortPosition            =
Camera.main.WorldToViewportPoint(transform.position);
Vector3                    viewPortXDelta              =
Camera.main.WorldToViewportPoint(transform.position            +
Vector3.left/2);
Vector3                    viewPortYDelta              =
Camera.main.WorldToViewportPoint(transform.position            +
Vector3.up/2);
```

In the previous code:

- We comment the previous code.

- We create two new vectors: **viewPortXDelta** and **viewPortYDelta**.

- **viewPortXDelta** will be used to determine the relative size of the sprite along the x axis (i.e., its width). Note that we use **Vector3.left/2** because we want to know the distance between the center of the sprite and its edges (i.e., half its width).

- **viewPortYDelta** will be used to determine the relative size of the sprite along the y axis (i.e., its height). Note that we use **Vector3.up/2** because we want to know the distance between the center of the sprite to its edge (half its height).

Note that our sprite, at present, has a scale of 1 on all axes; so the magnitude (length) of the vectors **Vector3.up** or **Vector3.left** will effectively describe the width or height of this sprite; however, if the scale had been **2** on the x axis, for example, we would then need to use **Vector3.left** instead of **Vector3.left/2 (i.e., Vector3.left/2** multiplied by 2).

- Please add the following code in the same **Update** function (new code in bold), just after the previous code:

```
float deltaX = viewPortPosition.x - viewPortXDelta.x;
float deltaY = -viewPortPosition.y + viewPortYDelta.y;


viewPortPosition.x = Mathf.Clamp(viewPortPosition.x, 0+deltaX, 1-
deltaX);
viewPortPosition.y = Mathf.Clamp(viewPortPosition.y, 0+deltaY, 1-
deltaY);
transform.position                                               =
Camera.main.ViewportToWorldPoint(viewPortPosition);
```

In the previous code:

- We declare two variables called **deltaX** and **deltaY**; these will be used to determine the actual distance, in the viewport, between the center of the sprite and its edges.

- We then clamp the position of the sprite using the values that we have calculated earlier; so the minimum x position will be the left side of the screen + half the width of the sprite; the same is done with the y position; all of these changes are done in the viewport referential (i.e., values ranging between 0 and 1)

- As we have done before, these new coordinates are then translated to world view coordinates.

Please save your code and check that it is error-free, and test your game; as you move towards the edges of the screen, you should now see that the player is properly "clamped" to each side of the screen, and that the full triangle is now displayed.

Figure 171: Clamping the player to the bottom-left corner

That's it!

APPLYING DAMAGE TO THE PLAYER

In this section, we will create code to implement a feature whereby, when the moving targets collide with the player, they destroy the player; in this case, the level should also be restarted automatically.

The process will be as follows:

- We will add collision capabilities to our player.

- We will then detect collision with moving targets.

- We will finally restart the level in case of a collision.

So let's get to it:

- Please add a **PolygonCollider2D** to the player: select the **player** in the **Hierarchy**, then select **Component | Physic2D| PolygonCollider2D** from the top menu. This will add a **Polygon2DCollider** to the object, as illustrated on the next figure.

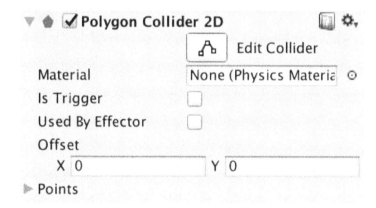

Figure 172: Adding a polygonal collider to the player

In the next sections, the player may be hit by other objects; so the mechanism involved in destroying the player and restarting the game may need to be performed several times (depending on the object that collided with the player); so to centralize this process and to make our code more efficient, we will create a function that manages this aspect of the game (i.e., player colliding with other objects), and add it to a script linked to the player. This way, upon collision with any object, this function will be called accordingly.

- Please create a new script called **ManagePlayerHealth**.

- Add the following code at the beginning of the class.

```
using UnityEngine.SceneManagement;
```

- Add the following functions at the end of the script (i.e., before the last closing curly bracket).

```
void OnCollisionEnter2D(Collision2D coll)
{
    if (coll.gameObject.tag == "target")
    {
        Destroy (coll.gameObject);
        DestroyPlayer ();
    }


}
void DestroyPlayer()
{
    SceneManager.LoadScene (SceneManager.GetActiveScene().name);
}
```

In the previous code:

- We detect collisions with targets.

- In case the player collides with a target, the target is destroyed, and the function called **DestroyPlayer** is called.

- The function **DestroyPlayer** reloads the current scene.

We can now apply this script:

- Please save your script and check that it is error-free.

- Drag and drop this new script (**ManagePlayerHealth**) on the object called **player** in the **Hierarchy**.

- Once this is done, you can test your scene and check that upon colliding with a moving target, that the scene is restarted.

ADDING ARTIFICIAL INTELLIGENCE

So at this stage, the game works relatively well, and we could also add a bit more challenge to it. So, to make this game more challenging to the player, we will add a few NPCs that will move and attack the player.

The NPC that we will add will be moving horizontally from left to right and it will shoot at the player whenever it is in front of the player (or close to it). It will consist of a simple triangle (the same as we have used for the player), that shoots projectiles towards the player, if the latter is detected.

- From the **Project** window, please drag and drop the asset called **Triangle** to the **Scene** view (or **Hierarchy** view), as illustrated on the next figure.

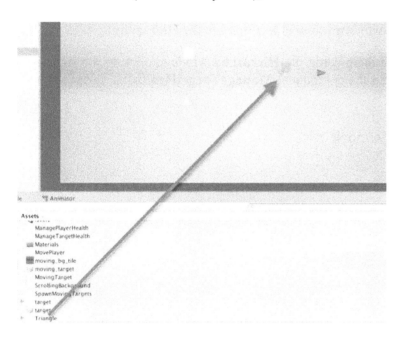

Figure 173: Recycling the triangle to create an NPC.

- This will create a new object called **Triangle** in the **Hierarchy** window.

- Please rename this object **npc1**.

- Using the **Inspector**, change the rotation of this object to **(0, 0, 180)**, so that it looks like the next figure.

Figure 174: Rotating the NPC

- Add a **Polygon Collider2D** to this object: select the object **npc1**, and then select the option **Components | Physics2D | PolygonCollider2D** from the top menu.

- Change its tag to **target**, as we have done previously using the **Inspector** window.

At this stage, we just need to make sure that this object, (i.e., **npc1**), can be destroyed in the same way as the targets that we have created earlier. So we will reuse the script called **ManageTargetHealth**, that was previously employed for the other targets.

- Please add the script **ManageTargetHealth** to the object **npc1** (i.e., drag and drop the script from the **Project** window to the object **npc1** in the **Hierarchy**).

- Select the object **npc1**, and then, using the **Hierarchy** window, click to the right of the attribute **Explosion** for the component **ManageTargetHealth**, as illustrated on the next figure.

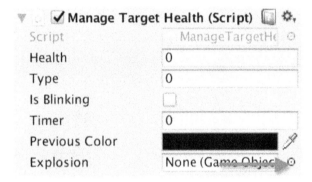

Figure 175: Adding an explosion

- Using the new window, search and select the prefab called **explosion**.

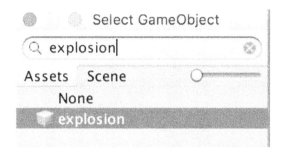

Figure 176: Choosing an explosion for the NPC

Next, we will create a new script that will be attached to the NPC; in this script, we will add some code that moves the NPC from right to left, and that also ensures that the NPC shoots at the player when it is in front of the player.

- Please create a new script called **MoveNPC**.

- Add the following code at the beginning of the class (new code in bold):

```
public class MoveNPC : MonoBehaviour {
public GameObject bullet;
public float direction = 1.0f;
public float timer;
```

In the previous code:

- We declare three variables.

- The variable **bullet** will be used as a placeholder for the bullet that we want to instantiate when the NPC shoots.

- The variable **direction** will be used to determine in what direction the NPC will be moving.

- The variable **timer** will be employed to determine when the NPC changes direction (e.g., from right to left or vice-versa).

- Please add the following code to the **Update** function.

```
timer += Time.deltaTime;
transform.Translate (Vector3.left *direction* Time.deltaTime *
2);
if (timer >= 2) {direction *= -1; timer = 0;}
```

In the previous code:

- We increase the variable **timer** by one, every seconds.

- Every second, we also move the NPC horizontally; it is moved to the left initially, as the value of the variable **direction** is **1** at the beginning.

- Then, after 2 seconds, the **direction** is reversed, and the **timer** is initialized back to **0**; so changes in the direction will occur every two seconds.

We can now save our script:

- Please save your code, and check that it is error-free.

- You can then drag and drop this script (i.e., **MoveNPC**) on the object **npc1**.

Once this done you can test the scene:

- Please deactivate the object **target** (i.e., f this is not already done).

- Move the object **npc1** to the upper boundary of the screen, as illustrated on the next figure.

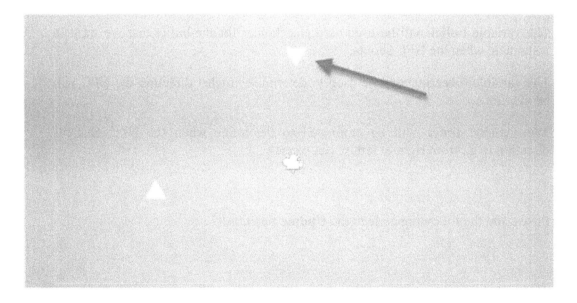

Figure 177: Moving the NPC

- As you play the scene, you should see that the NPC moves from left to right, as illustrated on the next figure.

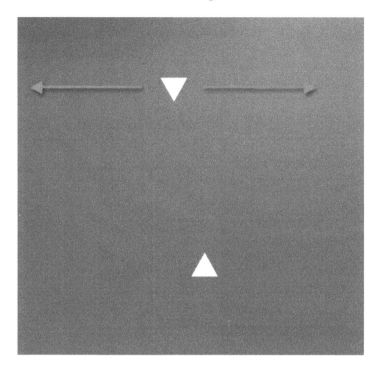

Figure 178: Testing the NPC's movement

Ok, so now that the NPC can move properly, we will add a feature whereby it shoots at the player when in front of the player. For this purpose, we will proceed as follows:

- Detect when the **NPC** is in front of the player.

- Shoot (i.e., instantiate a bullet prefab that moves towards the player).

- Ensure that the shooting stops after a few milliseconds, when the player is no longer in front of the NPC.

So let's start with this feature:

- Please open the script **MoveNPC**.

- Please add the following code to the function **Update** (new code in bold).

```
void Update ()
{
    timer += Time.deltaTime;
    transform.Translate (Vector3.left *direction* Time.deltaTime
* 2);
    if (timer >= 2) {direction *= -1; timer = 0;}
    detectPlayer ();
```

This function (i.e., **detectPlayer**) will be called to check if the player is in front of the NPC.

Now let's declare this function by adding the following code to the class, just after the function **Update**.

```
void detectPlayer()
{
    float          playerXPosition      =          GameObject.Find
("player").transform.position.x;
    if (transform.position.x   <   (playerXPosition   +   1)   &&
transform.position.x > (playerXPosition - 1)) Shoot();
}
```

In the previous code, we calculate the player's position on the **x-axis** and we then call the function called **shoot** if the player is in front of the NPC.

We just need to implement the function called **Shoot** now.

- Please add the following code at the end of the class, just after the previous function:

```
void Shoot()
{
    GameObject     b     =     (GameObject)(Instantiate   (bullet,
transform.position + transform.up*1.5f, Quaternion.identity));
    b.GetComponent<Rigidbody2D> ().AddForce (Vector3.down   *
1000);
}
```

In the previous code

- We define a new function called **Shoot**.

- We create a new object called **b** that is based on the variable **bullet** (the variable **bullet** will be initialized later using the **Inspector**).

- This projectile (i.e., the object called **b**) is then propelled downwards, by accessing its **Rigidbody2D** component and by then exerting a downwards force.

Please save your script and check that it is error-free.

Once this is done, we can now initialize the variable **bullet** defined in this script from the **Inspector**:

- Please, select the object **npc1** in the **Hierarchy**.

- Using the **Inspector**, click to the right of the attribute called **Bullet** for the script **MoveNPC**, as described on the next figure.

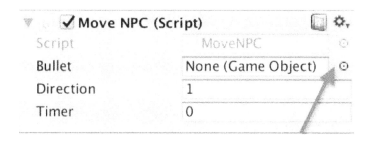

Figure 179: Selecting a bullet for the NPC (part 1)

- Using the new window, search and select the prefab called **bullet**.

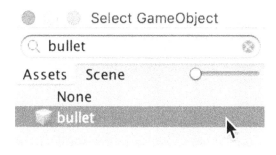

Figure 180: Selecting a bullet for the NPC (part 2)

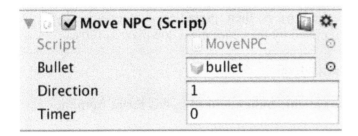

Figure 181: Selecting a bullet for the NPC (part 3)

Now that it is done, you can test the scene and check that the NPC fires bullets in the direction of the player when the player is in front of the NPC.

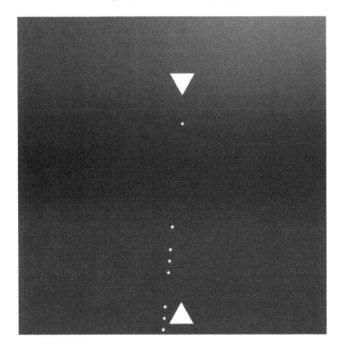

Figure 182: The NPC firing at the player

Now, this works well; however, there are a few things that we could improve, including:

- A slower firing rate for the NPC.

- Collision detection with the NPC's bullets.

- Restarting the level when the player has been shot.

Now, to start with, we will make sure that the game restarts if the player is hit by a bullet; to do so, we just need to add a tag to the bullets fired by the NPC, and then modify the script called **ManagePlayerHealth** to detect collision with these bullets. So, let's proceed:

- Please select the prefab called **Bullet** in the **Project** window.

- Create a new tag called **bullet**, as we have done earlier.

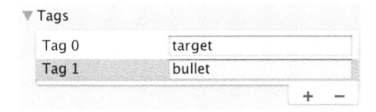

Figure 183: Creating a new tag for bullets

- Apply this tag to the prefab called **bullet**.

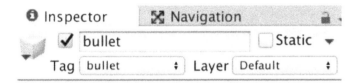

Figure 184: Applying the new tag to the bullet prefab

- Once this is done, please open the script **ManagePlayerHealth**.

- Modify the function **OnCollisionEnter2D** as follows (new code in bold):

```
void OnCollisionEnter2D(Collision2D coll)
{
    if (coll.gameObject.tag == "target" || coll.gameObject.tag
== "bullet")
    //if (coll.gameObject.tag == "target")
    {
        Destroy (coll.gameObject);
        DestroyPlayer ();
    }
}
```

In the previous code, we check that the object colliding with the player is either a moving target or a bullet.

Please save your code, check that it is error-free, and then test the scene.

Now that this is working, we can look at the NPC's firing rate: as you test the scene, you may notice that the firing rate of the NPC is quite high; so you can either leave it as it is or modify it, by amending the script **MoveNPC** as follows:

- Please open the script **MoveNPC**.

- Add the following code at the beginning of the class.

```
public bool startShootingTimer = false;
public bool canShoot = true;
public float shootingTimer;
```

- In the previous code, we create three variables that will be used to determine when the NPC can shoot again.

- Please add this code at the beginning of the **Update** function:

```
if (startShootingTimer)
{
    shootingTimer += Time.deltaTime;
    if (shootingTimer >= .5)
    {
        startShootingTimer = false;
        canShoot = true;
        shootingTimer = 0;
    }
}
```

In the previous code:

- If the NPC has just fired a bullet (i.e., **startShootingTimer** is true), the timer is ticking and its value is increased every second by one.

- If the timer reaches 500 milliseconds, then the timer stops ticking (i.e., **startShootingTimer** is false), and the player can shoot again.

- The timer is also reset to 0.

Now, we just need to modify the function **Shoot**, so that the **timer** starts just after the NPC has fired a bullet and also so that the NPC cannot shoot another bullet for the next 500 milliseconds (i.e., as long as the timer has not reached 500 milliseconds).

- Please modify the function called **Shoot**, in the script **MoveNPC**, as follows (new code in bold):

```
void Shoot()
{
    if (canShoot)
    {
        GameObject  b  =  (GameObject)(Instantiate  (bullet,
transform.position + transform.up * 1.5f, Quaternion.identity));
        b.GetComponent<Rigidbody2D> ().AddForce (Vector3.down
* 1000);
        canShoot = false;
        startShootingTimer = true;
    }

}
```

As you save and complete the code, you may test the scene and check that the NPC fires at a lower rate.

There is one more thing that we could modify in our game: as it is, several of the moving targets may fall on the NPC; however, we could decide to ignore collisions between these boulders and the NPC, otherwise, these targets may accumulate at the top of the screen. To do so, we will employ a built-in function called **IgnoreCollision** that will be used on every new moving target, so that collisions between NPCs and moving targets are ignored.

So let's proceed:

- Please create a new C# script called **IgnoreCollision**.

- Open this script.

- Add the following code to the function **Start** (new code in bold):

```
void Start ()
{
    Physics2D.IgnoreCollision    (GetComponent<BoxCollider2D>(),
GameObject.Find ("npc1").GetComponent<PolygonCollider2D> ());
}
```

In the previous code, we use the function **Physics2D.IgnoreCollision** to ignore collisions between the collider from the moving target (this object will be attached to this script) and the collider from the object with the name **npc1**. Although this function has some limitations when used with more than two objects (and we will see how this can be solved later), it is fine for the time being.

Please save your code, and check that the moving targets are not colliding anymore with the NPCs.

Once this is working, the next step will be to instantiate several NPCs at random positions; for example, we could instantiate one of these NPCs at the top of the screen, every 5 seconds; for this purpose, we will proceed as follows:

- We will create an empty object called **NPCSpawner**, that will be in charge of spawning NPCs.

- We will then set-up the **NPCSpawner** object so that NPCs are spawned at regular intervals.

So let's get started:

- Please create a prefab from the object called **npc1** (i.e., drag and drop the object **npc1** to the **Project** window); this will create a prefab called **npc1**.

Figure 185: The new prefab called npc1

- You can delete (or deactivate) the object called **npc1** from the **Hierarchy** window now.

- Please create a new empty object and rename it **NPCSpawner**.

- Create a new C# script called **SpawnNPCs** and drag and drop it to the object **NPCSpawner** in the **Hierarchy**.

We can now modify this script:

- Please open the script **NPCSpawner**.

- Add this code at the beginning of the class (new code in bold).

```
public class NPCSpawner : MonoBehaviour {
    public GameObject npc1;
    private float timer, respawnTime;
```

- In the previous code, we declare two variables that will be used to spawn NPCs at regular intervals.

- Please add this code to the **Update** function.

```
void Update ()
{
    timer += Time.deltaTime;
    if (timer >= 1)
    {
        timer = 0;
        SpawnNPC (npc1);


    }
}
```

- In the previous code, we create a timer that is used to spawn a new NPC every second.

- Please add this code at the end of the class (i.e., just before the last closing curly bracket):

```
void SpawnNPC(GameObject typeOfNPC)
{
    float range = Random.Range (-10, 10);//Screen.width);
    Vector3      newPosition     =     new     Vector3
(GameObject.Find("player").transform.position.x    +    range,
transform.position.y, 0);
    GameObject    newNPC    =    (GameObject)(Instantiate    (npc1,
newPosition,  Quaternion.identity));
    newNPC.transform.Rotate (new Vector3 (0, 0, 180));
    newNPC.name = "npc1";


}
```

In the previous code:

- We declare a variable called **range**, with a random value that will range between -10 and +10.

- This random value is then used to instantiated a new NPC for which the **x coordinate** is based on the x coordinate of the player +/- 10; this is similar to the code used to instantiate moving targets.

- The name of the new NPCs that has been instantiated is set to **npc1**.

You can now save your script and set-up the **NPCSpawner** object:

- Please, save your script.

- Using the **Hierarchy**, please select the object **NPCSpawner**.

- In the **Inspector**, you will see a field called **NPC1** for the component called **NPCSpawner**, as illustrated in the next figure.

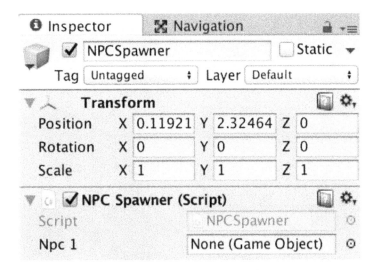

Figure 186: Setting-up the object Spawner (part 1)

- Please drag and drop the prefab **npc1** from the **Project** window, to the field **NPC1**, as illustrated in the next figure.

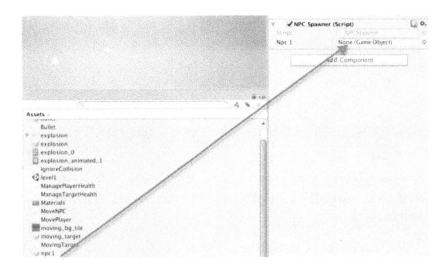

Figure 187: Setting-up the object Spawner (part 2)

- Finally, please move the object **NPCSpawner** close to the top part of the screen, as illustrated on the next figure.

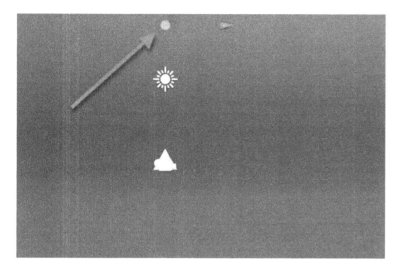

Figure 188: Moving the object NPCSpawner

As you play the scene, you will see that the NPCs are spawn at random positions.

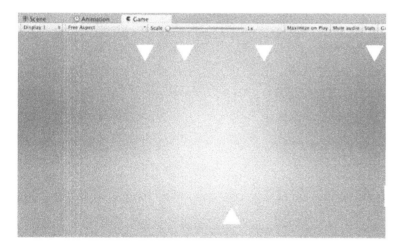

Figure 189: Spawning NPCs

You may notice that the moving targets collide with some of the NPCs; this is because we have previously used a function that ignores collision between two objects (i.e., the object **npc1** and a moving target); however, at this stage we would like to ignore collisions between more than two objects. This is because we now have <u>not just one, but</u> several objects called **npc1**.

So in the next section, we will be using a new technique to ignore collisions between more than two objects; this will involve **layers**. Layers are a way to group objects by adding them to a virtual group called a **layer**; we can then apply specific rules or features to all objects that are included in a specific layer; in our case we will specify that we should be ignoring collisions between objects belonging to two different layers; so, we will do as follows:

- Create a new layer, and add the falling (moving) targets to this layer.

- Create a second new layer, and add each NPC to this new layer.

- Make sure that collisions are ignored between the objects on the first layer and the objects on the second layer.

So let's start!

First we will create a layer for the NPCs and add any NPC based on the prefab **npc1** to this layer:

- Please select the prefab called **npc1** in the **Project** window.

- Then, open the **Inspector** window and locate the section called **Layer**, at the top of the **Inspector** window, as described on the next figure.

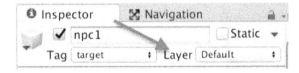

Figure 190: Adding a layer (part 1)

- Click on **Default** (to the right of the label **Layer**); this will display a list of existing layers.

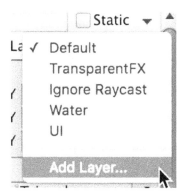

Figure 191: Adding a layer (part 2)

- You can then select the option **Add Layer** from the drop-down menu.

- In the new window, please type the name of the new layer called **NPC** to the right of the label **User Layer 8**.

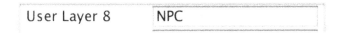

Figure 192: Adding a layer (part 3)

- Once this is, done, select the prefab **npc1** in the **Project** window.

- Using the **Inspector** window, click on **Default** (to the right of the label **Layer**); this will display a list of existing layers.

- This time, a list that includes your new layer (i.e., **NPC**) should appear; please select the layer called **NPC**.

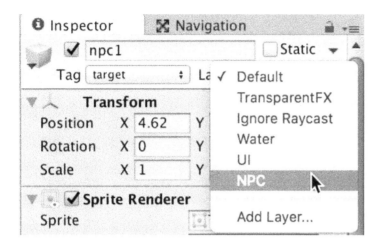

Figure 193: Applying a new layer

So by performing this action, we have specified that each object based on the prefab **npc1** will be on the layer called **NPC**.

Now we just need to specify a layer for the prefab called **moving_target**.

- Please select the prefab called **movingTarget** in the **Project** window.

- Then, open the **Inspector** window and locate the section called **Layer** (as we have done previously), at the top of the **Inspector** window, as described on the next figure.

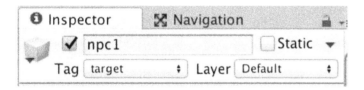

Figure 194: Creating a new layer for moving targets (part 1)

- Click on **Default** (to the right of the label **Layer**); this will display a list of existing layers.

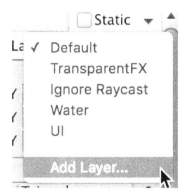

Figure 195: Creating a new layer for moving targets (part 2)

- Select **Add Layer**.

- In the new window, type the name of the new layer called **Target** to the right of the label **User Layer 9**.

Figure 196: Creating a new layer for moving targets (part 3)

- Once this is, done, please select the prefab **movingTarget** in the **Project** window.

- Using the **Inspector** window, click on the drop-down menu (to the right of the label **Layer)**; this will display a list of existing layers.

- This time a list that includes your new layer should appear; please select the layer called **Target**, as illustrated in the next figure.

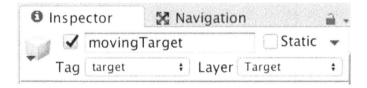

Figure 197:Applying a new layer to the moving targets

- So by performing this action, we have specified that each object based on the prefab **movingTarget** will be on the layer called **Target**.

Last but not least, we need to tell Unity that collisions should be ignored between objects belonging to these two new layers (i.e., objects that belong to the layers called **NPC** and **Target**); this will be done using scripting:

- Please open the script called **IgnoreCollisions**.

- Modify the **Start** function as follows:

```
void Start ()
{
    //if        (GameObject.Find        ("npc1")        !=        null)
Physics2D.IgnoreCollision        (GetComponent<BoxCollider2D>(),
GameObject.Find ("npc1").GetComponent<PolygonCollider2D> ());
    int layer1 = GameObject.Find ("npc1").layer;
    int layer2 = gameObject.layer;
    Physics2D.IgnoreLayerCollision(layer1, layer2, true);
}
```

In the previous code:

- We comment the first line that was originally used to ignore collisions between the object called **npc1** and the moving targets, since we will now use layers for this purpose.

- We then define the index of the two layers that we have created previously (i.e., **NPC** and **Target**). Note that to obtain the ids of these layers, we refer to objects that have been added to these layers. So to find the id of the layer **Target**, we refer to the layer on which the NPC called **npc1** has been added; the same is done for the moving targets (i.e., the object linked to this script).

- These layer indices are expressed as integers.

- **layer2** is the index of the layer (called **Target**) linked to the object (or prefab) that is attached to this script (i.e., **moving_target**)

- **layer1** is the index of the layer (called **NPC**) linked to the object (or prefab) named **npc1**.

Please save your code, and test the scene; you should see that the moving targets do not collide with the NPCs anymore.

LEVEL ROUNDUP

Summary

In this chapter, we have managed to add some interesting features, including artificial intelligence, applying damage to the player, and keeping the player in the field of view. Finally we also learned about layers and how to use them to ignore collisions between more than two objects.

Checklist

You can consider moving to the next stage if you can do the following:

- Understand how to create and apply layers.

- Understand how to ignore collision through scripting .

- Understand how to convert world coordinates to the camera viewport's coordinates.

Quiz

Now, let's check your knowledge! Please answer the following questions (the answers are included in the resource pack) or specify whether they are correct or incorrect.

1. Coordinates in the viewport range from 1 to 100.

2. The following code will convert world coordinates to viewport coordinates:

```
Camera.main.WorldToViewportPoint
```

3. Assuming that npc1 is on a layer called NPC, the following code will return the id of the layer called NPC.

```
int layer1 = GameObject.Find ("npc1").layer;
```

4. The following code will ignore collisions between objects belonging to the first layer and objects belonging to the second layer.

```
Physics2D.IgnoreLayerCollision(layer1, layer2, false);
```

5. By default, all new objects in Unity are allocated the layer called **Unity-Default**.

6. An object can be allocated to several layers.

7. The following code will create a variable that ranges from -10 to +10.

```
float range = Random.Range (-10, 10)
```

8. A polygon collider can be added to an object using the menu **Components | Polygon | PolygonCollider2D**.

9. For a particular script, the function **Start** is called when the script is loaded.

10. For a particular script, the function **Start** is called only when the game is loaded.

Answers to the Quiz

1. FALSE.

2. TRUE

3. TRUE.

4. TRUE.

5. FALSE.

6. FALSE.

7. TRUE.

8. FALSE.

9. TRUE.

10. FALSE.

Challenge 1

For this chapter, your challenge will be to modify the attributes of the game to make it more or less challenging:

- Modify the frequency at which the NPCs are spawn.
- Modify the speed at which the player moves.

CHAPTER 9: SPACE SHOOTER (PART 4): POLISHING-UP THE GAME

In this section, we will polish-up our game by adding a few features that will increase the game play, as well as the game flow; after completing this chapter, you will be able to:

- Improve AI by respawning NPCs given that specific conditions are fulfilled.

- Increase the difficulty of your game over time.

- Add a temporary shield to the player.

- Add sound effects.

IMPROVING AI

In this section, we will improve the AI in several ways:

- NPCs will be spawned after 5 seconds.

- The difficulty of the game will increase with time; as time elapses, the NPCs will be spawned more frequently and the falling targets will be generated more frequently also.

So let's get started:

- Please create a new empty object and call it **gameManager**.

- Create a new C# script and rename it **ManageShooterGame**.

- Open this script and modify it as follows.

- Add the following code at the beginning of the class (new code in bold).

```
public class ManageShooterGame : MonoBehaviour {
    public float timer;
    public float difficulty;
    public float timerThresold;
```

- In the previous code, we declare three variables that will be used to increase the difficulty of the game after a specific threshold has been reached by the timer.

- Add the following code in the **Start** function.

```
void Start ()
{
    timer = 0;
    difficulty = 1;
    timerThresold = 5;//difficulty increases after 5 seconds
}
```

- In the previous code: we initialize the time and set the initial **difficulty** level to **1**; the threshold is set to **5**, which means that the difficulty will increase every 5 seconds.

- Please add the following code in the **Update** function.

```
void Update ()
{
    timer += Time.deltaTime;
    if (timer >= timerThresold)
    {
        difficulty++;
        print ("Difficulty level: " + difficulty);
        timer = 0;
    }
}
```

- In the previous code, we update the variable **timer**, so that the difficulty level is increased every time the threshold (i.e., 5 seconds for now) has been reached. The difficulty level is also displayed in the **Console** window, for testing purposes.

- Please save this script (i.e., **manageShooterGame**), check that it is error-free, and then drag and drop it on the objet called **gameManager** in the **Hierarchy** window.

Now we just need to use this difficulty level for the scripts that spawn the moving targets or the NPCs. The idea is that the frequency at which these are spawn will be based on the difficulty level; the higher the difficult level, and the more frequently these objects will be spawn.

So let's modify these scripts:

- Please open the script called **SpawnMovingTarget**, and modify its **Update** function as follows (new code in bold).

```
timer += Time.deltaTime;
float range = Random.Range (-10, 10);//Screen.width);
Vector3          newPosition         =         new          Vector3
(GameObject.Find("player").transform.position.x       +       range,
transform.position.y, 0);
//if (timer >= 1 )
float                        respawnTime                        =
5/GameObject.Find("gameManager").GetComponent<ManageShooterGame>(
).difficulty;
if (timer >= respawnTime)
{
```

In the previous code:

- We create a variable **respawnTime** that is calculated based on the difficulty level; so at the start, **respawnTime** will be 5 and then 2.5, etc.; so objects will be respawn twice as fast every time the level of difficulty increases by one; this will make the game extremely challenging over time.

- We then use this **respawnTime** variable to know when the prefab should be instantiated.

You can now save your script, and we can then perform similar modifications for the NPCs.

- Please open the script **SpawnNPC**, and modify its **Update** function as follows (new code in bold).

```
//if (timer >= 1 )
float                          respawnTime                          =
5/GameObject.Find("gameManager").GetComponent<ManageShooterGame>(
).difficulty;
if (timer >= respawnTime)
{
```

- This code is identical to the one we have used to respawn the moving targets.

- You can now save your code.

Note that you can modify the variable **respawnTime** by multiplying it by a number of your choice. As it is, the game will quickly become very challenging as the spawning frequency is doubled every 5 seconds.

ADDING A TEMPORARY SHIELD TO THE PLAYER

While the player can shoot projectiles, given the frequency at which the NPCs are spawn, it would be great for the player to avail of a shield, even temporarily.

So, in this section, we will create a feature whereby:

- A bonus object will be instantiated randomly.

- After collecting this bonus, the player will avail of a shield and be invincible for 5 seconds.

- While it is invincible, a blue circle will be displayed around the player.

This will involve the following:

- Creating a tag for the bonus.

- Detecting collision with this bonus based on its tag.

- Creating a shield, based on a sprite.

- Initially deactivate the shield (i.e., make it invisible).

- Creating a timer to determine for how long the shield should be active.

- Activate the shield (i.e., make it visible) after the bonus has been collected, and ignore collisions with bullets or targets while the shield is active.

- Deactivate the shield when the timer has reached 5 seconds.

So let's implement this feature:

- Please create a new sprite: from the **Project** window, select **Create | Sprites | Circle**.

- Rename this asset **shield**.

Figure 198: Creating a new shield

- Drag and drop this asset (i.e., the shield) to the **Hierarchy** view; this will create a new object called **shield**.

- Using the **Hierarchy**, drag and drop this object (i.e., the shield) on top of the object called **player**, so that it becomes a child of the object **player**, as illustrated on the next figure.

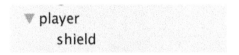

Figure 199: Adding the shield as a child of the object player

- Once this is done, you can click on the object called **shield** in the **Hierarchy**, and then look at the **Inspector** window.

- In the **Inspector** window, set the position of this object (i.e., the shield) to **(0, 0, 0)** and its scale attributes to **(1, 1, 1)**.

You can also change the color and transparency of the sprite for this object as follows:

- Using the **Inspector**, for the **Component** called **Sprite Renderer**, click on the white rectangle to the right of the attribute called **Color**.

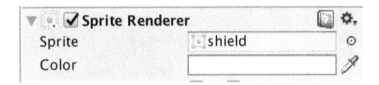

Figure 200: Changing the color of the shield

- This will open a new window; using this window you can pick a blue color of your choice, and also set the **opacity** to **70**, as illustrated on the next figures.

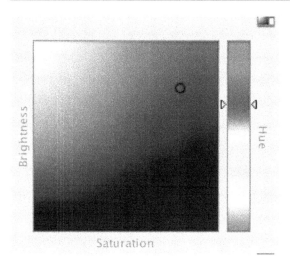

Figure 201: Painting the shield in blue

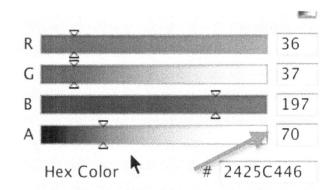

Figure 202: Setting the opacity to 70

- Once this is done, the player should look like the following figure:

Figure 203: The player and its shield

Next, we will create a prefab that will be used as a bonus to be collected by the player to activate its shield.

- In the **Project** window, please duplicate the prefab called **movingTarget** (i.e., select the prefab and then press **CTRL + D**).

- Rename the duplicate **bonus**.

Figure 204: Creating a new prefab for the bonus

- Once this is done, please click on the prefab called **bonus** that you have just created in the **Project** window, so that we can modify some of its properties.

- Using the **Inspector** window, create a new tag called **bonus** and apply it to this object, as we have done previously for other objects.

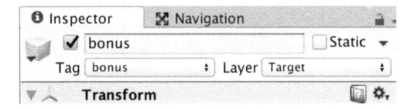

Figure 205: Adding a tag to the bonus prefab

- Please change the color of the sprite for this prefab to green using its **Sprite Renderer** component in the **Inspector**.

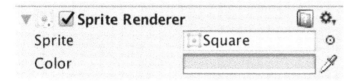

Figure 206: Changing the color of the bonus

So, this new prefab will behave the same way as the moving platforms, in the sense that, once spawned, it will move downwards; however, this **bonus** prefab has a different tag called **bonus**, so that he player can collect it; the **bonus** prefab also has a distinctive color (i.e., green) so that the player can tell it apart from the falling targets.

So now that we have created this prefab, we will need to spawn it and to ensure that when it is collected by the player, that the player's shield is activated accordingly.

So we will need to modify a few of the existing scripts: the script that spawns moving targets, and the other script that manages the player's health.

- Please open the script **SpawnMovingTargets**.

- Add the following code at the beginning of the class (new code in bold).

```
public GameObject newObject;
public GameObject bonus;
```

- Modify the function **Update** as follows (new code in bold).

```
if (timer >= respawnTime)
{
    float typeOfObjectSpwan = Random.Range(0,100);
    GameObject t;
    if (typeOfObjectSpwan >= 50)
    {
        t = (GameObject)(Instantiate (newObject, newPosition,
Quaternion.identity));
        t.GetComponent<ManageTargetHealth>      ().type      =
ManageTargetHealth.TARGET_BOULDER;
    }
    else t = (GameObject)(Instantiate (bonus, newPosition,
Quaternion.identity));
    //GameObject t = (GameObject)(Instantiate (newObject,
newPosition, Quaternion.identity));
    //t.GetComponent<ManageTargetHealth>      ().type      =
ManageTargetHealth.TARGET_BOULDER;
    timer = 0;
}
```

In the previous code:

- We generate a random number between 0 and 100; this number will be used to determine what object should be spawn; here, we are effectively specifying a probability of 50% chance for bonuses to be spawn and a 50% chance for moving targets to be spawn. This is a very simple way to apply probabilities (and random behaviors) to your games.

- If the random number id **50 or more**, we instantiate a moving target. Otherwise, we instantiate a bonus.

Note that **Random.Range** will generate numbers from a range that includes the boundaries of this range; in our case the number generated will range between 0 and 100 inclusive, which would include 101 possibilities; so to be more accurate, we could adjust the upper boundary of the range to 99, which would result in 100 possibilities.

- The previous code used to instantiate a moving target is commented.

That's it!

Please save your script and check that it is error-free.

Next, we can modify the script that manages the player's health.

- Please open the script **ManagePlayerHealth**.

- Modify the beginning of the class as follows:

```
public float timerForShield;
public bool startInvincibility;
void Start ()
{
    GameObject.Find      ("shield").GetComponent<SpriteRenderer>
().enabled = false;

}
```

In the previous code:

- We declare two variables: **timerForShield** and **startInvincibility**.

- We also make sure that the shield is not displayed at the start of the game by **not** rendering the corresponding sprite.

We can now modify the collision detection to account for the shield (and the temporary invincibility).

- Please modify the function **OnCollisionEnter2D**, in the script **ManagePlayerHealth**, as follows (new code in bold):

```
if ((coll.gameObject.tag == "target" || coll.gameObject.tag ==
"bullet") && !startInvincibility)
{
    Destroy (coll.gameObject);

    DestroyPlayer ();
}

if (coll.gameObject.tag == "bonus")
{
    Destroy (coll.gameObject);
    startInvincibility = true;
    GameObject.Find      ("shield").GetComponent<SpriteRenderer>
().enabled = true;
}
```

In the previous code:

- The player will sustain damage only when it is not invincible (i.e., when the shield is not active).

- We also check that the player has collided with a bonus.

- If this is the case, the bonus is destroyed, the player becomes invincible (for the time-being) and the shield is displayed. The variable **startInvincibility** is used to start a timer that will determine when this invincibility will stop.

Finally, we just need to modify the **Update** function to be able to implement the timer, and to check how long the shield should be active.

- Please modify the **Update** function in the script **ManagePlayerHealth** as follows (new code in bold):

```
void Update ()
{
    if (startInvincibility)
    {
        timerForShield += Time.deltaTime;
        if (timerForShield >= 20)
        {
            timerForShield = 0;
            startInvincibility = false;
            GameObject.Find
("shield").GetComponent<SpriteRenderer> ().enabled = false;
        }
    }
}
```

In the previous code:

- We check whether the player is invincible (i.e., if a bonus shield has been collected).

- If this is the case, the value of the timer is increased every second, until it reaches 20 seconds.

- In this case, the timer is reset to 0, the invincibility is set to **false**, and the shield is no longer displayed onscreen.

Last but not least, we need to add the bonus prefab to the object **targetSpawner**.

- Please select the object **targetSpawner** in the **Hierarchy**.

- Then drag and drop the prefab **bonus** from the **Project** window, to the field called **bonus** for the component called **SpawnMovingTargets**, as described on the next figure.

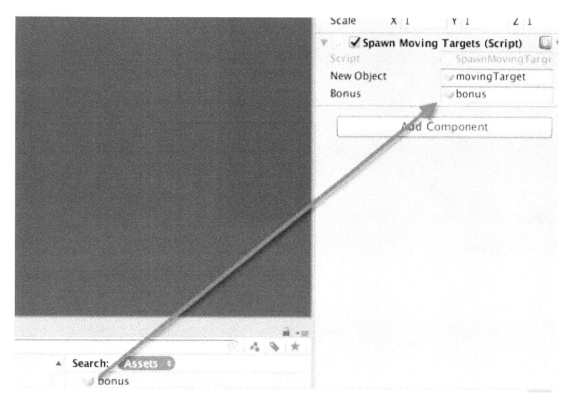

Figure 207: Adding the bonus to the targetSpawner object

Once this is done, you can now test your game: after collecting a bonus, the shield should appear for 20 seconds, allowing you to be invincible for that duration.

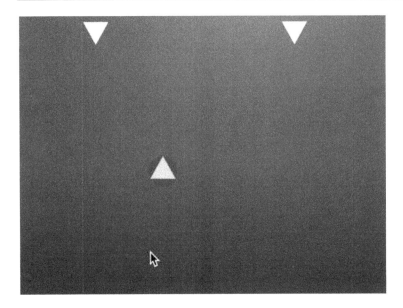

Figure 208: Using the shield

ADDING A SCORE

Now that our gameplay is improved thanks to randomly instantiated NPCs and an increasing difficulty, we could add and display a score. This will consist of a **UI Text** object that will be updated from a script every time the player manages to hit a target.

- Please create a new **UI Text** object; from the main menu, select: **GameObject | UI | Text**. This will create a new object called **Text**, along with a parent object called **Canvas**.

Figure 209: Adding a UI Text object

- To know where this object is in relation to the game screen, you can just double click on it in the **Hierarchy**.

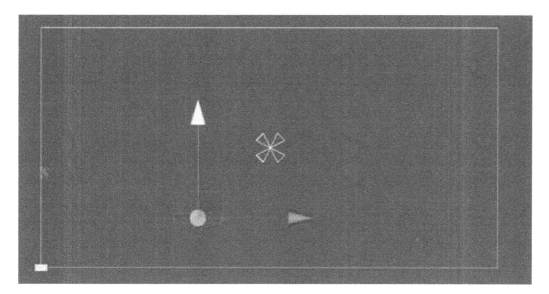

Figure 210: Locating the UI Text object

- Then, in the **Scene** view, move this object, to the top-left corner of the white rectangle that defines the game screen.

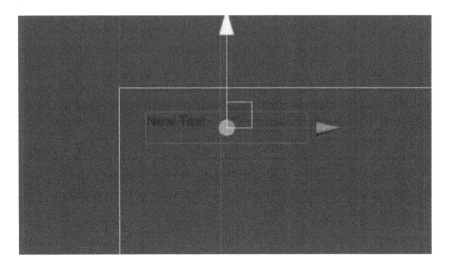

Figure 211: Moving the UI text object

We can now change some of the properties of this object (e.g., color and size):

- After selecting the object called **Text** in the **Hierarchy**, please use the **Inspector** window to change the color of its text to **white** (in the component called **Text**).

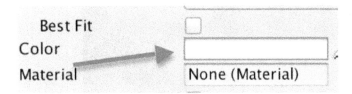

Figure 212: Changing the color of the text

- Please modify its alignment as described in the next figure:

Figure 213: Modifying the alignment of the Text object

- You can also rename this object **scoreUI**, using the **Hierarchy** window.

Once this is done, we just need to calculate the score and display it in the **UI Text** object.

- Please, open the script called **ManagePlayerHealth**.

- Add the following code at the start of the script (new code in bold):

```
using UnityEngine;
using System.Collections;
using UnityEngine.SceneManagement;
using UnityEngine.UI;
```

- Add the following code at the beginning of the class (new code in bold).

```
public float timerForShield;
public bool startInvincibility;
public int score;
void Start ()
{
    score = 0;
    GameObject.Find      ("shield").GetComponent<SpriteRenderer>
().enabled = false;
    GameObject.Find  ("scoreUI").GetComponent<Text>  ().text  =
"Score:" + score;

}
```

In the previous script:

- We declare a new variable called **score**.

- At the beginning of the scene, we set this variable (i.e., **score**) to **0**.

- We also initialize the text displayed by the **UI Text** component.

Please add the following code at the end of the class, just before the last closing curly bracket.

```
public void increaseScore()
{
    score++;
    GameObject.Find  ("scoreUI").GetComponent<Text>  ().text  =
"Score:" + score;
}
```

In the previous script:

- We create a new function called **increaseScore**.

- In this function, we increase the **score** by **1**.

- We also update the **UI Text** object to reflect the change in the **score**.

Please save this script, and check that it is error-free.

The next thing we need to do is to call this function when the bullet fired by the player has hit a target; this will be managed in the script called **Bullet**.

Note that the function **increaseScore** is public, which means that it will be accessible from outside its class, and as a result, from the script called **Bullet**.

So let's modify the script called **Bullet**:

- Please open the script called **Bullet**.

- Add the following code to the function **OnCollisionEnter2D** (new code in bold).

```
coll.gameObject.GetComponent<ManageTargetHealth>().gotHit(10);
GameObject.Find        ("player").GetComponent<ManagePlayerHealth>
().increaseScore ();
Destroy (gameObject);
```

- Please save your code.

You can now check the game to see whether the score is displayed and updated accordingly as your bullets hit different targets.

ADDING AUDIO

The last thing we will do is to add audio to our game whenever the player is hit, or s/he fires bullets. For this purpose, we will import two sound effects, and play them accordingly.

Please import the audio files **explosion.wav** and **bullet.wav** from the resource pack to Unity's **Project** window.

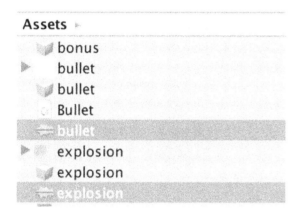

Figure 214: Importing audio

The two audio files were created using the site http://www.bfxr.net/, which is a free tool to create your own sound effects.

Next, we will create the necessary components to be able to play these sounds, and we will start with the sound for the bullet.

- Please select the object called **player** in the **Hierarchy**.

- From the top menu, select **Component | Audio | Audio Source**; this will add an **Audio Source** component to your object.

Whenever you need to play a sound, an **Audio Source** is needed, and it is comparable to an mp3 player in the sense that it plays audio clips that you need to select, the same way you would select a particular track on your mp3 player.

- Please, drag and drop the audio file called **bullet** from the **Project** window to the **Audio Clip** attribute of the **Audio Source.**

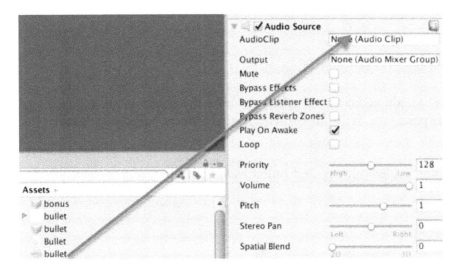

Figure 215: Adding an audio source

- You can then set the attribute **Play on Awake** to **false** (i.e., unchecked) so that this sound is not played automatically at the start of the scene, as illustrated on the next figure.

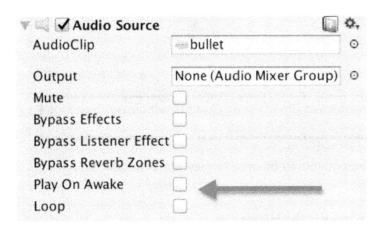

Figure 216: Setting the attributes of the sound effect

Next, we will write code that will access this **Audio Source** and play the clip, whenever the player fires a bullet.

- Please open the script called **MovePlayer**.

- Add the following code to the function **Update** (new cold in bold).

```
if (Input.GetKeyDown (KeyCode.Space))
{
    GameObject   b   =   (GameObject)(Instantiate   (bullet,
transform.position + transform.up*1.5f, Quaternion.identity));
    b.GetComponent<Rigidbody2D>   ().AddForce   (transform.up   *
1000);
    GetComponent<AudioSource> ().Play ();
}
```

In the previous code, we access the **AudioSource** component that is linked to the object **player** (i.e., the object linked to this script), and we play the clip that is included in this **AudioSource** (i.e., **bullet**).

Please save your code, test the scene, and check that the audio clip is played whenever you press the space bar.

Next, using the same principle, we will generate the sound of an explosion when the player is hit.

Now, because the **Audio Source** will need to play several sounds (a different sound depending on whether the player fires a bullet or is hit), we will need to specify which track needs to be played, so we will modify our script accordingly.

- Please open the script **MovePlayer**.

- Add the following line at the beginning of the script:

```
public AudioClip fireSound;
```

- This code declares an audio clip; because it is public, it will be accessible from the **Inspector**, and as a result, we will be able to set (or initialize) this variable by dragging and dropping objects to its placeholders in the **Inspector** window.

- Please save your script, switch to Unity, select the **player** object and display the **Inspector** window.

- You should see that a variable called **fireSound**, that acts as placeholder, is now available in the component called **Move**.

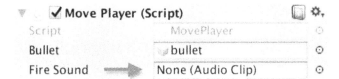

Figure 217: Initializing the audio clips (part1)

- Please drag and drop the sound **bullet.wav** from the **Project** view, to the variable **fireSound** in the **Inspector**, as illustrated in the next figure.

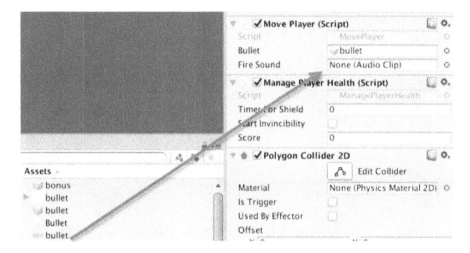

Figure 218: Initializing the audio clips (part 2)

Now, it's time to modify the script further to tell the system which audio clip to play and when.

- Please open the script **MovePlayer**.

- Add the following code to the **Update** function (new code in bold):

```
if (Input.GetKeyDown (KeyCode.Space))
{
    GameObject    b    =    (GameObject)(Instantiate    (bullet,
transform.position + transform.up*1.5f, Quaternion.identity));
    b.GetComponent<Rigidbody2D>    ().AddForce    (transform.up    *
1000);
    GetComponent<AudioSource> ().clip = fireSound;
    GetComponent<AudioSource> ().Play ();
}
```

In the previous code:

- We specify that we should play the clip called **fireSound** (which contains the audio **bullet.wav**); this track is now the default (or active) track for the **Audio Source**.

- We then play the track that we have selected.

Next, we will use a similar technique to play a different sound when the player is hurt.

- Please open the script called **ManagePlayerHealth**.

- Add the following lines at the beginning of the script:

```
public AudioClip hitSound;
```

- This code declares an audio clip; because it is public, it will be accessible from the **Inspector**, and as a result, we will be able to set (or initialize) this variable by dragging and dropping objects to its placeholders in the **Inspector** window.

- Add the following code to the function **DestroyPlayer** (new code in bold).

```
void DestroyPlayer ()
{
    GetComponent<AudioSource> ().clip = hitSound;
    GetComponent<AudioSource> ().Play ();
    SceneManager.LoadScene (SceneManager.GetActiveScene().name);
}
```

Once this is done, we just need to initialize the variable **hitSound** from the **Inspector** window.

- Please save your script, switch to Unity, select the **player** object and display the **Inspector** window.

- You should see that a variable called **hitSound**, for the component **ManagePlayerHealth**, that acts as placeholder, is now available.

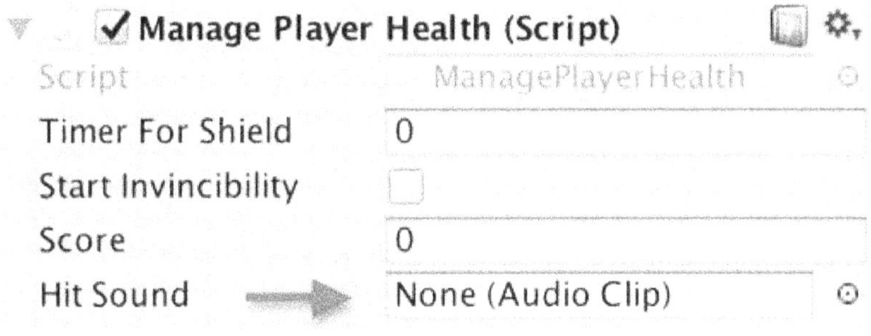

Figure 219: Initializing the audio clips (part1)

- Please drag and drop the sound **explosion.wav** from the **Project** view, to the variable **hitSound** in the **Inspector**, as illustrated in the next figure.

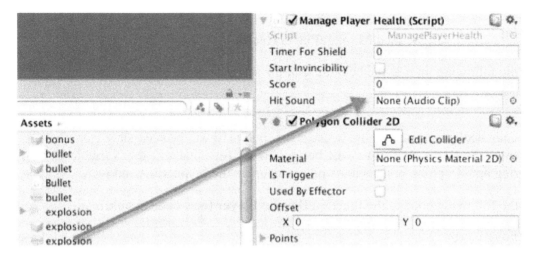

Figure 220: Initializing the audio clips (part 2)

You can now test your scene: when the player is hit, the explosion sound should be played.

CHAPTER 10: SPACE SHOOTER: FREQUENTLY ASKED QUESTIONS

This chapter provides answers to the most frequently asked questions about the features that we have covered in the previous sections. Please also note that some <u>videos are also available on the companion site</u> to help you with some of the concepts covered in this book.

USER INTERACTION

How can I detect keystrokes?

You can detect keystroke by using the function **Input.GetKey**. For example, the following code detects when the key E is pressed; this code should be added to the **Update** function.

```
If (Input.GetKey(KeyCode.E)){}
```

How can I play sound?

To play a sound, you need to add an **Audio Source** component to an object; when this is done, you can either play its default audio clip, or select which audio clip should be played.

```
GetComponent<AudioSource>().Play();//plays the default sound
GetComponent<AudioSource>().clip = clip1;//selects the clip
GetComponent<AudioSource>().Play();//plays clip selected
```

How can I display text onscreen?

To display text onscreen you will need to create a **UI Text** object, and then access it through a script. For example:

```
GetComponent<Text>().text = "New Text";
```

FIRING OBJECTS

How can I ensure that a projectile will not be subject to gravity?

If a projectile includes a Rigidbody2D component, you can make sure that it is not subject to gravity by setting its **gravity scale** attribute to 0.

How can I set a projectile in movement?

To set a projectile in movement, you need to apply a force to it. For example, to move it up the screen, the following code could be used.

```
GetComponent<Rigidbody2D> ().AddForce (transform.up * 1000);
```

IMPROVING GAMEPLAY

How can I create random numbers?

You can use the function called **Random.Range** to create a random number; for example, the following code will create a number between -10 and +10.

```
Random.Range (-10, 10)
```

How can I make some attributes temporary (e.g., invincibility)?

You can use a timer that can determine from when and for how long a variable should have a specific value; the timer can start at 0 and then increase until it has reached a specific threshold; when this is the case, a new value can be set for the variable. The following code snippet illustrates how this can be done.

```
void Update()
{
    timer+=Time.deltaTime;
    float threshold = 5.0f;
    if (timer > thresold)
    {
        ...
    }
{
```

CHAPTER 11: CREATING A WORD GUESSING GAME

In this section, we will start by creating a word guessing game with the following features:

- A word will be picked at random from an existing list.

- The letters of the word will be hidden.

- The players will try to guess each letter by pressing a letter on their keyboard.

- Once a letter has been discovered, it will then be displayed onscreen.

- The player has a limited number of attempts to guess the word.

So, after completing this chapter, you will be able to:

- Read words from a text file.

- Pick a random word.

- Process and assess the letters pressed by the player.

- Display the letters that were correctly guessed by the player.

- Track and display the score.

- Check when the player has used too many guesses.

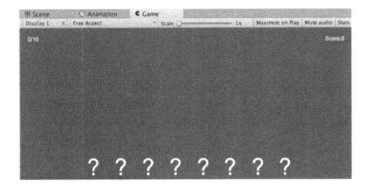

Figure 221: The final game

CREATING THE INTERFACE FOR THE GAME

So, in this section, we will start to create the core of the word guessing game; it will consist of text fields initially blank, and located in the middle of the screen.

So, let's get started:

- Please launch Unity and create a new **Project** (**File | New Project**).

Figure 222: Creating a new project

- In the new window, you can specify the name of your project, its location, as well as the **2D** mode (as this game will be in **2D**).

Figure 223: Specifying the name and location for your project

- Once this is done, you can click on the button called **Create** (located at the bottom of the window) and a new project should open.

- Once this is done, you can check that the 2D mode is activated, based on the 2D logo located in the top right-corner of the **Scene** view, as illustrated in the next figure.

Figure 224: Activating the 2D mode

First, we will remove the background image for our **Scene**. If you look at your **Game** view, it may look like the following figure.

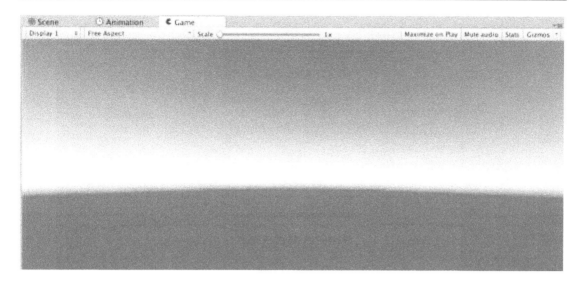

Figure 225: The initial background

If it is the case, then please do the following:

- From the top menu, select: **Window | Rendering | Lighting Settings**.

- Then delete the **Default Skybox** that is set for the attribute called **SkyBox** (i.e., click on the attribute to the right of the label **Skybox** and press **DELETE** on your keyboard).

- You can also set the environment lighting source color to **grey**.

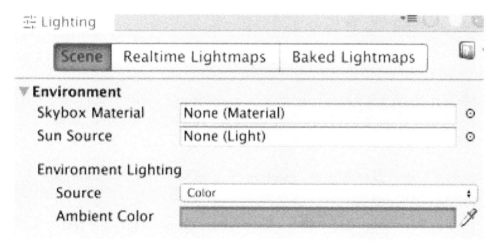

Figure 226: Lighting properties

- Once this is done, your **Game** view should look like the following.

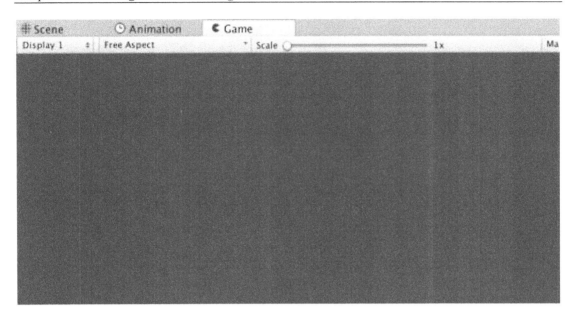

Figure 227: The Game view after deleting the SkyBox

We will now create a text field that will be used for the letters to be guessed.

- From the top menu, please select **GameObject | UI | Text**. This will create a **UI Text** object called **text**, along with a **Canvas** object.

- Please rename this text object **letter**.

Figure 228: Creating a new letter

Select this object (i.e., letter) in the **Hierarchy**, and, using the **Inspector** window, please set its attributes as follows:

- For the component **Rect Transform**: **Position = (PosX:0, PosY:0, PosZ:0);** **Width = 100** and **Height = 100**.

- For the component **Text**: **Font-size = 80; Color = white; please empty the text**.

- For the component **Text**: **vertical alignment = center; horizontal alignment = middle**.

Once this is done, we will create a prefab from this object, so that we can instantiate it later on (i.e., create objects based on this prefab).

- Please drag and drop the object **letter** from the **Hierarchy** window to the **Project** window.

- This will create a new prefab called **letter**.

Next, we will create a **gameManager** object; this object will be in charge of setting the layout for the game and processing the user's entries; in other words, it will be responsible for running and managing the game.

- Please create a new empty object (**GameObject | Create Empty**).

- Rename this new object **gameManager**.

Next, we will create a script that will be attached to the **gameManager** object; this script will be in charge of running the game (e.g., displaying letters, processing user inputs, etc.).

- From the **Project** window, select **Create | C# Script**.

- Rename the new script **GameManager**.

- You can then open this script.

In this script, we will display several letters in the middle of the screen.

- Please add this code at the beginning of the class.

```
public GameObject letter;
```

In the previous code we create a new **public** variable called **letter**; it will be accessible from the **Inspector** since it is public, and it will be set (or initialized) with the **letter** prefab that we have created earlier. This variable will be used to generate new letters based on that template (i.e., the prefab).

- Please check that the code is error free in the **Console** window.

- Drag and drop the script **GameManager** from the **Project** window on the object called **gameManager** located in the **Hierarchy**.

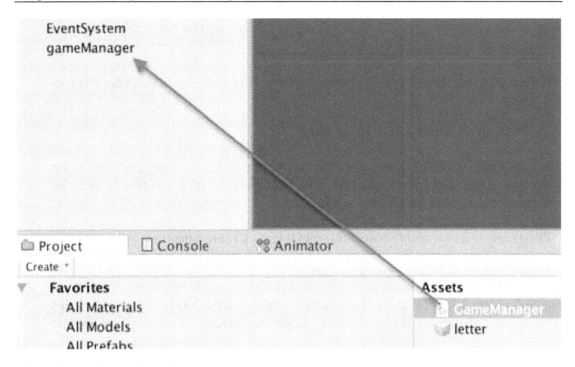

Figure 229: Adding a script to the game manager

- Once this is done, you can select the object called **gameManager** in the **Hierarchy**.

- Using the **Inspector** window, you will see that this object now includes a new component called **GameManager** with an empty field called **letter**.

Figure 230: A new component added to the game manager

- Please drag and drop the prefab called **letter** from the **Project** window to this empty field in the **Inspector** window, as described in the next figure.

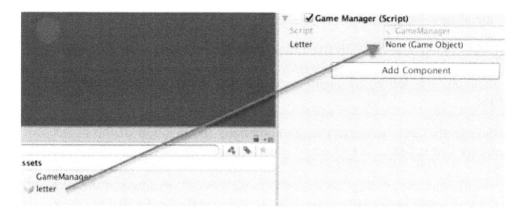

Figure 231: Initializing the letter variable with a prefab

Once this is done, we can start to write a function that will create the new letters.

- Please open the script **GameManager**.

- Add the following code at the end of the class (i.e., just after the function **Update**).

```
void initLetters()
{
    int nbletters = 5;
    for (int i = 0; i < nbletters; i++) {
        Vector3 newPosition;
        newPosition = new Vector3 (transform.position.x + (i *
100), transform.position.y, transform.position.z);
        GameObject  l  =  (GameObject)Instantiate  (letter,
newPosition, Quaternion.identity);
        l.name = "letter" + (i + 1);
        l.transform.SetParent(GameObject.Find
("Canvas").transform);

    }
}
```

In the previous code:

- We define that we will display five letters using the variable **nbLetters**; this number is arbitrary, for the time being, so that we can ensure that we can display letters onscreen; this number of letters will, of course, vary later on, based on the length of the word to be guessed.

- We then create a loop that will loop five times (once for each letter).

- In each iteration, we define the position of the new letter using the variable **newPosition**.

- This position of the letter is calculated by combining the position of the object **gameManager** that is linked to this script (i.e., **transform.position**) plus the size of the letter (i.e., **100**; this size/width was set-up earlier-on with the **Inspector** using the **width** attribute) multiplied by the variable **i**; so the position of the first letter on the x-axis will be **transform.position + 0**, the second one will be at the x position **transform.position + 100**, and so on.

- We instantiate a letter and also set its name.

- Finally, we set the parent of this new object to be the object called **Canvas**; this is because, as a **UI Text** object, this object needs to be associated to a canvas in order to be displayed onscreen; this is usually done by default as you create a new **UI Text** object with the editor in Unity; however, this needs to be done manually here, as this object is created and added to the **Scene** from a script.

Finally, please add the following code to the **Start** function.

```
initLetters();
```

As you play the **Scene**, you should see that new letters have been created in the **Hierarchy**.

Figure 232: The newly-created letters

If you double-click on one of them (e.g., **letter1**) in the **Hierarchy**, you should see where they are located and their layout in the **Scene** view.

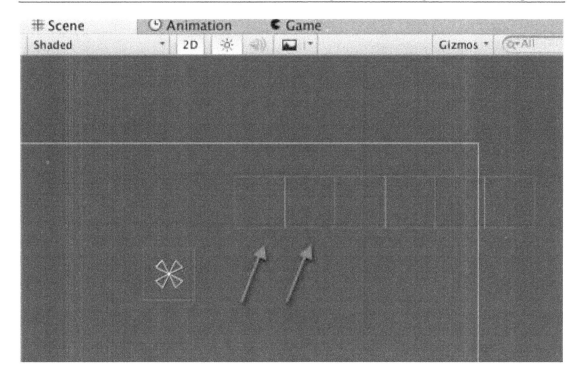

Figure 233: The layout of the letters

Now, because the position of the letters is based on the position of the game manager, you may notice, as for the previous figure, that the letters are not centered properly. So we need to ensure that these letters are properly aligned vertically and horizontally. For this purpose, we will do the following:

- Create an empty text object located in the middle of the screen.

- Base the position of each letter on this object.

- Ensure that all letters are now properly aligned.

So let's proceed:

- Please create a new **UI Text** object (**GameObject | UI | Text**) and rename it **centerOfScreen**.

- Select this object in the **Hierarchy**.

- Using the **Inspector**, in the component called **RectTransform**, change its position to **PosX=0** and **PosY=0**; you can leave the other attributes as they are.

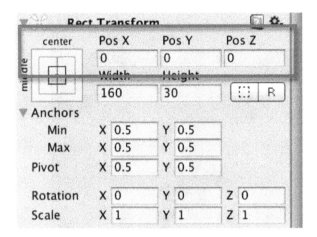

Figure 234: Changing the position attributes

Because this object is a **UI** object, setting its position to (0,0) will guarantee that it will be displayed in the center of the screen; this is because the coordinates of the UI object (for the component **RectTransform**) are based on the view/camera. So **PosX=0** and **PosY=0**, in this case, corresponds to the center of the screen; using an empty object would have been different as the coordinates would be world coordinates and not related to the screen/view.

- Using the **Inspector**, in the component called **Text,** delete the default text, so that this **UI Text** is effectively an empty field.

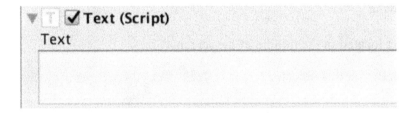

Once this is done, we can modify the code in the script **GameManager** to center our letters.

- Please open the script **GameManager**.

- Add the following code to the start of the class (new code in bold).

```
public GameObject letter;
public GameObject cen;

void Start () {
    cen = GameObject.Find ("centerOfScreen");
    initLetters ();
}
```

- In the previous code, we declare a new variable called **cen** that will be used to refer to the object **centerOfScreen**.

- In the function **initLetter** that we have created earlier-on, please modify this line

```
newPosition = new Vector3 (transform.position.x + (i * 100),
transform.position.y, transform.position.z);
```

… with this code…

```
newPosition = new Vector3 (cen.transform.position.x + (i * 100),
cen.transform.position.y, cen.transform.position.z);
```

In the previous code, we now base the position of our letter on the center of the screen.

- Please save your script, and check that it is error-free.

- Play the **Scene**, and you should see, in the **Scene** view, that the letters are now aligned vertically; however, they are slightly offset horizontally, as illustrated in the next figure.

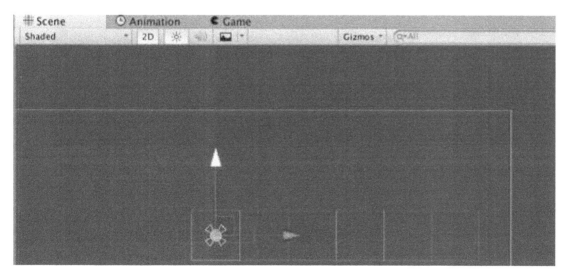

Figure 235: Aligning the letters

So there is a last change that we can include in our script, so that each letter is centered around the center of the screen; this will consist in offsetting the position of each letter based on the center of the screen as follows, so that the middle of the word matches with the center of the screen.

- Please open the script **GameManager** and, in the function called **initLetter**, replace this line:

```
newPosition = new Vector3 (cen.transform.position.x + (i * 100),
cen.transform.position.y, cen.transform.position.z);
```

with this line...

```
newPosition = new Vector3 (cen.transform.position.x + ((i-
nbletters/2.0f)       *100),       cen.transform.position.y,
cen.transform.position.z);
```

In the previous code, we offset the position of each letter based on the center of the screen; so the x-coordinate of the first letter will be **-250**, the x-coordinate of the second letter will be **-150**, and so on.

You can save your script, play the **Scene**, and look at the **Scene** view; you should see that the letters are now properly aligned, as illustrated on the next figure.

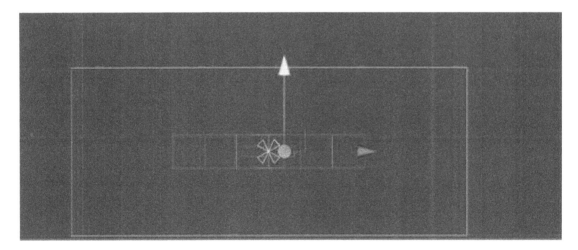

Figure 236: The letters are now properly aligned

If you would like to see what the letters would look like, you can, while the game is playing, select each newly-created letter in the **Hierarchy** and modify its **Text** attribute in the **Inspector** (using the component **Text**), as illustrated in the next figure.

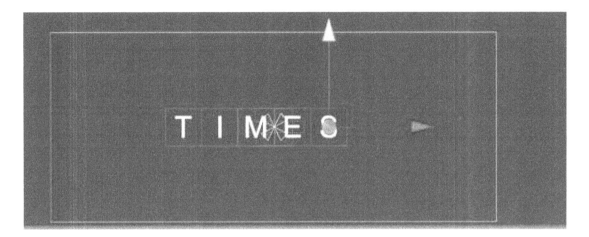

Figure 237: Changing the text of each letter at run-time

DETECTING AND PROCESSING THE USER INPUT

Perfect. So at this stage, we have a basic interface for our game, and we can display letters onscreen. So, in this section, we will implement the main features of the game, that is:

- Create a new word to be guessed.

- Count the number of letters in this word.

- Display corresponding empty text fields.

- Wait for the user to press a key (i.e., a letter) on the keyboard.

- Detect the key pressed by the user.

- Display the corresponding letters in the word to be guessed onscreen.

So let's start.

- Please open the script called **GameManager**.

- Add the following code at the start of the class (new code in bold).

```
public GameObject letter;
public GameObject cen;

private string wordToGuess = "";
private int lengthOfWordToGuess;
char [] lettersToGuess;
bool [] lettersGuessed;
```

In the previous code:

- We declare four new variables.

- **wordToGuess** will be used to store the word to be guessed.

- **lengthOfWordToBeGuessed** will store the number of letters in this word.

- **lettersToGuess** is an array of **char** (i.e., characters) including every single letter from the word to be discovered by the player.

- **letterGuessed** is an array of Boolean variables used to determine which of the letters in the word to guess were actually guessed correctly by the player.

Next, we will create a function that will be used to initialize the game.

- Please add the following function to the class.

```
void initGame()
{
    wordToGuess = "Elephant";
    lengthOfWordToGuess = wordToGuess.Length;
    wordToGuess = wordToGuess.ToUpper ();
    lettersToGuess = new char[lengthOfWordToGuess];
    lettersGuessed = new bool [lengthOfWordToGuess];
    lettersToGuess = wordToGuess.ToCharArray ();
}
```

In the previous code:

- We declare a function called **initGame**.

- In this function, we initialize the variable **wordToGuess**; this will be the word **Elephant** for the time being.

- We then capitalize all the letters in this word; as we will see later in this chapter, this will make it easier to match the letter typed by the user (which usually is upper-case) and the letters in the word to guess.

- We then initialize the array called **lettersToGuess** and **lettersGuessed**.

> Note that for Boolean variables, the default value, if they have not been initialized, is **false**. As a result, all variables in the array called **lettersGuessed** will initially be set to false (by default).

- Finally, we initialize the array called **lettersToGuess** so that each character within corresponds to the letters in the word to guess; for this, we convert the word to guess to an array of characters, which is then saved into the array called **lettersToGuess**.

Once this function has been created, we will need to process the user's input; for this purpose, we will create a function that will do the following:

- Detect the letter that was pressed by the player on the keyboard.

- Check if this letter is part of the word to guess.

- In this case, check if this letter has **<u>not</u>** already been guessed by the player.

- In this case, display the corresponding letter onscreen.

Let's write the corresponding code.

- Please add this code at the start of the script

```
using UnityEngine.UI;
```

- Please add the following function to the script **GameManager**:

```
void checkKeyboard()
{
    if (Input.GetKeyDown(KeyCode.A))
    {
        for (int i=0; i < lengthOfWordToGuess; i++)
        {
            if (!lettersGuessed [i])
            {
                if (lettersToGuess [i] == 'A')
                {
                    lettersGuessed [i] = true;

    GameObject.Find("letter"+(i+1)).GetComponent<Text>().text   =
"A";
                }
            }
        }
    }
}
```

In the previous code:

- We declare the function called **checkKeyBoard**.

- We then create a loop that goes through all the letters of the word to be guessed; this is done from the first letter (i.e., at the index 0) to the last one.

- We check if this letter has already been guessed.

- If it is **not** the case, we check whether this letter is **A**.

- If this is the case, we then indicate that this letter (i.e., the letter **A**) was found.

- We then display the corresponding letter onscreen.

Last but not least, we just need to be able to call these two functions to initialize the game and to also process the user's inputs.

- Please add the following code to the **Start** function (new code in bold).

```
void Start () {
     cen = GameObject.Find ("centerOfScreen");
     initGame ();
     initLetters ();
}
```

Please make sure that the function **initGame** is called before **initLetters** (as illustrated in the previous code) in the **Start** function; this is because, as we will see later, the function **initLetters** will use some of the information that has been set in the function **initGame** (i.e., the number of letters). So in order for our game to work correctly, the function **initGame** should be called before the function **initLetters**.

- Please add the following code to the **Update** function.

```
void Update () {
     checkKeyboard ();
}
```

The last change we need to add now is linked to the number of letters to be displayed; as it is, the number is set to 5 by default; however, we need to change this in the function called **initLetters**, so that the number of **UI Text** objects that corresponds to the letters in the word to be guessed reflects the length of the word that we have just created.

- Please modify the function **initLetters** as follows (new code in bold).

```
void initLetters()
{
     int nbletters = lengthOfWordToGuess;
```

So at this stage, we have all the necessary functions to start our game; so you can save the script, check that it is error free and play the **Scene**. As you play the **Scene**, if you press the **A** key on the keyboard, the letter **A** should also be displayed onscreen, as it is part of the word **Elephant**.

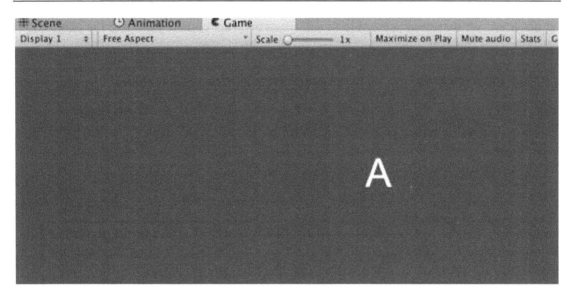

Figure 238: Detecting the key pressed

So, this is working properly, and we could easily add more code to detect the other keys; this would involve using the code included in the function **checkKeyboard**, and copying/pasting it 25 times to be able to detect the other 25 keys/letters, using the syntax **Input.GetKeyDown**, once for each key. So the code could look as follows:

```
if (Input.GetKeyDown(KeyCode.A))
{
...
}
if (Input.GetKeyDown(KeyCode.B))
{
...
}


if (Input.GetKeyDown(KeyCode.Z))
{
...
}
```

Now, this would be working perfectly, however, this would also involve a lot of repetitions (copying 24 times the same code); so to make the code more efficient, we will use a slightly different way of detecting the key pressed by the player. This method will involve the following:

- Check if a key was pressed.

- Check if this key is a letter.

- Proceed as previously to check whether this letter is part of the word to be guessed.

Please create a new function called **checkKeyBoard2**, as follows:

```
void checkKeyboard2()
{
    if (Input.anyKeyDown)
    {
        char letterPressed = Input.inputString.ToCharArray ()
[0];
        int    letterPressedAsInt    =    System.Convert.ToInt32
(letterPressed);
        if (letterPressedAsInt >= 97 && letterPressed <= 122)
        {
            for (int i=0; i < lengthOfWordToGuess; i++)
            {
                if (!lettersGuessed [i])
                {
                    letterPressed    =    System.Char.ToUpper
(letterPressed);
                    if    (lettersToGuess    [i]    ==
letterPressed)
                    {
                        lettersGuessed [i] = true;

    GameObject.Find("letter"+(i+1)).GetComponent<Text>().text    =
letterPressed.ToString();
                    }
                }
            }
        }
    }
}
```

In the previous code:

- We detect whether a key has been pressed using the keyword **Input.anyKeyDown**.

- If this is the case, we save the key (i.e., the letter) that was pressed into the variable called **letterPressed**. For this, given that any key pressed on the keyboard is stored as a string, we need to convert this string value to a character; the character recorded in the variable **letterPressed** will effectively be the first character of the string that corresponds to the key pressed by the player.

- Once this is done, we convert the letter pressed (i.e., character) to an integer value.

- We then check, using the integer value associated with the key pressed, that the key is a letter; this corresponds to an integer value between **97** and **122**.

- Once this final check is complete, we do the exact same as we have done earlier in the function **checkBoard** that we have created previously (i.e., this is the same code).

The last thing we need to do is to call the function **chekBoard2** instead of the function **checkBoard** by amending the **Update** function as follows (new code in bold):

```
void Update () {

    //checkKeyboard ();
    checkKeyboard2 ();

}
```

That's it!

Once this is done, please save your code, check that it is error-free and test the **Scene**. As you press the keys **E**, **L**, **P** and **A**, you should see that they now appear onscreen.

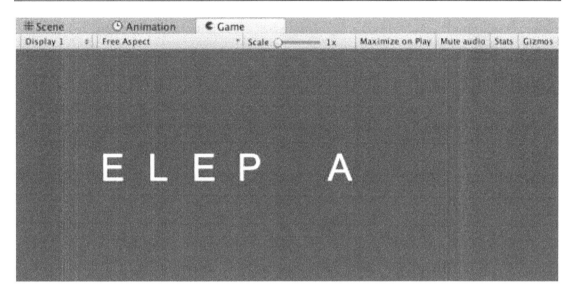

Figure 239: Detecting all the keys pressed

CHOOSING RANDOM WORDS

At this stage, the game works properly and the letters that the player has guessed are displayed onscreen; this being said, it would be great to add more challenge by selecting the word to guess at random from a list of pre-defined words. So in the next section, we will learn to do just that; we will start by choosing a word from an array, and then from a text file that you will be able to update yourself without any additional coding.

So let's get started.

- Please open the script **GameManager**.

- Add the following code at the beginning of the class.

```
private string [] wordsToGuess = new string [] {"car",
"elephant","autocar" };
```

- In the previous code, we declare an array of string variables and we add three words to it.

- Add the following code to the function **initGame** (new code in bold).

```
//wordToGuess = "Elephant";
int randomNumber = Random.Range (0, wordsToGuess.Length);
wordToGuess = wordsToGuess [randomNumber];
```

In the previous code:

- We comment the previous code.

- We create a random number that will range from **0** to the **length of the array**. So in our case, because we have three elements in this array, this random number will range from 0 to 2 (i.e., from **0** to **2**).

- We then set the variable called **wordToGuess** to one of the words included in the array called **wordsToGuess**; this word will be picked at random based on the variable called **randomNumber**.

You can now save you script, and check that it is error-free.

There is a last thing that we could do; because the word is chosen at random, the player will not have any idea of the length of this word; so to give an indication of the number of letters to be guessed, we could display questions marks for all the letters to be guessed, onscreen as follows:

- Please select the prefab called **letter** from the **Project** window.

- Using the **Inspector**, and the component called **Text** change its text to **?**, as described in the next figure.

Figure 240: Changing the default charcater for letters

- Lastly, we can also deactivate the object called **letter** that is in the **Hierarchy**.

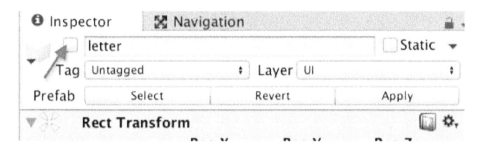

Figure 241: Deactivating the letter object

You can now play the **Scene**, and you should see questions marks where letters need to be guessed.

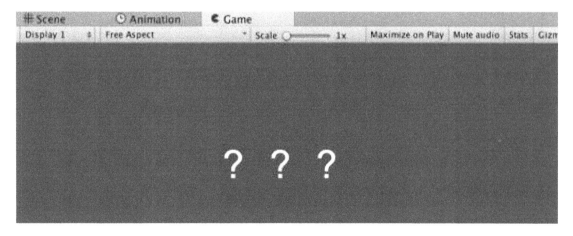

Figure 242: Displaying question marks

TRACKING THE SCORE AND THE NUMBER OF ATTEMPTS

So at this stage, we have a game were we generate random words that need to be guessed by the player. So we will start to finalize our game by adding the following features:

- A starting screen.

- A game-over screen.

- Display the number of guesses.

- Set and display the maximum number of attempts.

- Detect if all the letters in the word to be guessed were found.

- Restart the level with a new word whenever the previous word has been guessed.

- Load the game-over screen if the maximum number of attempts has been reached.

First, we will create s new splash-screen for our game; it will consist of a new **Scene** with a button to proceed to the game. In this splash-screen, we will also initialize the score to 0.

- Please save the current scene as **chapter1**: select **File | Save Scene As…**.

- Create a new scene: from the **Project** view, select **Create | Scene**, and rename it **chapter1_start**.

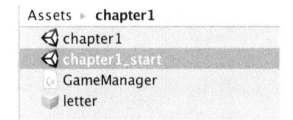

Figure 243: Creating a new Scene

- In the **Project** window, double-click on this new scene.

- If the skybox appears in the background, you can, as we have done in the previous sections, remove it by changing the **Lighting** options (i.e., **Window | Rendering | Lighting Settings**).

Once this is done, we can create a button that will be used to start the game:

- Please, select **GameObject | UI | Button**; this will create a new button along with its corresponding **Canvas**.

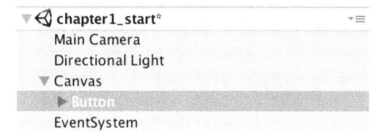

Figure 244: Creating a new button

- Select this button in the **Hierarchy**.

- Using the **Inspector** window, and the component called **RectTransform**, change its position to (**PosX = 0;PosY = 0**).

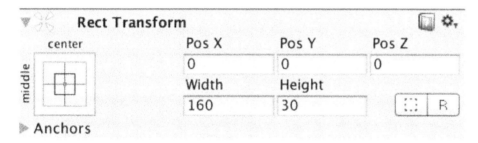

Figure 245: Changing the position of the button

- Using the **Hierarchy**, select the object called **Text** that is a child of the object called **Button,** as illustrated in the next figure.

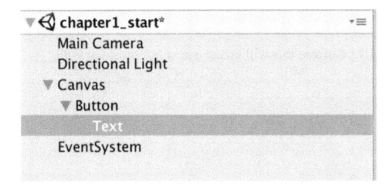

Figure 246: Setting the text for the button

- Using the **Inspector**, in the component called **Text**, change the text attribute to >> **Start** <<, as described in the next figure.

Figure 247: Changing the text for the button

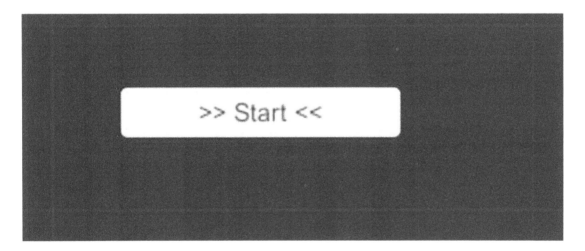

Figure 248: The button with the new text

Next, we need to create a script (and the associated empty object) that will be used to trigger an action when the button is pressed.

- Please create a new empty object (**GameObject | Create Empty**) and rename it **manageButtons**.

- Then, from the **Project** window, select: **Create | C# Script**.

- Rename the new script **ManageButtons** and open it.

We can now add the code that will initialize the score; the new code will also be used to launch the game when the button is pressed.

- Please add the following code at the start of the class (new code in bold):

```
using UnityEngine;
using System.Collections;
using UnityEngine.SceneManagement;
public class ManageButtons : MonoBehaviour {
```

In the previous code we import the library called **SceneManagement**, as we will be using the class **SceneManager** in the next code to load a new **Scene**. The class **SceneManager** is part of the library called **SceneManagement**.

- Please modify the **Start** function as follows:

```
void Start ()
{
    PlayerPrefs.SetInt ("score", 0);
}
```

In the previous code, we declare and initialize a variable called **score**; this variable is saved in the **User Preferences**, which means that it will be accessible throughout the game (i.e., from any scene).

- Please create the following function just before the end of the class:

```
public void startWordGame()
{
    SceneManager.LoadScene ("chapter1");
}
```

In the previous code, we define the function **startWordGame**; when this function is called, the scene called **chapter1** is loaded.

Next, we will link the button to the function **startWordGame**.

- Please save the script and check that it is error-free.

- Once this is done, drag and drop the script **ManageButtons** from the **Project** window to the empty object **manageButton** in the **Hierarchy**, as illustrated in the next figure.

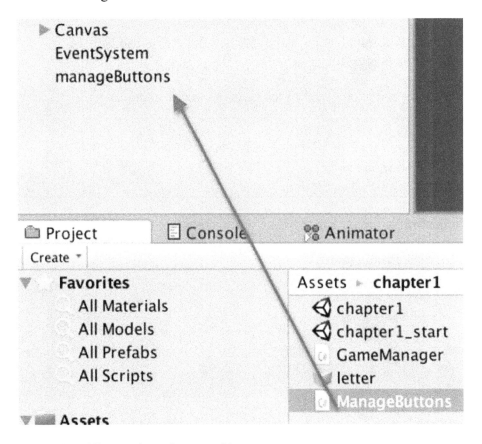

Figure 249: Adding a script to the empty object

You can then select the object **manageButtons** in the **Hierarchy** and look at the **Inspector** window; you should see that the component **ManageButtons** has been added.

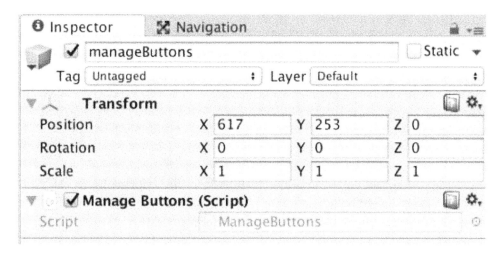

Figure 250: Checking the new component

Next, we will set-up the button so that the function **startWordGame** is called whenever this button is pressed.

- Please select the object called **Button** in the **Hierarchy**.

- Using the **Inspector**, in the section called **Button**, click on the + sign that is below the label **List is Empty**.

Figure 251: Handling clicks (part 1)

Once this is done, this section should now include a new field called **None Object**, as illustrated on the next figure.

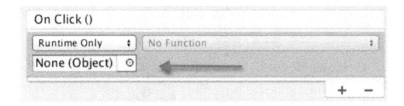

Figure 252: Handling clicks (part 2)

You can then drag and drop the object called **manageButtons** from the **Hierarchy** to the section called **None (Object)** for this object.

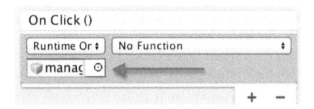

Figure 253: Handling clicks (part 3)

Following this, you can then click on the drop-down menu called "**No Function**" and select: **ManageButtons | startWordGame**. By doing so, we specify that if the button is pressed, the function **startWordGame** from the script **ManageButtons** should be called.

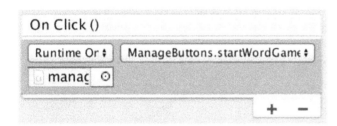

Figure 254: Handling clicks (part 4)

Last but not least, we just need to make sure that all scenes to be played in the game are part of the build settings; this is a way to declare the scenes that should be loaded to Unity.

- Please open the **Build Settings** by selecting **File | Build Settings**.

- Drag and drop the scenes **chapter1** and **chapter1_start** from the **Project** view to the **Build Settings** window.

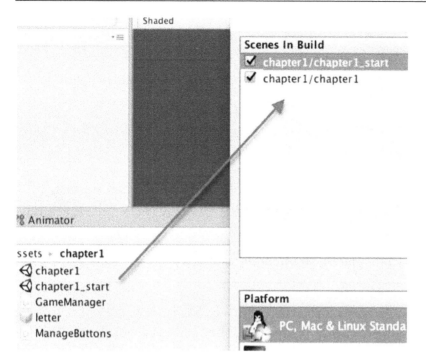

Figure 255: Updating the Build Settings

You can now, play the scene (i.e., **chapter1_start**) and check that the game starts after you press the **START** button.

Next, we will be focusing on recording the number of attempts made by the player. So we will create some code that will track how many guesses the player has made, in the view to evaluate if the player has reached the maximum number of attempts (to be defined later in this section).

- Please save the current scene (**CTRL +S** or **APPLE + S**).

- Open the scene called **chapter1**.

- Open the script called **GameManager**.

- Add the following code at the beginning of the class.

```
private int nbAttempts,maxNbAttempts;
```

- Add the following code to the **Start** function:

```
nbAttempts = 0;
maxNbAttempts = 10;
```

- Please add the following code the function **checkKeyboard2** (new code in bold):

```
if (letterPressedAsInt >= 97 && letterPressed <= 122)
{
     nbAttempts++;updateNbAttempts();
```

In the previous code, we increase the value of the variable **nbAttempts**, and we then refresh the user interface by calling the function **updateNbAttempts**, that we will define in the next paragraph.

- Please create the new function **updateNbAttempts** as follows:

```
void updateNbAttempts()
{
     GameObject.Find ("nbAttempts").GetComponent<Text> ().text =
nbAttempts + "/" + maxNbAttempts;
}
```

In the previous code, we update the text of the **Text UI** object **nbAttempts** (that we have just created) so that it displays the number of attempts made by the player.

- Please add the following line to the **Start** function.

```
updateNbAttempts();
```

- Please save your script, and check that it is error-free.

Finally, we just need to create a **UI Text** object called **nbAttempts** where the number of attempts will be displayed.

- Please create a new **UI Text** component (**GameObject | UI | Text**) and rename it **nbAttempts**.

- Change its **color** to **white**, change its **font-size** to **20**, empty its text, and, using the **Move** tool, place this object in the top-left corner of the white rectangle that defines the viewable area for the player, as described on the next figure.

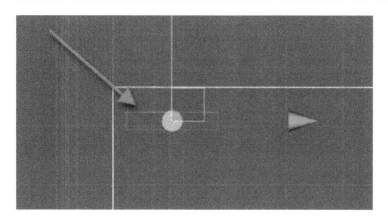

Figure 256: Modifying the user interface

Once this is done, you can test the scene and check that the user interface is updated every time you make a guess (i.e., when you press a letter on the keyboard).

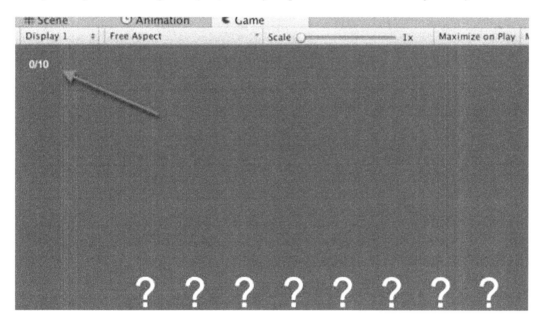

Figure 257: Displaying the number of attempts

Next, we will update the score. So the process will be similar to what we have done previously, as we will:

- Create a **UI Text** object that will display the **score**.

- Increase the **score** whenever a letter has been found.

- Update the text of the corresponding **UI Text** object.

So let's gets started:

- Using the **Hierarchy** window, please duplicate the object called **nbAttempts** and rename the duplicate **scoreUI**.

- Move this object (i.e., **scoreUI**) to the top-right corner of the screen.

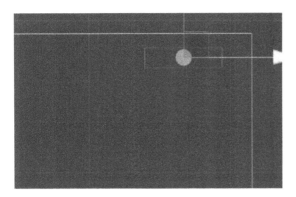

Figure 258: Displaying the score

Once this is done, we can update our script:

- Please open the script called **GameManager**.

- Add this code at the beginning of the class.

```
int score = 0;
```

- Add the following function just before the end of the class (before the last closing curly bracket) so that we can update the score onscreen.

```
void updateScore()
{
    GameObject.Find  ("scoreUI").GetComponent<Text>  ().text  =
"Score:"+score;
}
```

- Add the following code to the **Start** function.

```
updateScore();
```

- Modify the function **checkKeyboard2** as follows (new code in bold):

```
if (lettersToGuess [i] == letterPressed)
{
     lettersGuessed [i] = true;
     GameObject.Find("letter"+(i+1)).GetComponent<Text>().text  =
letterPressed.ToString();
     score = PlayerPrefs.GetInt ("score");
     score++;
     PlayerPrefs.SetInt ("score", score);
     updateScore ();
}
```

In the previous code, we just increase the score by one every time the player has guessed a letter correctly; the score accessed from the **Player Preferences**; it is increased by one then saved in the **Player Preferences**, and the interface is then updated accordingly through the function **updateScore**.

- Please save your code, and check that it is error-free. As you play the scene the **score** should be displayed in the top-right corner, as illustrated in the next figure.

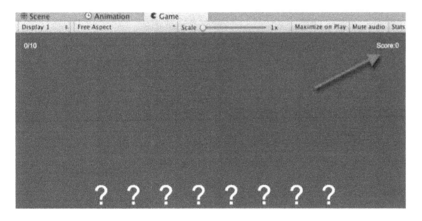

Figure 259: Displaying the score

Now, the last thing we need to do is to check whether the player has guessed the word using less than the maximum number of attempts allowed; if this is the case, a **win** scene will be displayed; otherwise, if the player has failed to guess the word within the maximum number of attempts allowed, a scene called **lose** will be displayed instead. So first, we will create these two scenes (i.e., win and lose).

- Please duplicate the scene called **chapter1_start**: in the **Project** view, select the **Scene** called **chapter1_start**, and press **CTRL + D**.

- This will create a duplicate.

- Please rename the duplicate **chapter1_lose**.

- Open this **Scene** (i.e., **chapter1_lose**).

- Select the object called **Text** in the **Hierarchy**.

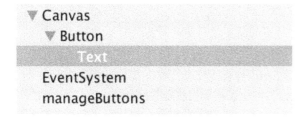

Figure 260: Changing the label of the button

- Using the **Inspector**, for the component called **Text**, change the attribute **text** to
>> **RESTART** <<.

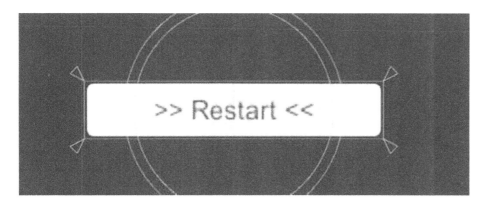

Figure 261:Changing the label of the button

If you wish, you can also add a **UI Text** object with the text "**You Lost**", as follows.

- Create a new **UI Text** object and rename it **message**.

- Using the **Inspector**, change this object's width to **600** and its height to **200**.

- Align its text so that it is centered vertically and horizontally, using the section called **Paragraph** in the component called **Text**.

- Change the font-size to **100**.

- Change the font-color to **white**.

- Center the text both horizontally and vertically.

> Please make sure that there is no overlap between the **UI Text** object and the button, otherwise clicks on the button may not be detected.

- Change the text to "**YOU LOST!**".

- The scene should look like the next figure.

Figure 262: Displaying the game-over screen

You can now save the scene.

Last but not least, we will modify the script called **ManageButtons** so that the score is only initialized in the splash-screen.

- Please open the script **ManageButttons**.

- Modify the **Start** function as follows (new code in bold):

```
void Start ()
{
    if (SceneManager.GetActiveScene().name == "chapter1_start")
PlayerPrefs.SetInt ("score", 0);
}
```

In the previous code, the score is initialized only if we are in the scene called **chapter1_start** (i.e., the splash-screen).

Now that the scene called **lose** has been created, we can modify the code used in the game scene so that the **lose** scene is loaded when the number of guesses is more than the maximum allowed.

- Please save the current scene (i.e., press **CTRL + S**).

- Open the scene **chapter1**.

- Open the script called **GameManager**.

- Add the following code at the beginning of the class.

```
using UnityEngine.SceneManagement;
```

- Add the following code to the function **checkKeyboard2** (new code in bold).

```
if (letterPressedAsInt >= 97 && letterPressed <= 122)
{
    nbAttempts++;updateNbAttempts ();
    if (nbAttempts > maxNbAttempts)
    {
        SceneManager.LoadScene ("chapter1_lose");
    }
}
```

In the previous code, we check whether we have reached the maximum number of attempts; in this case, the scene called **chapter1_lose** is loaded.

- Please save your script and check that it is error-free.

We can now add the scene **chapter1_lose** to the **Build Settings** (i.e., select **File | Build Settings**) as we have done for the other scenes.

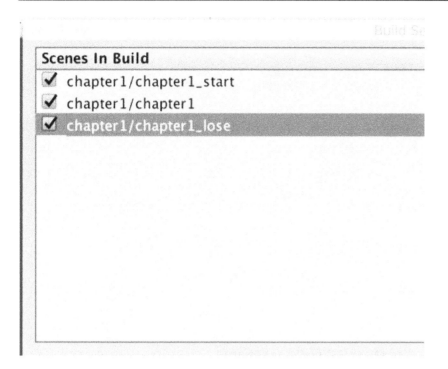

Figure 263: Adding a Scene to the Build Settings

Once this is done, you can play the scene; as you reach the maximum number of attempts, the **lose** scene should be displayed.

Next, we will create code that will assess whether the player has managed to guess all the letters in the word. For this purpose, we will do the following:

- Create a function that will be called whenever the player has correctly guessed a letter.

- This function will check if all the letters were guessed accurately.

- In this case, it will save the word to be guessed, and then display it in the **win** scene.

So let's create this function:

- Please open the script **GameManager**.

- Add the following script at the end of the class.

```
void checkIfWordWasFound()
{
     bool condition = true;
     for (int i = 0; i < lengthOfWordToGuess; i++)
     {
          condition = condition && lettersGuessed [i];
     }
     if (condition)
     {
          PlayerPrefs.SetString                ("lastWordGuessed",
wordToGuess);
          SceneManager.LoadScene ("chapter1_well_done");
     }
}
```

In the previous code:

- We define a function called **checkIfWordWasFound**.

- We then declare a Boolean variable called **condition** that will be used to determine if all the letters were found.

- This variable called **condition** is initially set to true.

- We then go through each variable of the array called **letterGuessed** to check the letters that were guessed correctly by the player. If one of the word's letters was not found (i.e., even just one), the variable called **condition** will be set to false.

- The following code effectively performs a logical **AND** between all the variables of the array **lettersGuessed**, as all of them need to be true (i.e., found) for the variable **condition** to be **true**; so this is the same as saying "**if letter1 was guessed, and letter2 was guessed and letter3 was guessed, …, and the last letter was guessed then the condition is true**"

```
condition = condition && lettersGuessed [i];
```

- If the variable **condition** is **true**, we then save the word that was guessed in the player preferences, so that it can be accessed and displayed in the next scene.

- We then load the **win** scene (that we yet have to create).

We can now add a call to this function from the **checkKeyboard2** function, as follows (new code in bold):

```
score++;
PlayerPrefs.SetInt ("score", score);
updateScore ();
checkIfWordWasFound ();
```

So, we just need to create that new scene:

- Please save your code and check that it is error free.

- Using the **Project** window, duplicate the scene called **chapter1_lose** (**CTRL + D**) and rename the duplicate **chapter1_well_done**.

- Open the new scene called **chapter1_well_done**.

- Using the **Inspector**, duplicate the object called **Text** (the one used to display the message "**YOU LOST**") and rename the duplicate **wordGuessed**.

- Using the **Move** tool, move the object **wordGuessed** below the button that is already in the scene, as in the next figure.

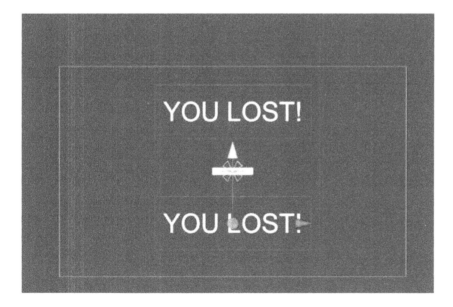

Figure 264: Moving the new UI Text

- We can change the text of the **UI Text** called **Text**, so that it now displays the text "**YOU WON**".

- We can also empty the text of the **UI Text** object **wordGuessed** so that the interface looks like the next figure.

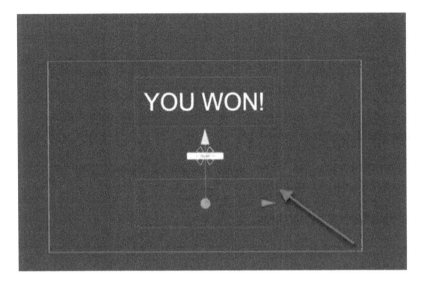

Figure 265: Modifying the GUI

We will now create a script that will be attached to the object **wordGuessed** and that will display the actual word that was just guessed by the player.

- Please create a new C# script called **DisplayLastWordGuessed**.

- Drag and drop this script on the object called **wordGuessed**.

- Open this script.

- Add this code at the beginning of the script.

```
using UnityEngine.UI;
```

- Modify its **Start** function as follows:

```
void Start ()
{
    GetComponent<Text>().text      =      PlayerPrefs.GetString
("lastWordGuessed");
}
```

- Please save your script and your scene.

- Add your scene to the **Build Settings**.

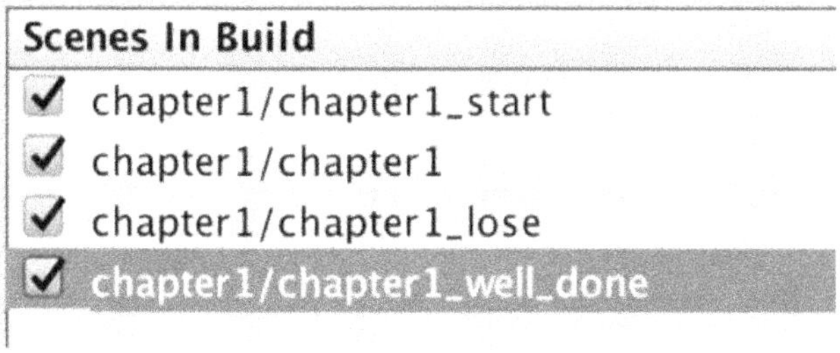

Scenes In Build

☑ chapter1/chapter1_start
☑ chapter1/chapter1
☑ chapter1/chapter1_lose
☑ chapter1/chapter1_well_done

Figure 266: Adding the last Scene to the Build Settings

We can now open the main scene **chapter1**, and test the transition to the **win** scene.

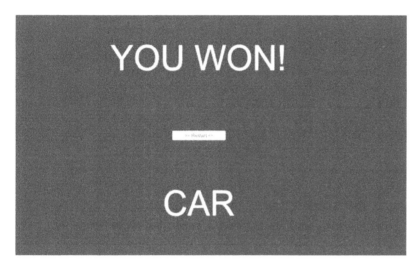

Figure 267: Displaying the win screen

CHOOSING WORDS FROM A FILE

At this stage, the word game is pretty much functional with words selected at random; this being said, the words that we are using are part of an array that we need to update manually; if you were to include 100 words, you would need to enter them manually, which could be time-consuming. So in this section, we will use a technique that consists of selecting a word from a pre-existing list of words saved in a text file. Because such files are available on the Internet, you could virtually create a word guessing game in several languages, by just modifying the file that contains these words.

So we will proceed as follows:

- Import a file with that includes a list of words.

- Add this file to a folder in Unity, where it can be accessed from a script.

- Access this file from our script.

- Pick a random word from this file.

So let's get started.

- Please create a new folder in the **Assets** folder, and call it **Resources**: select the **Assets** folder in the **Project** window, and then select **Create | Folder** from the **Project** window.

- Rename this folder **Resources**.

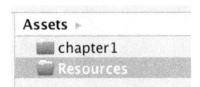

Figure 268: Adding a new folder

- Once this is done, please import the file called **words.txt** from the resource pack that you have downloaded from the companion website to the folder **Resources** that you have just created.

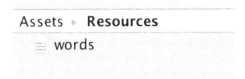

Figure 269: Importing the word file

Next, we will modify our code:

- Please open the script **GameManager**.

- Add the following code just before the end of the class.

```
string pickAWordFromFile()
{
    TextAsset    t1    =    (TextAsset)Resources.Load("words",
typeof(TextAsset));
    string s = t1.text;
    string[] words = s.Split ("\n"[0]);
    int randomWord = Random.Range (0, words.Length + 1);
    return (words[randomWord]);
}
```

In the previous code:

- We create a variable of type **TextAsset** that will point to the text file that we have just imported.

- We then store the text from this file in a variable called **s**.

- Since this file consists of one word per line, we split this string into lines, so that the variable **words** now contains an array of all the words (i.e., lines) included in the file.

Note that the command **string.Split()** will split a string based on a specific character; in our case it is the **end of line** which is symbolized in computer terms by "**\n**".

- The syntax **words = s.Split ("\n"[0]);** means that we split the string called **s** based on the separator "**end of line**" (i.e., **\n**).

Last but not least, we just need to pick one of these words at random.

- Please modify the function called **initGame** as follows.

```
//wordToGuess = wordsToGuess [randomNumber];
wordToGuess = pickAWordFromFile ();
```

That's it.

You can now try the game again and check that it works.

There are a few things that you could then modify, for example:

- You could set the number of attempts to the number of letters in the word to be guessed.

- You could also display the word that was to be guessed in the **lose** scene.

- Finally, you could also use sound effects to provide feedback on whether the letter that was selected was correct.

LEVEL ROUNDUP

In this chapter, we have learned to create a simple word guessing game where the player can guess the letters of a particular word. Along the way, we have learned a few interesting skills including: generating random numbers, reading words from a file, using player preferences to save information between scenes, or detecting the player's input. So, we have covered considerable ground to get you started with your first word game!

Checklist

You can consider moving to the next stage if you can do the following:

- Create random numbers.

- Access a text file from a script.

- Update the text of **UI Text** object from a script.

- Create an array of string or Boolean variables.

- Detect the keys pressed by the player.

Quiz

Now, let's check your knowledge! Please specify whether the following statements are true or false.

1. The following code will declare an array of integers.

```
int [] i = new int [];
```

2. The following code will declare and initialize an array of string variables:

```
string    []    wordsToGuess    =    new    string    []    {"car",
"elephant","autocar" };
```

3. The following code will check whether the player has pressed the key called A.

```
if (Input.GetKeyDown(A))
```

4. The following code will display the number of characters in the string **Hello**.

```
string s = "Hello";
print(s.Length);
```

5. A **char** variable can be used to store a name with more than two letters.

6. A **string** variable can be used to store a name with more than two letters.

7. The following code will generate a random number between 0 and 100.

```
float randomNumber = Random.Number (0, 100);
```

8. The first element of an array starts at the index 1.

9. The first element of an array starts at the index 0.

10. The following code will store the score in the player preferences:

```
PlayerPrefs.SetInt ("score",score);
```

Answers to the Quiz

1. TRUE.

2. TRUE.

3. FALSE.

4. TRUE.

5. FALSE.

6. TRUE.

7. TRUE.

8. FALSE.

9. TRUE.

10. TRUE.

Challenge 1

Now that you have managed to complete this chapter and that you have created your first level, you could improve it by doing the following:

- Set the number of attempts to the number of letters in the word to be guessed.

- Display the word that was to be guessed in the **lose** scene.

Challenge 2

Another interesting challenge could be as follows:

- Create a text file of your choice with a word on each line.

- Use this word file instead for your game.

CHAPTER 12: CREATING A MEMORY GAME

In this section, we will learn how to create a memory game similar to the Simon Game, whereby the player needs to remember a sequence of colors associated to a sound. As the game progresses, the sequence will become longer, hence, increasing the challenge for the player.

After completing this chapter, you will be able to:

- Generate sound effects from Unity and modify their frequency.

- Detect when a player has pressed a button.

- Generate colors at random.

- Generate a sequence of colors and sound.

- Record the sequence entered by the player and compare it to the correct sequence.

INTRODUCTION

In this chapter, we will learn how to create visual and sound effects. We will also create a process by which a sequence of colors is created, and then compared to the sequence entered by the player.

The game will consist of four colored boxes that the player will need to press to reproduce a sequence created randomly by the game.

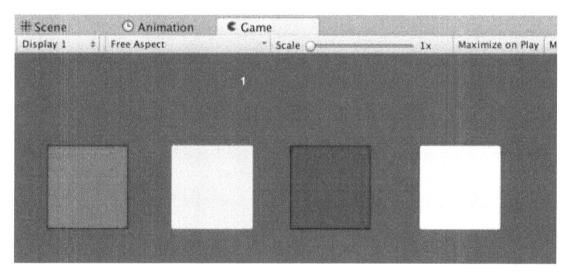

Figure 270: A preview of the game

CREATING THE INTERFACE AND THE CORE OF THE GAME

In this section, we will create the interface for the game; it will consist of four buttons of different colors that the player can click on.

So' let's proceed:

- Please save your current scene (**File | Save Scene**).

- Create a new scene for this new game (**File | New Scene**).

- Rename this new scene **chapter2** (**File | Save Scene As**).

- If the skybox appears by default, you can, as we have done in the previous chapter, remove it using the menu **Window | Rendering | Lighting Settings**.

Once this is done, we can start to create the buttons that will be used for our game.

- Please create a new button: from the top menu, select **GameObject | UI | Button**. This will create a new object called **Button**, and a parent object called **Canvas**.

- Rename the object called **Button** to **red**.

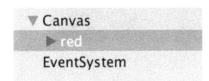

Figure 271: Adding a button

- Please select the object called **red**, and, using the **Inspector**, change its color to **red**, by modifying the **color attribute** of its component called **Image**, as per the next figure.

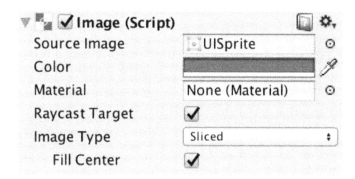

Figure 272: Changing the color of the button

- We can also change its size, so that it looks like a square: please change the **width** and **height** of this object (for the component **Rect Transform**) to **160**.

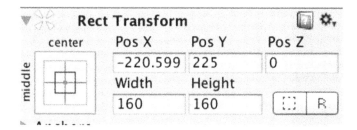

Figure 273: Modifying the size of the button

Last, we will empty the label of this button.

- Using the **Hierarchy**, select the object called **Text** that is a child of the button called **red**.

Figure 274: Emptying the label of the button (part 1)

- Using the **Inspector**, empty the attribute called **text** for its component called **Text**, as per the next figure.

Figure 275: Emptying the label for the button (part 2)

So, at this stage, your button should look like the one illustrated in the next figure.

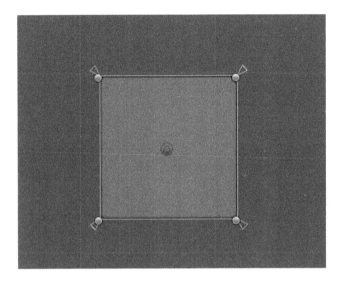

Figure 276: Displaying the red button

So the next step for now is to create the three other buttons by **duplicating** the **red** button:

- Please select the object called **red** in the **Hierarchy** window.

- Duplicate it three times so that you have three duplicates.

- Rename the duplicates **green**, **blue**, and **yellow**.

Figure 277: Duplicating the red button

- Using the **Move** tool, move each duplicate apart, as illustrated on the next figure.

Figure 278: Aligning the buttons

- For each of the duplicates: select the corresponding button in the **Hierarchy**, and change its color to **green**, **blue**, and **yellow**, so that the color that you choose matches the name of the corresponding object. You can change the color of a button by selecting this object, and by using the **Inspector** to modify its **Image component**, as described in the next figure.

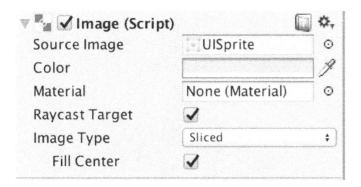

Figure 279: Changing the color of a button

- Once this is done, your **Scene** view may look like the next figure.

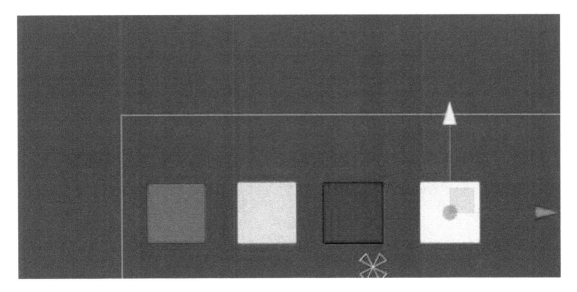

Figure 280: Four buttons with colors

DETECTING WHEN BUTTONS HAVE BEEN PRESSED

Next, we will create an empty object and a script that will be used to detect when a button has been pressed.

- Please create an empty object (**GameObject | Create Empty**) and rename it **manageBt**.

- Create a new C# script called **TouchButton**.

- Add this script (i.e., drag and drop it) to the empty object called **manageBt**.

- Select the object called **red** in the **Hierarchy**.

- For this object and in its component called **Button**, click on the + sign located under the label "**List is Empty**", as illustrated in the next figure.

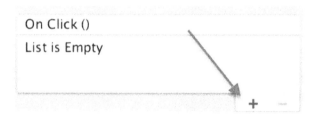

- You can then drag and drop the object called **manageBt** from the **Hierarchy** to the empty field that you have just created, as illustrated on the next figure.

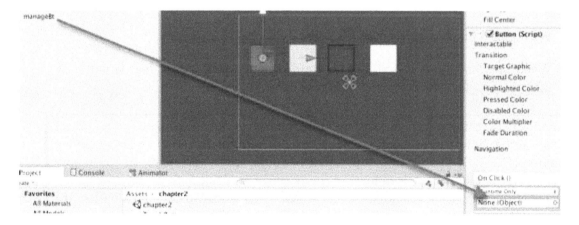

Figure 281: Managing the clicks on buttons (part 1)

- The component called **Button** should then look as illustrated on the next figure.

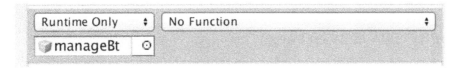

Figure 282: Managing the clicks on buttons (part 2)

Now, we just need to modify our script **TouchButton**, to create a function that will be called whenever the player clicks on the button.

- Please open the script called **TouchButton**.

- Add the following code at the beginning of the class.

```
using UnityEngine.EventSystems;
```

- This line is necessary, as we will be using some of the classes from the library called **EventSystems** in the next code.

- Add this new function to the script (i.e., just before the last closing curly bracket).

```
public void touchButton()
{
    print         ("You        have        pressed        "        +
EventSystem.current.currentSelectedGameObject.name );
}
```

In the previous code:

- We define a function called **touchButton**.

- When this function is called, it displays the name of the object that is currently selected (i.e., the button that we have clicked);

We would usually employ the syntax **gameObject.name** to obtain the name of an object linked to a script; however, in this particular case, this script is linked to an empty object (i.e., **manageBt**), so calling **gameObject.name** would return the name of the empty object (i.e., **manageBt**), which is not useful for us, since we want to determine the button that was pressed; so instead, because an event is generated when we click on a button, we use this event to determine the button we have just clicked on; hence the code **EventSystem.current.currentSelectedGameObject.name**.

- Please save your code and check that it is error-free.

The last thing we need to do is to specify that the function called **touchButton** should be called whenever the **red** button is clicked. For this, we will proceed as follows:

- Select the object called **red** in the **Hierarchy**.

- In the **Inspector** window, for the attribute **Button**, locate the section called **On Click**() and select the drop-down menu called **No Function**, as illustrated on the next figure.

On Click ()

Figure 283: Selecting the function to be called

- Then, from the drop-down menu, select **TouchButton | touchButton** to specify that the function called **touchButton** should be called if we click on this button.

You can now play the scene and check that, after pressing the red button, a message appears in the **Console** window.

So now, we just need to repeat the previous steps for the three other buttons.

To save you time, and instead of repeating the same actions three times, you could proceed as follows:

- Select the three buttons **green**, **blue** and **yellow** in the **Hierarchy** (e.g., left-click + **SHIFT**).

- Because all three objects are selected, the changes that we are about to make will be applied to all three.

Figure 284: Selecting the three buttons

- In the **Inspector**, in the component called **Button**, click on the + sign located under the label "**List is Empty**", as illustrated in the next figure.

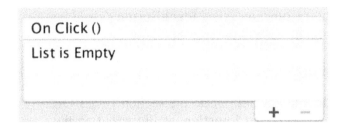

Figure 285: Adding an event

- You can then drag and drop the object called **manageBt** from the **Hierarchy** to the empty field that we just created.

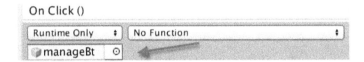

Figure 286: Adding the manageBt object

- Then select **TouchButton | touchButton** to specify that the function called **touchButton** should be called if we click on this button.

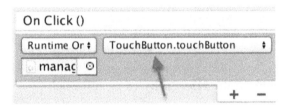

Figure 287: Selecting the corresponding function

To check that this has been applied to all three buttons you can just play the scene, press on any of the four buttons, and check that a corresponding message appears in the **Console** window, as illustrated in the next figure.

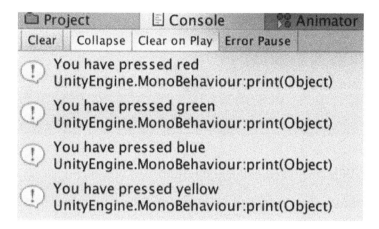

Figure 288: Displaying a message for each button

MANAGING THE GAME

Ok, so at this stage, we have four buttons and we can detect when the player clicks on them. So the next steps will be to:

- Create a **game manager** object.

- This object (and its associated script) will manage different aspects of the game.

- The actions performed by this manager will depend on states that we will define and that will help to know whether we are waiting for a user input, processing the user's input, or just displaying a new sequence of colors.

First, we will give a label to all four buttons, this is so that they can be identified later-on in our scripts.

- Please select the object called **red** in the **Hierarchy**.

- In the **Inspector** window, click on the drop-down menu called **Untagged**, that is located to the right of the label called **Tag**.

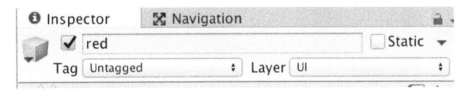

- Select the option **Add Tag** from the drop-down menu.

Figure 289: Selecting a new tag

- In the new window, press on the + button that is just below the label "**List is Empty**".

Figure 290: Creating new tags (part 1)

- This will a placeholder for the new tag that we want to create.

- Create a new tag by entering **1** to the right of the label called **Tag 0.**

- Repeat the previous steps to create three additional tags: **2**, **3**, and **4**.

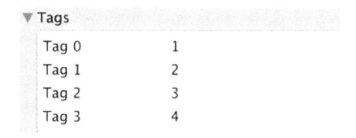

Figure 291: Creating new tags (part 2)

Next, once these tags have been created, we can apply them to the different buttons.

- Please select the button called **red** in the **Hierarchy**.

- Using the **Inspector** window, click to the right of the label called **Tag** and select the tag called **1** from the drop-down menu, as illustrated on the next figure.

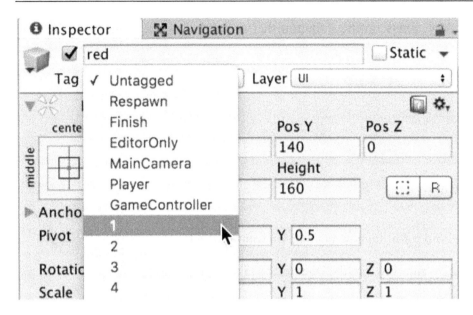

Figure 292: Selecting a tag for each button (part 1)

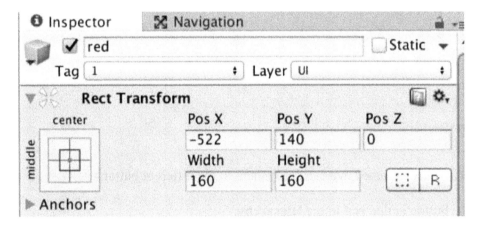

Figure 293: Selecting a tag for the buttons (part2)

Once this is done, you can repeat the last steps to allocate the other tags as follows:

- **Green box**: Tag = 2;

- **Blue box**: Tag = 3;

- **Yellow box**: Tag = 4.

HANDLING CLICKS

Next, we will create a function that will be called whenever a button is pressed. In the previous sections, the handling of the clicks on the buttons was performed by the script **TouchButton**; so we will link this script **TouchButton** to the game manager, so that every time a button is pressed, the game manager is called and receives the name or the tag of the button that was pressed.

- Please create a new C# script called **ManageAudioGame**.

- Create a new empty object called **gameManager**.

- Drag and drop the script **ManageAudioGame** to the object **gameManager**.

- Add the following code at the beginning of the class:

```
int colorSubmitted;
```

In the previous code, we declare the variable **colorSubmitted**, which will store the tag of the button that was just pressed.

- Add the following function just before the end of the class (just before the last closing curly bracket).

```
public void submitColor(int newColor)
{
    print ("You have pressed color " + newColor);
    colorSubmitted = newColor;
}
```

In the previous code:

- We define a function called **submitColor**.

- This function has a parameter called **newColor** that will be used to determine the color of the button that was pressed.

- So when this function is called, it will display the tag number of the button that was just pressed in the **Console** window.

Please save your script.

Next, we just need to be able to call the function **submitColor** every time a button has been pressed, so we will need to modify the script called **TouchButton** accordingly.

- Please open the script **TouchButton**, and modify it as follows (new code in bold).

```
public void touchButton()
{
    //print        ("You       have       pressed      "      +
EventSystem.current.currentSelectedGameObject.name );
    int                    colorNumber                   =
(int)(int.Parse(EventSystem.current.currentSelectedGameObject.tag
));
    GameObject.Find
("gameManager").GetComponent<ManageAudioGame>       ().submitColor
(colorNumber);
}
```

In the previous code:

- We comment the line that displayed the color of the box pressed, as we will display a similar message in the function called **submitColor** in the script **ManageAudioGame**.

- We declare a new variable called **colorNumber**; this number will be set using the tag of the button that was just pressed.

- Because the tag is a **string** value (i.e., text), we use the function **int.Parse** to convert it to an **integer** type.

We also use the expression **(int)** to cast (or convert) it to an **int** type; this is because although we have already converted the **string** to an **int**, Unity needs to ensure that what is on the right side of the equal sign is of the same type as what is on the left side of the equal sign. So by adding a casting in the form of **(int)**, we ensure that values on both sides of the equal sign are of the same type. This is called **casting**.

Before we can test our scene, please ensure that both the scripts **TouchButton** and **ManageAudiogame** are error-free, and also that the script **ManageAudioGame** has been added (i.e., dragged and dropped) to the object **gameManager**.

- You can now test your scene, and press on any of the buttons, and you should see a corresponding message displayed in the **Console** window, as illustrated in the next figure.

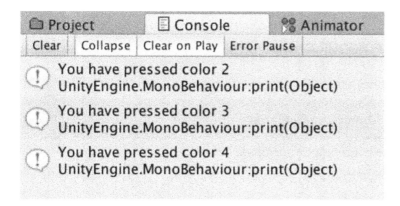

Figure 294: Displaying the tag of the active button

CREATING DIFFERENT STATES FOR OUR GAME

Next, we will declare the different states that will apply to our game.

- Please open the script called **ManageAudioGame**.

- Add the following code at the beginning of the class.

```
private const int STATE_PLAY_SEQUENCE = 1;
private const int STATE_WAIT_FOR_USER_INPUT = 2;
private const int STATE_PROCESS_USER_INPUT = 3;
```

In the previous code:

- We declare three constants; these are variables that will not change throughout our game. Although they are integers, their name will be easier to remember than numbers.

- All these variables are there to define a state in which the game will be at any given time.

So the game will be in one of these states.

- **Playing a sequence of colors**: once a new color has been created, the new sequence that includes all the colors generated is played. Every turn, one new color is added to the sequence.

- **Waiting for the user's input**: After a new sequence has been played/displayed by the game, the player needs to click on the boxes in the correct order to reproduce this sequence.

- **Processing the user's input**: Once the user has pressed the different buttons, the game will need to process this information to determine whether the player has remembered and played the previous sequence correctly.

Once this is done, the game will either add a new color to the sequence, or restart from the beginning.

The core of our game will be based on all these states; so we will now modify the **Update** functions to mirror these different states.

- Please add the following code at the beginning of the class:

```
private int currentState;
```

- Please add the following code in the **Start** function:

```
currentState = STATE_PLAY_SEQUENCE;
```

In the previous code, we just specify that at the start of the game, the game will play the new sequence.

- Please modify the **Update** function as follows:

```
void Update ()
{
    switch (currentState)
    {
        case STATE_PLAY_SEQUENCE:
        break;

        case STATE_WAIT_FOR_USER_INPUT:
        break;

        case STATE_PROCESS_USER_INPUT:
        break;

        default:
        break;
    }
}
```

In the previous code:

- We create a switch statement; this is comparable to branching instructions based on a specific variable; in our case, we will execute code based on the value of the variable called **currentState**.

- So if **currentState** is **STATE_PLAY_SEQUENCE**, we will go to the corresponding section called **STATE_PLAY_SEQUENCE**.

- The idea of this structure is that all branches are mutually exclusive which means that you can be in only one state at any time. So the game will either be playing a new sequence of colors, waiting for the user input, or assessing the user input.

PLAYING A SEQUENCE OF COLORS

Next we will be dealing with the state called **STATE_PLAY_SEQUENCE**; in this state, the game should do the following:

- Pick a color at random.

- Add it to the existing sequence of colors.

- Play the new sequence of colors (including the last color) and light-up the corresponding boxes sequentially.

- Note that if we are at the start of the game, only the new color that has been generated will be displayed (i.e., corresponding boxed lit up).

For this purpose, we will need to do the following:

- Generate a new color at random.

- Store the sequence of colors in an array.

- Hide all the boxes currently displayed onscreen.

- Display (and subsequently hide) each individual box that is part of this sequence.

First, let's create a function that will generate a random number.

- Please add the following code at the beginning of the class:

```
int [] sequenceOfColor = new int[100];
int indexOfColor = 0;
```

In the previous code, we define the array that will be used to store the sequence created by the game.

- Please add the following code to the **Start** function:

```
void Start ()
{
    currentState = STATE_PLAY_SEQUENCE;
    sequenceOfColor = new int[100];
}
```

In the previous code, in addition to specifying the current state, we initialize the array **sequenceOfColor**; as it is, it should handle up to 100 items.

- Please add the following code just before the end of the class:

```
public void generateNewColor()
{
    int r = Random.Range (1, 4);
    sequenceOfColor [indexOfColor] = r;
    indexOfColor++;
}
```

In the previous code:

- We declare a function called **generateColor**.

- We create a new random number with a value that can range between **1** and **4**.

- We then add this number to the array that stores the sequence of colors generated by the game.

- We then increment the index of the array **indexOfColor**. This is so that the next time a color is created, it will be added at the index (or position) **index** in the array.

Next, we will create a function that will hide all the boxes; this is because we want to clear the screen before displaying each of the boxes that are part of the sequence.

- Please add the following code at the beginning of the script **ManageAudioGame** (new code in bold).

```
using UnityEngine;
using System.Collections;
using UnityEngine.UI;
```

In the previous code, we introduce the **UI** library, since will be using some of its element (i.e., **Text**).

- Please add the following code at the end of the class (i.e., before the last closing curly bracket).

```
void hideBoxes()
{
    for (int i = 1; i <= 4; i++)
    {
        GameObject.FindWithTag                    (""            +
i).GetComponent<Image>().enabled = false;
    }
}
```

In the previous code:

- We loop through the four boxes that we have created earlier (i.e., the boxes that are onscreen).

- We identify each of these boxes using their tag.

- For each box, we disable the **Image** component, which means that the box will not be visible.

Next, we will need another function that displays a particular box; this is so that we can display individually each of the colors included in the sequence generated by the game.

- Please add the following function at the end of the class **ManageAudioGame** (i.e., just before the last closing curly bracket).

```
public void displayBox(int index)
{
    GameObject.FindWithTag                    (""            +
index).GetComponent<Image>().enabled = true;
}
```

In the previous code:

- We declare a new function called **displayBox**, that will be used to display a particular box.

- We identify a box based on its tag.

- For this particular box, we enable the **Image** component, which means that the box will be visible.

Please save your script. At this stage, you can test the functions **hideBoxes** and **displayBox** by adding the following code to the **Start** function.

```
hideBoxes ();
displayBox (1);
```

- As you play the Scene, you should see that only the red box is displayed.

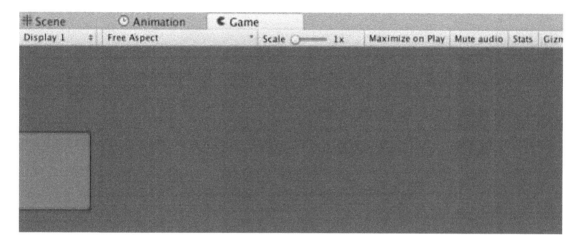

Figure 295: Testing the functions

CREATING A NEW SEQUENCE OF COLORS

Now that we can hide and display boxes, we will get to do the following:

- Pick a color/box at random.

- Add it to a new sequence.

- Display the sequence.

- Make sure that there is a delay between the display of each box, so that the sequence can be identified clearly by the player (i.e., otherwise, the sequence will be displayed too fast to be remembered).

- Wait for the player to reproduce this sequence by clicking on the corresponding boxes.

First, we will create a timer; this timer will be used to display each of the colors that are part of the sequence generated by the game.

- Please add the following code to the beginning of the class:

```
bool          newColorHasBeenGenerated,          allBoxesDisplayed,
startTimer,waitingTimerActivated,waitingTimeElapsed;
float timer, waitingTime, timeDelayBetweenDisplays;
int animationIndex, nbColorsSubmitted;
```

In the previous code, we declare a set of variables that will be used for the state called **STATE_PLAY_SEQUENCE**; each of these variables will be explained in the next sections.

- Please add the following code to the **Start** function:

```
newColorHasBeenGenerated = false;

startTimer = false;
waitingTimerActivated = false;
waitingTimeElapsed = false;
allBoxesDisplayed = false;
timer = 0;
waitingTime = 0;
animationIndex = 0;
timeDelayBetweenDisplays  = 2;
nbColorsSubmitted = 0;
```

In the previous code:

- We set the variable **newColorHasBeenpicked** to false.

- This variable is used to know whether the game has already picked a new color at random.

- We also declare a series of variables that will be explained in details later.

Once this is done, we can look at what the game should do in the state called **STATE_PLAY_SEQUENCE.**

- Please add the following code to the switch section that corresponds to the state **STATE_PLAY_SEQUENCE** (new cod in bold).

```
case STATE_PLAY_SEQUENCE:
if (!newColorHasBeenGenerated) {
    initTimer ();
    generateNewColor ();
    newColorHasBeenGenerated = true;
    allBoxesDisplayed = false;
    hideBoxes ();
}
```

In the previous code:

- We are in the state called **STATE_PLAY_SEQUENCE**, a state where the game is supposed to pick a new colored box at random, add this color to the existing sequence, and then play the full sequence (including the last color picked).

- If a new random color has not yet been picked, we proceed as follows.

- We call a function called **initTimer** that we yet need to define; this function will basically initialize the timer that will be used to make sure that there is enough time or delay between the display of each box in the sequence.

- We call the function **generateNewColor**; if you remember well, this function picks a color at random and adds it to a sequence.

- Next, we specify that we have picked a new color by setting the variable **newColorHasBeenGenerated** to **true**.

- Finally, we hide all the boxes and set the corresponding value of the variable **allBoxesDisplayed** to **false**.

So we can now add the function **initTimer** at the end of the class (i.e., before the last closing curly bracket), as follows:

```
void initTimer()
{
     startTimer = true;
     timer = 0;
     animationIndex = 0;
}
```

In the previous code:

- We set the variable **startTimer** to true, so that the timer can start ticking.

- Its initial value is **0**.

- The animation index is set to **0**; when we successively display a new sequence to the player, we effectively create an animation that includes several stages depending on the box in the sequence that is currently displayed as part of the animation. So we will start with the first element of the animation (i.e., the first box in the sequence).

We can now resume the structure of the state **STATE_PLAY_SEQUENCE**.

- Please add the following to the code that you have already included in the switch portion that corresponds to the state **STATE_PLAY_SEQUENCE**.

```
timer += Time.deltaTime;
if   (startTimer   &&   timer   >=   timeDelayBetweenDisplays   &&
!waitingTimerActivated) {
      timer = 0;
      hideBoxes ();
      displayBox (sequenceOfColor [animationIndex]);
      animationIndex++;
      if (animationIndex >= indexOfColor) {
            startTimer = false;
            animationIndex = 0;
            waitingTimerActivated = true;
      }
}
}
```

In the previous code:

- We increase the timer by one every seconds.

- This timer is used to determine when we should display the next part of the animation.

- This is the case when the timer has started (**startTimer** is true), and when we have reached the threshold called **timeDelayBetweenDisplays** (i.e., **timer >= timeDelayBetweenDisplays**).

- We also use a variable called **waitingTimerActivated**; this is employed to add a slight delay at the end of the animation; without this delay, the last color would be displayed too briefly; so we create a waiting timer that will be used once we have reached the end of the sequence, hence, in this particular case, we also require **waitingTimerActivated** to be false.

- When these three conditions are fulfilled, we do the following.

- The timer is reset to 0.

- We then hide all the boxes.

- We display the box at the current index (i.e., **animationIndex**) in the sequence.

- We increase the variable **animationIndex** by one.

- If we have reached the end of the animation (i.e., **animationIndex >= indexOfColor**), we reset the timer, as well as the **animationIndex**, and we also specify that we will add a slight delay at the end of the sequence by activating the waiting timer (i.e., **waitingTimerActivated = true**).

- Please add the following to the code that you have already included in the switch portion that corresponds to the state **STATE_PLAY_SEQUENCE**.

```
if (waitingTimerActivated)
{
    waitingTime += Time.deltaTime;
    if (waitingTime >= timeDelayBetweenDisplays)
    {
        waitingTime = 0;
        waitingTimerActivated = false;
        waitingTimeElapsed = true;
    }
}
```

In the previous code:

- This code is used when the waiting timer is activated at the end of the sequence.

- Once it is activated, we just increase its time every second.

- Whenever it has reached a specific threshold (i.e., **waitingTime >= timeDelayBetweenDisplays**) we then reset this timer.

- Then, the variable **waitingTimeActivated** is set to false (since the delay has already been applied).

Please add the following code just after the code that you have typed.

```
if (waitingTimeElapsed)
{
    currentState = STATE_WAIT_FOR_USER_INPUT;
}
```

In the previous code: if we have reached the end of the animation and applied the slight delay at the end (i.e., **waitingTimeElapsed = true**), then we move on to the next state where the user needs to repeat this sequence.

We can also add the code to re-initialize all the variables used in the animation in the **Start** function, as follows.

```
//hideBoxes ();
//displayBox (1);
indexOfColor = 0;
startTimer = false;
waitingTimerActivated = false;
waitingTimeElapsed = false;
allBoxesDisplayed = false;
timer = 0;
waitingTime = 0;
animationIndex = 0;
timeDelayBetweenDisplays  = 2;
newColorHasBeenGenerated = false;


//testing
sequenceOfColor = new int[] { 1, 2, 3, 4 ,2};
indexOfColor = 4;
```

The last part of the code creates a virtual sequence of colors and sets the variable **indexOfColor** to 4 (remember: for an array, the first element starts at the index 0, so here the index of the last element in this array is not 5 but **4**), indicating that the last element of the sequence (or array) is at the index **4**.

After making these changes, your Start function should look like the following code snippet:

```
void Start()
{
    currentState = STATE_PLAY_SEQUENCE;
    sequenceOfColor = new int[100];

    //hideBoxes ();
    //displayBox (1);
    indexOfColor = 0;
    startTimer = false;
    waitingTimerActivated = false;
    waitingTimeElapsed = false;
    allBoxesDisplayed = false;
    timer = 0;
    waitingTime = 0;
    animationIndex = 0;
    timeDelayBetweenDisplays = 2;
    newColorHasBeenGenerated = false;
    timeDelayBetweenDisplays = 2;
    nbColorsSubmitted = 0;

    //testing
    sequenceOfColor = new int[] { 1, 2, 3, 4, 2 };
    indexOfColor = 4;
}
```

You can now save your script and play the scene, you should see that all the boxes disappear and that a sequence of 5 random boxes is displayed onscreen.

WAITING FOR THE USER'S INPUT

So, at this stage we are able to generate a random color and to play a sequence; so the next step will be to wait for the user input; so, in this section, we will write code that will do the following:

- Wait for the user's input.

- Let the player select (i.e., click on) a sequence of boxes.

- Record the boxes that were selected by the player.

- Record the number of boxes selected.

- When the expected number of boxes has been reached (e.g., if the sequence includes two colors, we expect the player to choose two boxes), we will then check if the correct sequence was entered by the player by comparing it to the sequence previously generated by the game.

- In case the sequence entered by the player is correct, the game will restart the process by generating a new color, and add it to the previous sequence.

- In case the sequence entered by the player is incorrect, the game will restart with a sequence of just one color initially.

Please add the following code at the beginning of the class **ManageAudioGame**.

```
int [] sequenceOfColorsSubmitted = new int[100];
```

In the previous code, we declare an array that will be used to store the sequence of colors chosen by the player.

- Please modify the function **SubmitColor** as follows (the new code is in bold).

```
public void submitColor(int newColor)
{
    print ("You have pressed color " + newColor);
    if (currentState == STATE_WAIT_FOR_USER_INPUT)
    {
        colorSubmitted = newColor;
        sequenceOfColorsSubmitted      [nbColorsSubmitted]      =
newColor;

        nbColorsSubmitted++;
        if (nbColorsSubmitted == (indexOfColor))
        {
            currentState = STATE_PROCESS_USER_INPUT;
        }
    }
}
```

In the previous code.

- We record the color (or corresponding tag) of the box that was just selected by the player.

- We increase the index of the variable called **nbColorsSubmitted**, so that we know how many boxes the player has selected.

- Then, if the player has selected the required number of boxes, we then proceed to the state called **STATE_PROCESS_USER_INPUT**.

We can then make a few more changes.

- Please modify the **Update** function as follows (new code in bold).

```
if (waitingTimeElapsed)
{
    currentState = STATE_WAIT_FOR_USER_INPUT;
    nbColorsSubmitted = 0;
}
```

- Please, also add the following code to the **Update** function (new code in bold):

```
case STATE_WAIT_FOR_USER_INPUT:
if (!allBoxesDisplayed)
{
     setBoxColors ();
     allBoxesDisplayed = true;
}
```

In the previous code:

- We check whether all the boxes are displayed.

- This is because, in the previous state, the colors are displayed one by one; however, now the player needs to be able to choose the correct sequence; therefore, all boxes should now be displayed, so that the player can click on them.

- We call a function called **setBoxColors** that we yet have to define, that will display all the boxes.

Please add the following code to the class:

```
void setBoxColors()
{
     for (int i = 1; i <= 4; i++)
     {
          GameObject.FindWithTag                    (""            +
i).GetComponent<Image>().enabled = true;
     }
}
```

In the previous code, we display all boxes by activating their **Image** component.

PROCESSING THE USER'S INPUT

In this section, we will process the user's input.

- Please modify the **Update** function as follows (new code in bold) in the class **ManageAudioGame**:

```
case STATE_PROCESS_USER_INPUT:
    bool okResult = assessUserMove ();
    if (okResult) {
        animationIndex = 0;
        newColorHasBeenGenerated = false;
        timer = 0;
        waitingTimerActivated = false;
        waitingTimeElapsed = false;
        currentState = STATE_PLAY_SEQUENCE;
    }
    else
    {

        loadLoseLevel ();
    }
```

In the previous code:

- We are in the state where the game is processing the user's inputs.

- We create a Boolean variable that will store the result returned by the function **assessUserMove**; this function, that we yet have to define, will return **true** if the user has entered the correct sequence, and **false** otherwise.

- So if the player has entered the correct sequence (i.e., if **okResult** is true), then the **animationIndex** is set to **0** (so that the animation can start from the first element of the next sequence); we also re-initialize several of the variables linked to the state **STATE_PLAY_SEQUENCE**, including **newColorHasBeenGenerated**, **timer**, **waitingTimerActivated**, **waitingTimeElapsed**, and **currentState**.

- If the sequence is not correct, we then call a function called **loadLoseLevel**, that we yet have to define, and that will load a scene that indicates that the player has lost.

So next, we can start to create the function **assessUserMove**, so that we can check if the player has entered the correct sequence.

- Please add the following function at the end of the class (i.e., before the end of the last curly bracket).

```
public bool assessUserMove ()
{
    bool allPerfect = true;
    for (int i = 0; i < indexOfColor; i++) {
        int a = sequenceOfColor [i];
        int b = sequenceOfColorsSubmitted [i];
        if (a != b)
            allPerfect = false;
        //print ("Color1: " + a + "/" + b);
    }
    if (allPerfect)
    {print ("WELL DONE!");return true;}
    else {print ("NOT RIGHT!"); return false;}

}
```

In the previous code:

- We define a Boolean variable called **allPerfect** and set it to true. This variable will be used to determine if all the colors selected by the player were entered in the right sequence; if any error was made, this variable (i.e., **allPerfect**) will be set to false.

- We then loop through the colors entered by the player; the variable **indexOfColor** indicates the number of colors entered by the player; so we go from the first to the last color chosen by the player. The sequence of colors entered by the player is stored in the variable **sequenceOfColorsSubmitted** and the correct sequence of colors is submitted in the array **sequenceOfColor**; so we compare these two arrays at the current index (e.g.., for the first or the second color chosen).

- If the colors are different at the current index, then the variable **allPerfect** is set to false; so at the end of the loop, if one of the colors amongst the sequence chosen by the player is incorrect, the variable **allPerfect** is set to **false** and the value **false** is returned.

- Otherwise, the value **true** is returned.

Last but not least, we will create the function **loadLoseLevel** that will be called when the player has entered the incorrect sequence along with the corresponding scene.

- Please add the following code at the beginning of the class (new code in bold):

```
using UnityEngine;
using UnityEngine.UI;
using System.Collections;
using UnityEngine.SceneManagement;
```

- Please add the following code at the end of the class (i.e., just before the last closing curly bracket).

```
public void loadLoseLevel()
{
    PlayerPrefs.SetInt ("score", indexOfColor-1);
    SceneManager.LoadScene ("chapter2_lose");
}
```

In the previous code:

- We define the function **loadLoseLevel**.

- In this function, we save the score, which is basically the length of the sequence that the player has managed to reproduce. So, for example, if the player has managed to remember a sequence of two colors but has failed to remember (and to reproduce) the next sequence, then the score will be **2**. Because **indexOfColors** is incremented just before we start a new sequence, we need to subtract one from this number to calculate the correct score if the current sequence has not reproduced correctly.

- We then load the scene called **chapter2_lose** (that we yet have to create).

So before we check for incorrect answers, we can just check if the game works for correct inputs.

Please comment the following code in your script:

```
//sequenceOfColor = new int[] { 1, 2, 3, 4 ,2};
//indexOfColor = 4;
```

- Please save your script and check that it is error-free

- You can play the scene.

- The game will display one color, then wait for your input. As you click on the right color, it should now display two colors, and wait for your input again. You should also see the following (or similar) messages in the **Console** window.

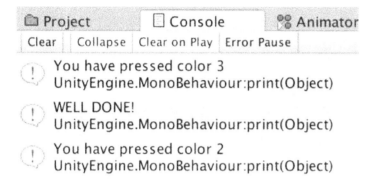

Figure 296: Testing the game

Now that you have checked that the game plays correctly, we can now create the scene called **lose**, so that the game also accounts for incorrect inputs; the new scene will include a text field that will be used to display the score as well as a button that the player will be able to click to restart the game.

- Please save the current scene.

- Create a new scene (**File | New Scene**).

- You can, as we have done in the past, remove the skybox from your scene (i.e., **Window | Lighting**).

- Add a **Text UI** object to the **Scene** (**GameObject | UI | Text**) and rename it **scoreUI**.

- You can center it in the middle of the screen using the **Scene** view or the **Inspector** (i.e., by modifying the attributes **PosX** and **PosY** for the component **Rect Transform**).

- You can also change the **font size** to **20**, and its alignment, as illustrated in the next figure.

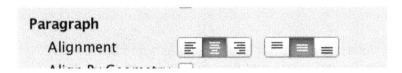

Figure 297: Changing the alignment of the text

When this is done, we just need to create a script that we will link to this object and that will display the score through the object called **scoreUI**.

- Please create a new C# script and call it **LoseScreen**.

- Add the following code at the beginning of the class (new code in bold).

```
using UnityEngine;
using System.Collections;
using UnityEngine.UI;
```

- Then modify the **Start** function as follows (new code in bold).

```
void Start ()
{
    GameObject.Find  ("scoreUI").GetComponent<Text>  ().text  =
"Score :" + PlayerPrefs.GetInt ("score");
}
```

In the previous code, we display the score using the object **scoreUI**.

- Please save your code and make sure that this script (i.e., **LoseScreen**) is added (or linked) to the object called **scoreUI**.

Next, we just need to create a button that the player can use to reload the main scene and restart the game.

- Please create a new button (i.e., select: **GameObject | UI | Button**).

- Modify the label of this button to **>> Restart <<** using the object **Text** that is a child of the object called **Button** in the **Inspector**, as illustrated in the next figure.

Figure 298: Changing the label of the button (part 1)

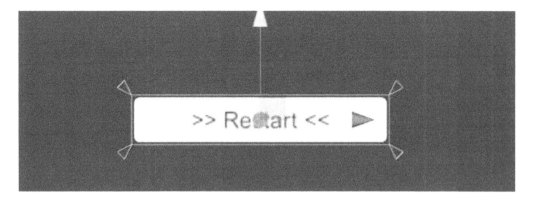

Figure 299: Changing the label of the button (part 2)

Once this is done, we just need to do the following, as we have done previously:

- Create an empty object.

- Create a new script with a function that should be called when the button is pressed.

- Link the button to this script.

So let's proceed:

- Please create a new empty object (**GameObject | Create Empty**) and rename it **manageBt**.

- Create a new script called **ManageBtChapter2**.

- Open this script.

- Add the following code at the beginning of the class (new code in bold).

```
using UnityEngine;
using System.Collections;
using UnityEngine.SceneManagement;
```

- Add the following function to this script.

```
public void restart()
{
    SceneManager.LoadScene ("chapter2");
}
```

Please save your script and drag and drop it to the object **manageBt**.

- Select the object called **Button** in the **Hierarchy**.

- Using the **Inspector**, click on the + button located below the label called **OnClick**.

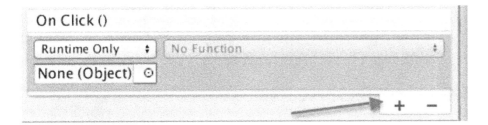

Figure 300: Managing events (part1)

- Drag and drop the object **manageBt** to the empty field called **NoneObject**.

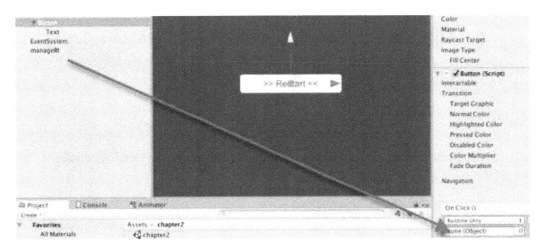

Figure 301: Managing events (part 2)

- And finally, select the option **ManageBtChapter2 | Restart** from the menu to the right of the label **Runtime Only**.

Figure 302: Managing events (part 3)

- Please save the current scene as **chapter2_lose** (**File | Save Scene As**).

The last thing we have to do is to add this scene to the **Build Settings**:

- Please open the **Build Settings** (**File | Build Settings**).

- You will see that all the scenes from the first chapter are included; for now, you can unselect them (or remove them).

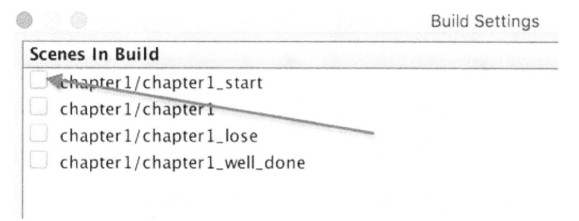

- You can then add the two scenes for this game (i.e., drag and drop them from the **Project** window), that is: **chapter2** and **chpater2_lose**, to the **Build Settings**.

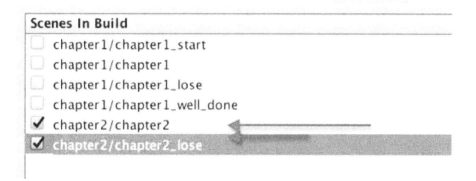

You can now save your scene, and open the scene **chapter2**, so that we can test what happens when the player enters an incorrect sequence.

- Please close the **Build Settings** window.

- Save your scene (**CTRL + S**).

- Open the scene **chapter2**.

- Play the scene.

As you play the scene, and enter an incorrect sequence, a new scene should appear with your score, and a button to restart the game, as illustrated in the next figure.

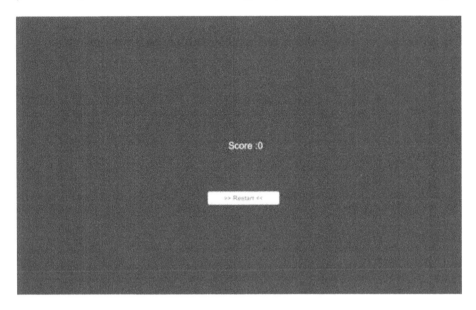

Figure 303: Restarting the game after an incorrect move

GENERATING SOUND EFFECTS

Ok, so the game works well at present; however, so that the users can obtain additional information on their move, we could add a few more features to our game, including:

- A Text field that displays the current score (or the number of colors that the player has managed to memorize so far).

- A specific sound for each of the colors, so that the player associates (and remembers) the colors associated to this sound.

So, first, let's create the onscreen text:

- Please open the scene called **chapter2**.

- Create a new **Text UI** object (i.e., select **GameObject | UI | Text**).

- Rename this object **nbMemorized**.

- Using the **Move** tool, you can move this object just above the boxes, as illustrated in the next figure.

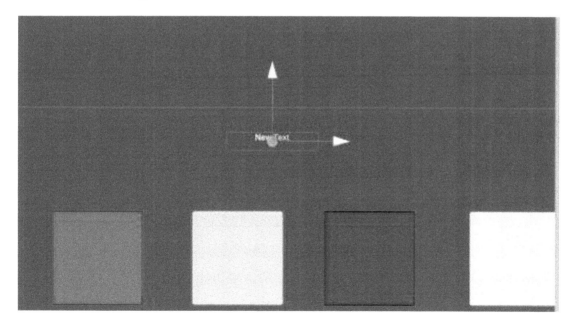

Figure 304: Moving the new text field

- Using the **Inspector**, in the component **Text**, please empty the attribute called **text**.

Figure 305: Emptying the text of the field

- You can also change its **color** to **white**, its **font size** to **20**, and its **alignment**, as illustrated on the next figure.

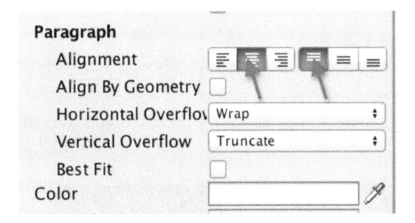

Figure 306: Changing the properties of the text.

Once this is done, we will create a function that displays the corresponding information in this text field.

- Please, open the script **ManageAudioGame**.

- Add the following function to this script.

```
public void updateUI()
{
    GameObject.Find ("nbMemorized").GetComponent<Text> ().text =
"" + indexOfColor;
}
```

- Please add the following code at the end of the **Start** function.

```
updateUI();
```

- Add the following code in the function **assessUserMove** (new code in bold).

```
if (allPerfect)
{
print ("WELL DONE!");
updateUI ();
return true;
}
else {print ("NOT RIGHT!"); return false;}
```

- In the previous code, we update the user interface when the user has guessed the sequence correctly.

- You can now save your script, play the scene, and check that your score is displayed at the top of the screen.

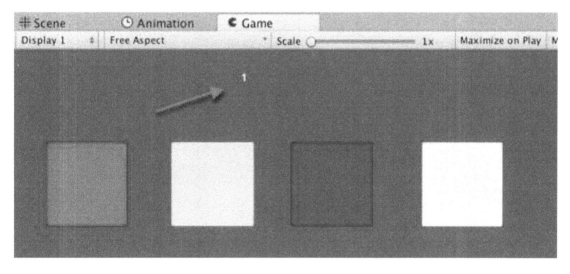

Figure 307: Checking the score

Once this is done, we can start to add some audio. For this, we will create a note for which the pitch will be linked to the label of the color being displayed, or the color chosen by the player. For this purpose, we will first create an **Audio Source** component, and then use it to generate a sound effect at run-time. So, let's get started!

- Please select the object **gameManager** in the **Hierarchy**.

- Add an **Audio Source** to it (i.e., select: **Component | Audio Source**).

- This should add an **Audio Source** component to the **gameManager** object.

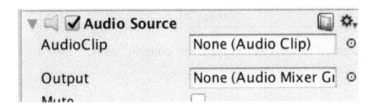

Figure 308: Adding an Audio Source

- Please import the sound called **bip** from the resource pack (i.e., drag and drop it from your file system to the **Project** window), and drag and drop it to the field called **AudioClip**.

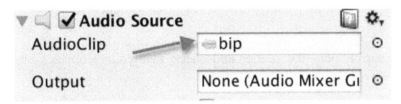

Figure 309: Adding a clip

- Also make sure that the option **Play on Awake** is set to **false**.

Figure 310: Amending the audio's properties

Once this is done, we can start to modify our script to be able to generate notes.

- Please open the script **ManageAudioGame**.

- Add the following function to it.

```
public void playNote(int index)
{
    float note = (float)index;
    GetComponent<AudioSource>().pitch = note;
    GetComponent<AudioSource>().Play();
}
```

In the previous code:

- We define a new note based on the tag of the corresponding box.

- The pitch of the sound is based on this note.

- We then play the sound at the pitch defined earlier.

Now that we have defined the function **playNote**, we can then call it whenever a box is displayed or when a box has been selected by the player.

- Please. add the following code at the beginning of the function **submitColor**.

```
playNote (newColor);
```

- Please add this code at the end of the function **displayBox**.

```
playNote(index);
```

- You can now save your script and test the scene; you will notice that a different sound is played every time a color is displayed or selected by the player.

If you would like to increase the quality of the audio played, you can also modify the function **playNote** as follows (new code in bold):

```
public void playNote(int index)
{
    float pitch = 0.5f;
    float note = (float)index;
    GetComponent<AudioSource> ().pitch = pitch * Mathf.Pow(2.0f,
(note)/12.0f);
    GetComponent<AudioSource>().Play();
}
```

In the previous code:

- We define a new pitch for the note to be played; the lower this number and the deeper the note.

- We also use some mathematics to calculate a new frequency based on the note and the tone.

You can now test your game, and hear the difference in the sound effects generated.

The last thing we need to do now is to be able to check whether the player is selecting the right color: at present we have to wait for the full sequence to be entered before completing the test. So, what we could do instead is to perform this check every time the player selects a box (instead of waiting for the player to enter a full sequence).

For this purpose, we will create a new function called **assessUserCurrentMove** and call it whenever the user has selected a box.

- Please open the script **ManageAudioGame**.

- Add the following function before the end of the class (i.e., before the last closing curly bracket).

```
public bool assessUserCurrentMove()
{
    if (sequenceOfColorsSubmitted    [nbColorsSubmitted-1]    ==
sequenceOfColor [nbColorsSubmitted-1])
            return (true);
    else
    return false;

}
```

In the previous code:

- We define the function **assessUserCurrentMove**.

- We check if the color chosen by the player matches the corresponding color in the sequence created by the game.

Next, we will just need to modify the function **submitColor** as follows (new code in bold):

```
if (currentState == STATE_WAIT_FOR_USER_INPUT)
{
     sequenceOfColorsSubmitted [nbColorsSubmitted] = newColor;
     nbColorsSubmitted++;
     bool rightMove = assessUserCurrentMove ();
     if (!rightMove) loadLoseLevel ();

     if (nbColorsSubmitted == (indexOfColor))
     {
          currentState = STATE_PROCESS_USER_INPUT;
     }

}
```

In the previous code, as we have done earlier, we check if the player's move is correct (i.e., right color selected) and then call the function **loadLoseLevel** otherwise.

You can test your scene and check that after an incorrect move, the game will display the scene called **lose**, without waiting for you to enter the complete sequence.

That's it!

LEVEL ROUNDUP

Well, this is it!

In this chapter, we have learned about creating a relatively simple memory game with interesting features such as: displaying or hiding objects, playing sounds and generating frequencies for this sound, creating a finite-state machine, arrays to store a sequence, and a timer to play this sequence. So, we have covered some significant ground compared to the last chapter.

Checklist

You can consider moving to the next chapter if you can do the following:

- Create a timer.

- Use switch statements to create different states for your game.

- Display or hide objects from your script.

Quiz

It's now time to check your knowledge with a quiz. So please specify whether the following statements are true or false.

1. When using switch case statements, it is a good practice to add a **break** statements for each case.

2. The following code will create a constant variable.

```
private const int STATE_PLAY_SEQUENCE = 1;
```

3. The following code will hide an object.

```
GameObject.FindWithTag ("myObject").GetComponent<Image>().enabled
= false;
```

4. The following code will play a note, even if the object linked to this script does not have any **Audio Source** component.

```
GetComponent<AudioSource>().pitch = 2;
GetComponent<AudioSource>().Play();.
```

5. The following code will add one to the variable time every seconds.

```
float time + = Time.time;
```

6. The following code will create a new array of integers.

```
Int [] sequenceOfColor = new int[] { 1; 2; 3; 4 ;2};
```

7. The following function will be accessible from anywhere in the game

```
void test(){}
```

8. The following variable will be accessible from the **Inspector**.

```
int myVariable
```

9. Using the **Inspector**, it is possible to apply changes simultaneously to all objects selected, provided that they share the same attribute that you want to modify.

10. If you are using buttons in your game, the following code, if linked to a button, will return its name, when the button is pressed.

```
EventSystem.current.currentSelectedGameObject.name
```

Answers to the Quiz

1. TRUE.

2. TRUE.

3. TRUE

4. FALSE.

5. TRUE.

6. FALSE.

7. FALSE.

8. FALSE.

9. TRUE.

10. TRUE.

Challenge 1

Now that you have managed to complete this chapter and that you have improved your skills, let's do the following.

- Modify the texture of each box so that, instead of displaying colored boxes, the game displays an image; this image would be different for each box.

- Add a splash-screen where the player can press on a start button to start the game; you can duplicate the scene **chapter2_lose** for this purpose.

CHAPTER 13: CREATING A CARD GUESSING GAME

In this section, we will create a simple card guessing game where the player has to remember a set of 20 cards and to match these cards based on their value.

After completing this chapter, you will be able to:

- Create a card game.

- Change the sprite of an object at run-time.

- Check when two cards picked by the player have the same value.

- Shuffle the cards.

INTRODUCTION

In this chapter, we will create a new card game as follows:

- The deck of cards will be shuffled.

- There will be two rows of cards (i.e., 10 cards in each row).

- All cards are initially hidden.

- The player needs to pick one card from the first row and then one card from the second row.

- If the cards are identical, it's a match, and they are then both removed.

- Otherwise both cards are hidden again.

- The player wins when s/he has managed to match (and subsequently remove) all the cards.

Figure 311: An example of the game completed

SETTING-UP THE INTERFACE

First, we will import the new deck of cards:

- Please save your current scene (**File | Save Scene**).

- Create a new scene (**File | New Scene**).

- Save this new scene as **chapter3**.

- As we have done before, you can remove the skybox used for the background (if any), using the menu **Window | Lighting**.

- Please locate the resource pack that you have downloaded in your file system, and import (i.e., drag and drop) the folder called **cards** to the **Project** window in Unity.

- As you will see, this folder includes a set of 68 cards that we will be using for our game, as illustrated in the next figure.

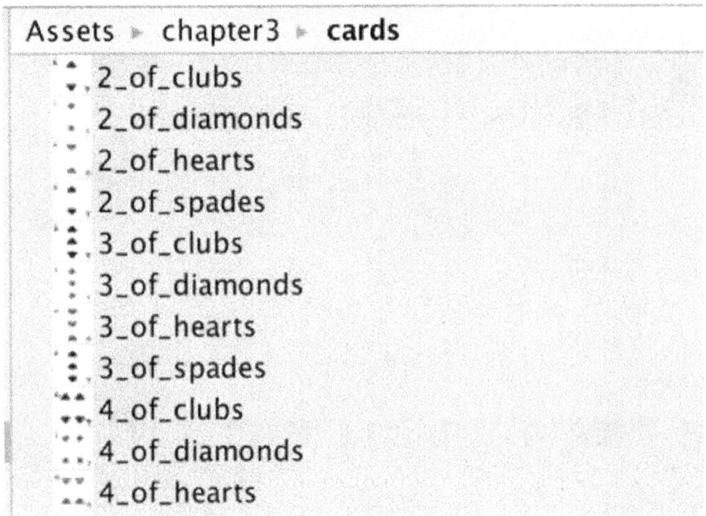

Figure 312: Importing the cards

- Once this is done, we just need to change some of the properties of these images so that they can be used as sprites in our game.

- In the **Project** window, and in the folder called **cards**, that contains the different images imported, please select all the cards (i.e., click on one card and then select **CTRL + A**).

- Using the **Inspector**, change the **Texture Type** of these images to **Sprite (2D and UI)** and leave the other options as default, as described on the next figure.

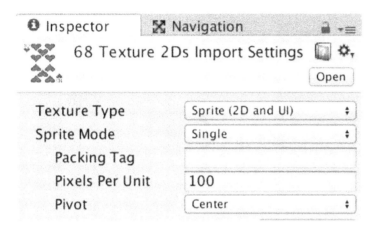

Figure 313: Changing the attribute Texture Type

- You can then press the **Apply** button located in the bottom-right corner of the window, as described on the next figure.

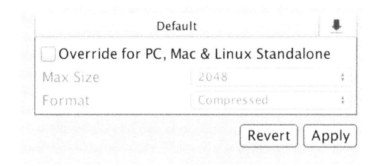

Figure 314: Applying changes

- It should take Unity a few seconds to convert these images.

Next, we will use one of these sprites to start to implement basic functionalities for our game.

- Please create a new square sprite: from the **Project** window select **Create | Sprites | Square**.

- Rename this new asset **tile** and drag and drop it to the **Scene** view, as illustrated on the next figure.

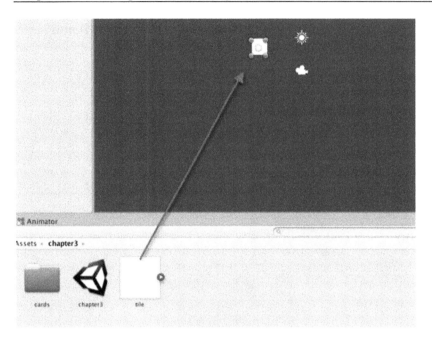

- This will create a new object called **tile** in the **Hierarchy**.

- You can change its position to **(0, 0, 0)** and add a **Box Collider 2D** component to it: from the top menu select **Component | Physics2D | Box Collider 2D**.

- This collider is needed so that we can detect clicks on this sprite.

Next, we will create a script that will process clicks on this sprite.

- Please create a new C# script called **Tile** (i.e., from the **Project** window, select **Create | C# Script**).

- Open this script.

- Add the following function to it.

```
public void OnMouseDown()
{
    print ("You pressed on tile");
}
```

- Save your script, and drag and drop it to the object called **tile** in the **Hierarchy**.

Once this is done, you can test the scene by playing the scene and by then clicking on the white rectangle (tile) that you have created; a message should appear in the **Console** window.

Next, we will just change the appearance of our tile by using one of the sprites that we have imported.

- Please select the object called **tile** in the **Hierarchy**.

- Using the **Inspector**, you will see that it has a component called **Sprite Renderer**, with an attribute called **Sprite**, as described on the next figure.

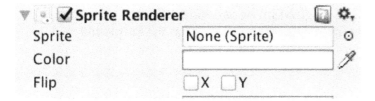

Figure 315: Identifying the Sprite Renderer component

- Drag and drop one of the images that you have imported from the **Project** window (i.e., from the folder called **cards**) to the attribute called **Sprite**, for example the **two of hearts**, as illustrated in the next figure.

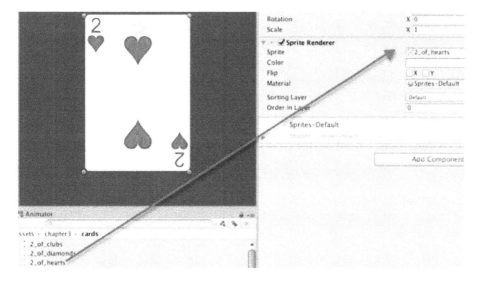

- Once this is done, you should see that the tile has now turned into a card, as per the previous figure.

Next, we will create the code that either hides or displays a card; for this purpose, we will be using two different sprites: the sprite for the card that is supposed to be displayed, and a blank sprite that symbolizes the back of each card, for when a card is supposed to be hidden.

- Please add the following code at the beginning of the class **Tile**.

```
private bool tileRevealed = false;
public Sprite originalSprite;
public Sprite hiddenSprite;
```

- Because the last two variables (i.e., **originalSprite** and **hiddenSprite**) are public, if you select the object called **tile** in the **Hierarchy** and look at the **Inspector**, you should now see that its component called **Tile** has two empty fields (or placeholders) called **originalSprite** and **hiddenSprite**.

- Please drag and drop the sprite called **2_of_hearts** from the **Project** window to the field **originalSprite**, and the sprite called **back_of_cards** to the field called **hiddenSprite**.

- The component should then look as in the next figure.

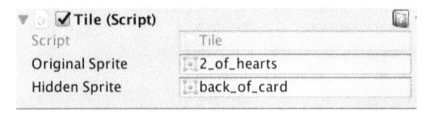

Figure 316: Setting the appearance of the card.

Next, we will create two functions called **hideCard** and **displayCard** that will either display or hide a card.

- Please open the script called **Tile**.

- Add the following code to it.

```
public void hideCard()
{
    GetComponent<SpriteRenderer> ().sprite = hiddenSprite;
    tileRevealed = false;
}
public void revealCard()
{
    GetComponent<SpriteRenderer> ().sprite = originalSprite;
    tileRevealed = true;
}
```

In the previous code, we create two functions that either display or hide a card by setting the sprite for this particular card to the **hiddenSprite** or the **originalSprite**. The variable **tileRevealed** is also amended to indicate whether the card is displayed or hidden.

- Next, add the following code to the **Start** function, so that all cards are initially hidden at the start of the game.

```
hideCard();
```

- Last, we can modify the function **OnMouseDown** as follows (new code in bold):

```
public void OnMouseDown()
{
    print ("You pressed on tile");
    if (tileRevealed)
        hideCard ();
    else
        revealCard ();
}
```

In the previous code:

- When the mouse is clicked, we check whether the card is currently revealed or hidden.

- If it is revealed, then we call the function **hideCard**.

- Otherwise, we call the function **revealCard**.

You can now save your code, and test the scene; you should see that the card is hidden at the beginning (i.e., the back of the card is displayed); then, as you click several times on the card, it should subsequently be hidden or revealed.

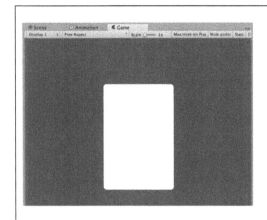

Figure 317: The card is hidden

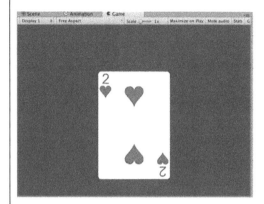

Figure 318: The card is displayed

- Lastly, we will scale down the card: using the **Inspector**, modify the scale property of the object **tile** to (0.5, 0.5, 1).

Now that the interaction with the card works, we can create a prefab from it, so that this prefab can be used to generate several similar cards.

- Please select the object **tile** in the **Hierarchy**.

- Drag and drop it to the **Project** window.

- This should create a new **prefab** called **tile**, as illustrated on the next figure.

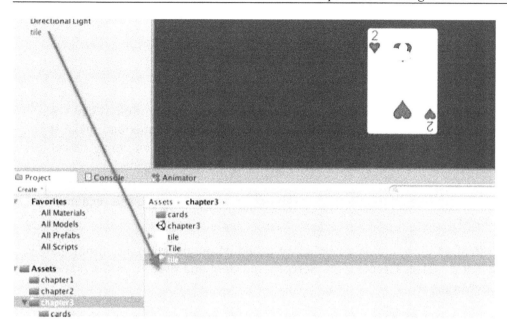

Figure 319: Creating a prefab from the card

- You can then delete or de-activate the object called **tile** in the **Hierarchy**.

CREATING A GAME MANAGER

So at this stage, we have managed to create a card (and a corresponding prefab) that we can either hide or reveal. So the next step will be to display several cards and make it possible for the player to match them. For this purpose, we will create an empty object **gameManager** that will manage the game, including adding cards to the game.

- Please create a new empty object (**GameObject | Create Empty**), and rename it **gameManager**.

- Using the **Project** view, create a new script called **ManageCards** (i.e., from the **Project** window, select **Create | C# Script**), and drag and drop it on the object called **gameManager**.

- Open the script called **ManageCards** (i.e., double-click on it in the **Project** window).

- Add this code at the beginning of the script (new code in bold).

```
public GameObject card;
void Start ()
{
     displayCards();
}
public void displayCards()
{
     Instantiate    (card,    new    Vector3    (0,    0,    0),
Quaternion.identity);
}
```

In the previous code:

- We declare a new variable called **card**, that is public (hence accessible from the **Inspector** window), and that will be used as a template for all the cards to be added to the game (i.e., it will be based on the template called **tile**).

- We also create a function called **displayCards**.

- This function instantiates a new card.

Before we can test this code, we just need to initialize the variable **card**, as follows:

- Please select the object **gameManager** in the **Hierarchy**.

- Drag and drop the prefab called **tile** to the field called **card**, in the component called **ManageCards**, as illustrated on the next figure.

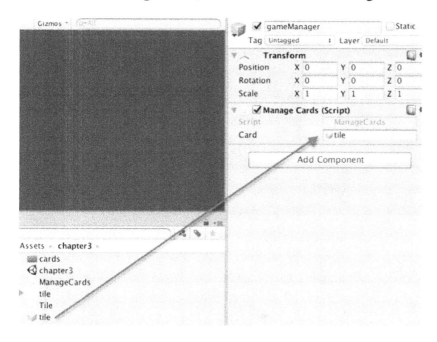

Figure 320: Initializing the variable called card

- Once this is done, you can test the game by playing the scene; you should see that a card has been added to the game, as described in the next figure.

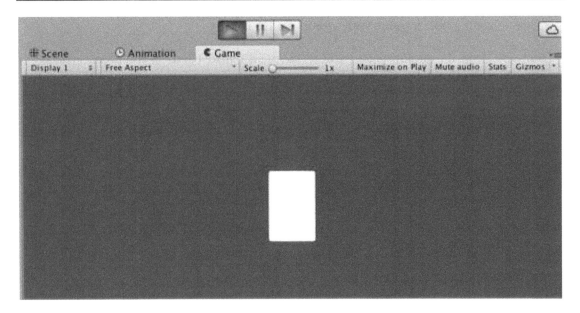

Figure 321: Testing the game

If you find it difficult to select (i.e., click on) some of the cards, it may be because their collider is too small and needs to be resized, hence collision and clicks might only be detected on a portion of the card rather than on the entire card.

To do so:

- Select the prefab called **tile** in the **Project**.

- Click on the button called **Open Prefab** in the **Inspector**.

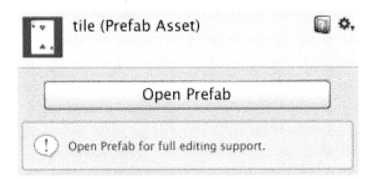

- In the Inspector, the component **Box Collider 2D**.

- You can the current boundary of the collider by clicking on the button called **Edit Collider**; it should show that the green area of the collider only covers a small area of the card.

So to increase the area covered by the collider, we will need to do the following.

- Modify the parameters as follows.

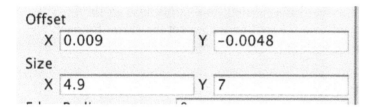

By changing the **Offset** and **Size** settings, we have effectively modified the boundary of the collider, and you can check it by clicking on the button called **Edit Collider**; it should now show that the green area of the collider covers most of the card.

You can now test the scene again and check that the clicks are detected easily.

Next, we will modify the script called **Tile**, to add a function that will set the sprite (or image) that should be displayed when this card is revealed; this is because in the next section, the cards will be allocated randomly; so we will no longer set the sprite for each card manually; instead, this will be done through our code.

- Please open the script called **Tile**.

- Add the following function to it.

```
public void setOriginalSprite(Sprite newSprite)
{
    originalSprite = newSprite;
}
```

In the previous code, we create a public function that will be accessible from outside this class and that will change the original sprite for this card to a sprite that is passed as a parameter to the function.

- Please save this script (i.e., the script called **Tile**).

- Please open the script **ManageCards**.

- Add the following function to the class.

```
void addACard(int rank)
{
    GameObject c = (GameObject)(Instantiate (card, new Vector3
(0, 0, 0), Quaternion.identity));
}
```

In the previous code:

- We declare a function called **addACard.**

- This function creates a new card.

- We can now modify the function called **displayCards** as follows:

```
public void displayCards()
{
    //Instantiate    (card,    new    Vector3    (0,    0,    0),
Quaternion.identity);
    addACard(0);
}
```

ADDING MULTIPLE CARDS AUTOMATICALLY

We will now create several cards on the go. The idea will be to display two rows of 10 cards each. The player will then need to match cards from the first row to cards on the second row. So the idea will be to:

- Create and add new cards based on the prefab created earlier.

- Arrange the cards so that they are aligned around the center of the screen and all visible onscreen.

- For each card, set the default sprite that should be displayed when the card is revealed.

- Shuffle the cards.

So the first step will be to add all of these cards.

If you look at the sprites that we have imported in the **Project** window, you will notice that their size is 500 by 725 pixels; we have also scaled-down these images using the **Inspector**, so their actual width in the game is 250 pixels; if you remember well, we used an import setting of 100 pixels per units pixels; this means that our cards will have a size of 2.5 (i.e., 250/100) in the game's units. So when creating our cards, we will need to make sure that their origins (or center) is at least 2.5 units apart (we will choose 3 units to be safe).

- In the script called **ManageCards**, please modify the function **AddAcard** as follows (new code in bold):

```
void addACard(int rank)
{
     //GameObject c = (GameObject)(Instantiate (card, new Vector3
(0, 0, 0), Quaternion.identity));
     GameObject c = (GameObject)(Instantiate (card, new Vector3
(rank*3.0f, 0, 0), Quaternion.identity));
}
```

In the previous code, we make sure that the x coordinate of the new card will be based on its rank; as we will be adding other cards, the first card's x coordinate will be 3 (i.e., 1 x 3), the second card's x coordinate will be 6 (i.e., 2 x 3), and so on.

- Next, we can modify the function called **displayCards** so that we can add a row of 10 cards, with the following code (new code in bold).

```
public void displayCards()
{
    //Instantiate    (card,    new    Vector3    (0,    0,    0),
Quaternion.identity);
    //addACard(0);
    for (int i = 0; i < 10; i++)
    {
        addACard (i);
    }
}
```

- Please save your code and play the scene; you will notice that 10 cards have been created; however, some of them are outside the screen; in other words, the cards need to be centered around the center of the screen.

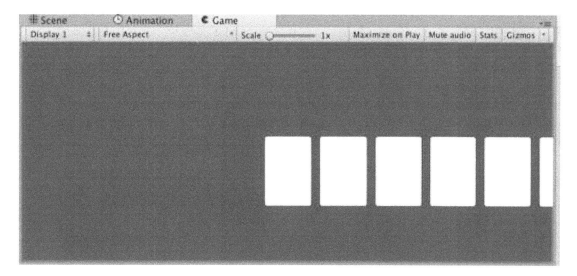

Figure 322: Displaying 10 cards

So, to solve this issue, we will do the following:

- Create an empty object that will be used as an anchor for the cards.

- Move this object to the center of the screen.

- Center the cards horizontally around this object.

So let's proceed.

- Please create an empty object and call it **centerOfScreen**.

- Using the **Inspector**, change its position to **(0, 0, 0)**.

- Open the script **ManageCards** and modify the function **addACard** as follows (new code in bold):

```
void addACard(int rank)
{

    GameObject cen = GameObject.Find("centerOfScreen");
    Vector3 newPosition = new Vector3 (cen.transform.position.x
+       ((rank-10/2)       *3),        cen.transform.position.y,
cen.transform.position.z);
    GameObject c = (GameObject)(Instantiate (card, newPosition,
Quaternion.identity));

    //GameObject c = (GameObject)(Instantiate (card, new Vector3
(0, 0, 0), Quaternion.identity));
    //GameObject c = (GameObject)(Instantiate (card, new Vector3
(rank*3.0f, 0, 0), Quaternion.identity));
}
```

As you save the code and play the scene, you should see that the cards are now centered; however, their size is too large for all of them to fit onscreen; so we will need to resize the cards accordingly.

Figure 323: Displaying 10 aligned cards

- Using the **Inspector**, change the scale of the **tile** prefab to **(0.3, 0.3, 0.3)**.

- Open the script called **ManageCards** and modify it as follows (new code in bold):

```
void addACard(int rank)
{

    float cardOriginalScale = card.transform.localScale.x;
    float scaleFactor = (500 * cardOriginalScale) / 100.0f;

    GameObject cen = GameObject.Find("centerOfScreen");
    //Vector3        newPosition       =       new       Vector3
(cen.transform.position.x       +       ((rank-10/2)       *3),
cen.transform.position.y, cen.transform.position.z);
    Vector3 newPosition = new Vector3 (cen.transform.position.x
+    ((rank-10/2)    *scaleFactor),    cen.transform.position.y,
cen.transform.position.z);

    GameObject c = (GameObject)(Instantiate (card, newPosition,
Quaternion.identity));
```

In the previous code:

- We save the initial scale of the card.

- We create a variable called **scaleFactor** that takes into account the original width of the card (i.e., **500**) as well as its original scale.

- This **scaleFactor** variable is taken into account when defining the x coordinate of each card.

Please save your code, and play the scene; you should see that now all cards are displayed within the camera's field of view, as illustrated in the next figure.

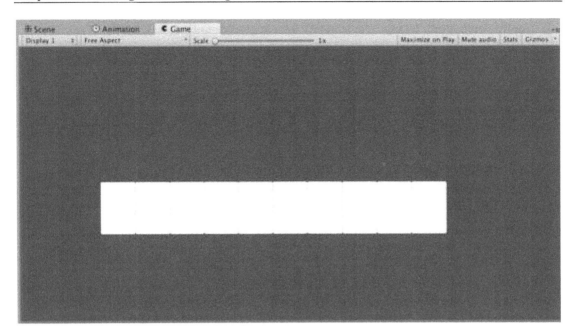

Figure 324: Displaying and scaling the cards

ASSOCIATING THE CORRECT IMAGE TO EACH CARD

At this stage, we can display the hidden cards, however, their value is the same (i.e., they are all showing the same sprite); if you play the scene and click on each of the images, they will all display the **2 of hearts**, as illustrated on the next figure.

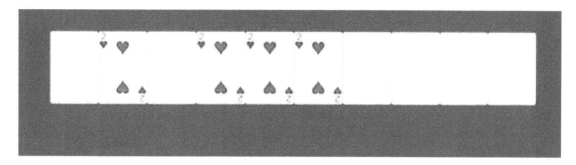

Figure 325: Displaying cards with a similar image

So, the idea now is to specify a corresponding sprite for each card; so we will do the following:

- Create 10 tags.

- Assign a tag to each of these cards based on their rank (e.g., first card from the left will use the tag called **1**, the second card from the left will use the tag called **2**, and so on).

- Associate an image to each card based on its tag (e.g., **ace for tag 1**, **two for tag 2**, and so on).

So let's proceed:

- Please select the prefab called **tile** in the **Project** window.

- Using the **Inspector**, click to the right of the label called **Tag**.

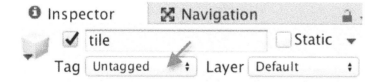

Figure 326: Checking tags already created

- If you have already completed the previous chapters, you should see that the tags **1**, **2**, **3**, and **4** have already been created; if not, we can create these in the next steps.

- Please click on **Add Tag**.

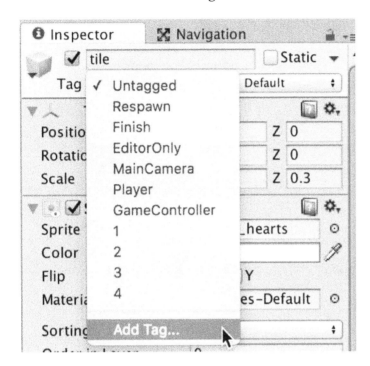

Figure 327: Creating tags

- In the next window, please click several times on the button +, as illustrated in the next figure.

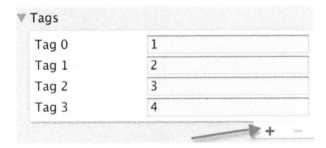

- This will create new fields that you can use to create additional tags, by typing a number (for a new tag) to the right of the fields which name starts with **Tag,** as illustrated on the next figure.

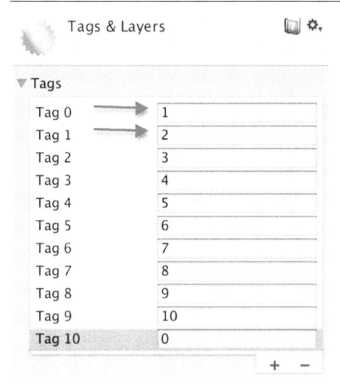

Figure 328: Creating the 11 tags

- Once this is done, you should have **11** tags ranging from **0** to **10**, as per the previous figure.

We can then use these tags from our code.

- Please open the script called **ManageCards**.

- Add the following code at the end of the function **addACard**.

```
c.tag = ""+rank;
```

- Please save your code.

As you play the scene, and if you click on one of the cards that has been created in the **Hierarchy**, you will see, using the **Inspector** that each card has a tag that ranges from **0** to **9**.

Note that tags cannot be created from a script; they have to have already been defined in the editor before they can be applied to objects in a script.

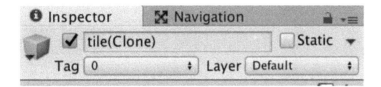

Figure 329:Checking the new tags

Next, we will work on the images that need to be displayed when a card is revealed. For this, we will access the images that we have imported in our project directly from our script; so the next steps will consist in:

- Moving all the images that we have imported to a "recognized" or "standard" folder that we can access from our script.

- Accessing the images from this folder.

- Associating a corresponding image based on the rank of the card created.

So let's proceed:

If you have already completed the previous chapters, then you would already have created a **Resources** folder (within the **Assets** folder), as illustrated in the next figure.

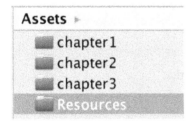

Figure 330: Checking the folder Resources

If this is not the case, we can create this folder as follows:

- In the **Project** window, select the folder called **Assets**.

- Then, from the **Project** window, select **Create | Folder**.

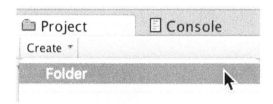

Figure 331: Creating a new folder

- Rename the new folder **Resources** (i.e., right-click on the folder and then select the option **Rename**).

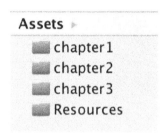

Figure 332: Renaming the folder

Now that this folder has been created, you can move the images that you have imported inside this folder, within Unity, as follows:

- Within Unity, navigate to the folder called **cards** where all the cards have been stored previously.

- Select all the cards (i.e., **CTRL + A**).

- Move these cards (i.e., drag and drop them) to the folder called **Resources**, as illustrated in the next figure.

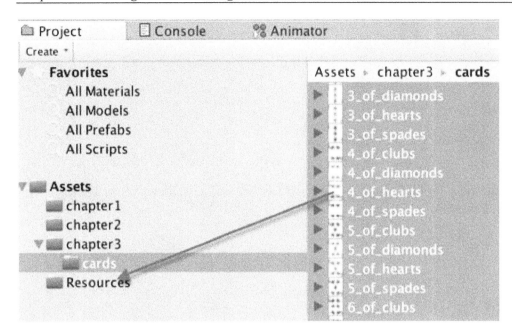

Figure 333: Moving the images to the Resources folder

- If you then check the content of the folder called **Resources**, you should see that the cards were moved successfully, as illustrated in the next figure.

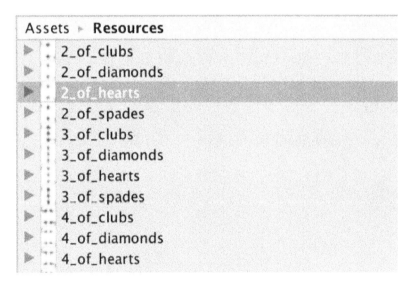

Figure 334: Checking that the cards have been copied properly

Next, we will modify the script **ManageCards** so that the correct images from the **Resources** folder are assigned to each card.

- Please open the script **ManageCards**.

- Add this code at the end of the function **addACard**.

```
c.name = "" + rank;
string nameOfCard = "";
string cardNumber = "";
if (rank == 0)
     cardNumber = "ace";
else
     cardNumber = "" + (rank+1);
nameOfCard = cardNumber + "_of_hearts";
Sprite s1 = (Sprite) (Resources.Load<Sprite>(nameOfCard));
print ("S1:" + s1);
GameObject.Find(""+rank).GetComponent<Tile>  ().setOriginalSprite
(s1);
```

In the previous code:

- The name of the sprite to be selected for a particular card will be in the form: **XX_of_hearts**; where **XX** can be a number (e.g., 1, 2, 3, 4, 5, 6, etc.) or a string (e.g., ace). So the purpose of this code is to form this word based on the card that we have just added and its rank; the first card should be the **ace of hearts**, the second card a **2 of heart**s, and so on.

- We set the name of the new card.

- We declare a variable called **nameOfCard** that will be used to save the name of the corresponding sprite for a particular card.

- We form the first part of the name of the card based on its rank.

- Once the name of the sprite to be used is formed properly and stored in the variable **nameOfCard**, we access the corresponding sprite and save it in the variable called **s1**.

- We then set the **originalSprite** variable for this card to the sprite **s1**.

You can now save your code, and test the scene. You should see that if you click on each of the cards, they will show the correct image.

Figure 335: Displaying all the cards.

SHUFFLING THE CARDS

Now we just need to be able to shuffle the cards; the idea will be to create two rows of cards with identical sets of cards but shuffled. So we will create a new function that will shuffle the cards for us, and then call it from the **Start** function, after the cards have been added to the game view.

To do so, we need to differentiate between the order in which the cards are picked (this will determine their position) and their value (this will determine the value of the card and the corresponding sprite).

- Please create the following function in the class **ManageCards**.

```
public int []  createShuffledArray()
{
    int [] newArray = new int [] {0,1,2,3,4,5,6,7,8,9};
    int tmp;
    for (int t = 0; t < 10; t++ )
    {
        tmp = newArray[t];
        int r = Random.Range(t, 10);
        newArray[t] = newArray[r];
        newArray[r] = tmp;
    }
    return newArray;
}
```

In the previous code:

- We declare a new function called **createShuffledArray**; it returns an array of integers for which the values are shuffled.

- We declare a new array of integers that includes the labels of all 10 cards; these values are ordered in ascending order.

- We then loop through this array and shuffle its content.

- Once this is done, we return an array that includes these values in a random order.

This shuffling function is based on the Fisher-Yates algorithm.

Next, we will need to modify the function **addACard** so that it accounts for a card's rank and its value:

- Please modify the definition of the function **addACard** as follows (new code in bold):

```
void addACard(int rank, int value)
```

- Modify the function **addACard** as follows (new code in bold):

```
c.tag = ""+(value+1);
c.name = "" + value;
string nameOfCard = "";
string cardNumber = "";
if (value == 0)
      cardNumber = "ace";
else
      cardNumber = "" + (value+1);
nameOfCard = cardNumber + "_of_hearts";
Sprite s1 = (Sprite) (Resources.Load<Sprite>(nameOfCard));
GameObject.Find(""+value).GetComponent<Tile> ().setOriginalSprite
(s1);
```

- Last, we will modify the function **displayCards** as follows (new code in bold):

```
int [] shuffledArray = createShuffledArray();
for (int i = 0; i < 10; i++)
{
      //addACard (i);
      addACard (i,shuffledArray[i]);
}
```

- Please save your script and test the game; you should see that, after clicking on some of the cards, that these cards have been shuffled, as described on the next figure.

Figure 336: Displaying the card (after shuffling)

If you find it difficult to select (i.e., click on) some of the cards, it may be because their collider is too small and needs to be resized, hence collision and clicks might only be detected on a portion of the card rather than on the entire card.

Last but not least, we want to create two rows of cards. So it will be the same as we have done so far, except that we will modify the function **addACard** so that we can specify the row where the card should be added (i.e., first or second row).

- Please change the definition of the function **addACard** as follows (new code in bold):

```
void addACard(int row, int rank, int value)
{
```

In the previous code, we have modified the function so that it takes a third parameter named **row**.

- Next, please modify the function **displayCards** as follows (new code in bold):

```
int [] shuffledArray = createShuffledArray();
int [] shuffledArray2 = createShuffledArray();
for (int i = 0; i < 10; i++)
{
//addACard (i);
      addACard (0, i, shuffledArray[i]);
      addACard (1, i, shuffledArray2[i]);


}
```

In the previous code:

- We declare another array of integers called **shuffledArray2**, that will be used for the second row of cards.

- In the **for** loop, we then call the function **addACard** to display both the first and the second row.

- When the function **addACard** is called, three parameters are passed: the **row** (0 or 1), the **rank** of the card (i.e., its **position** in the row), and its value (i.e., ace, 1, or 2, etc.).

Next, we can modify the function **addACard** as follows:

```
//Vector3 newPosition = new Vector3 (cen.transform.position.x +
((rank-10/2)      *scaleFactor),      cen.transform.position.y,
cen.transform.position.z);
float yScaleFactor = (725 * cardOriginalScale) / 100.0f;
Vector3 newPosition = new Vector3 (cen.transform.position.x +
((rank-10/2) *scaleFactor), cen.transform.position.y + ((row-2/2)
*yScaleFactor), cen.transform.position.z);
```

In the previous code:

- We comment the previous line that was used to set the new position of the card.

- We define a new variable called **yScaleFactor** that will be used to calculate the position of the card (especially its y coordinate).

- We then define the new position of the card using the parameter called **row** and the variable called **yScaleFactor** to centre it properly.

Next, we just need to change the naming of the new card.

- Please replace this code:

```
c.name = "" + value;
```

- ...with this code...

```
c.name = ""+row+"_"+value;
```

In the previous code, we specify that the cards from the first row have a name starting with 0 (**row = 0**) and that the cards from the second row have a name starting with 1 (i.e., **row = 1**).

- Please replace this code...

```
GameObject.Find(""+value).GetComponent<Tile> ().setOriginalSprite
(s1);
```

- ... with this code

```
GameObject.Find(""+row+"_"+value).GetComponent<Tile>
().setOriginalSprite (s1);
```

- Please save your code.

As you play the scene, you should now have two rows of cards, as illustrated on the next figure.

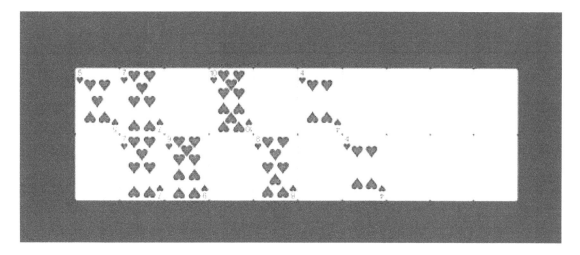

Figure 337: Displaying two rows of cards

> If you find it difficult to select (i.e., click on) some of the cards, it may be because their collider is too small and needs to be resized, hence collision and clicks might only be detected on a portion of the card rather than on the entire card.

So, in this case you can resize the collider as follows:

- Select the prefab called **tile** in the **Project** window.

- Scroll down to the component called **Box Collider 2D**.

- Change the size of the collider to (**x=5, y = 7**).

ALLOWING THE PLAYER TO CHOOSE CARDS FROM EACH ROW

So now that we can shuffle and display two rows of 10 cards, we just need to make it possible for the player to select a card from the first row, then a card from the second row, and then check if these cards are similar (i.e., have the same value) by comparing their tags and value.

Based on our code, we know that the cards from the first row have a name starting with **0** and that cards from the second row have a name starting with **1**, as illustrated in the next figure.

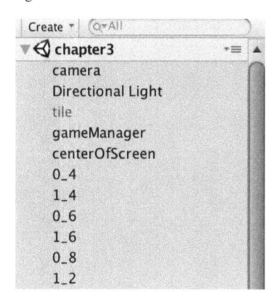

Figure 338: Naming the cards

If you find it difficult to select (i.e., click on) some of the cards, it may be because their collider is too small and needs to be resized, hence collision and clicks might only be detected on a portion of the card rather than on the entire card.

So we will proceed as follows:

- Display the cards (i.e., two rows).

- Allow the player to successively pick (i.e., click on) two cards.

- We will then check that whenever the player clicks on a card for the first time, that the name of this card includes **0** (i.e. that it belongs to the first row).

- We will also check that whenever the player clicks on a second card, that the name of this card includes **1** (i.e. that it belongs to the second row).

- After that we will compare their tags.

- If these cards have the same tag (i.e., the same value) then both will be destroyed.

Next, we can implement the code that checks how we handle clicks on cards.

- Please add the following code at the start of the script **ManageCards**.

```
private bool firstCardSelected, secondCardSelected;
private GameObject card1, card2;
```

- Please add the following code just before the end of the class.

```
public void cardSelected(GameObject card)
{
    if (!firstCardSelected)
    {
        firstCardSelected = true;
        card1 = card;
        card1.GetComponent<Tile> ().revealCard ();
    }
}
```

In the previous code:

- We declare a new function called **cardSelected**; this function will be used to monitor whether we have already selected the first card.

- If this is not the case, then the card that was passed as a parameter (i.e., the card currently selected – the first card -) is saved in the variable **card1**.

- We also display (i.e., reveal) the value of this card.

The hiding and revealing of the cards will now be handled by the game manager; so we will modify the function called **OnMouseDown** in the **Tile** class, as follows:

```
public void OnMouseDown()
{
     print ("You pressed on tile");
     /*if (tileRevealed)
           hideCard ();
     else
           revealCard ();*/
     GameObject.Find   ("gameManager").GetComponent<ManageCards>
().cardSelected (gameObject);
}
```

In the previous code:

- We comment the previous code.

- Now, when the player clicks on a card, the function called **cardSelected** (that we have defined earlier), is called.

- The card that the player has just selected is also passed as a parameter.

Next, we will further code the overall management of the game.

- Please add the following code at the beginning of the class called **ManageCards**.

```
private string rowForCard1, rowForCard2;
```

- Modify the function **cardSelected** as follows:

```
public void cardSelected(GameObject card)
{
    if (!firstCardSelected)
    {
        string row = card.name.Substring (0, 1);
        rowForCard1 = row;
        firstCardSelected = true;
        card1 = card;
        card1.GetComponent<Tile> ().revealCard ();
    }
    else if (firstCardSelected && !secondCardSelected)
    {
        string row = card.name.Substring (0, 1);
        rowForCard2 = row;
        if (rowForCard2 != rowForCard1)
        {
            card2 = card;
            secondCardSelected = true;
            card2.GetComponent<Tile> ().revealCard ();
        }
    }
}
```

In the previous code:

- If the player selects the first card, we record the name of the row for this card, we save this card in the variable **card1**, and we also reveal the card.

- Then, if the player is selecting the second card, we record the name of the row for this card, and check that it is a different row than the first card selected.

- If this is the case, then we save this card in the variable **card2**, and reveal this card also.

- We also check whether we have a match, using the function **checkCard** that we yet have to create.

You can save both scripts now (i.e., **Tile** and **ManageCards**), and test the scene; as you try to select two cards, you should only be able to choose one card from the first row and a second card from the second row (or vice versa).

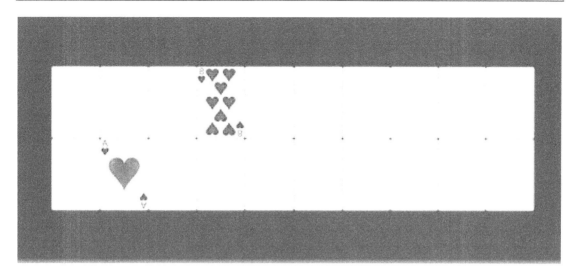

Figure 339: Picking one card from each row

CHECKING FOR A MATCH

Now we just need to determine when there is a match between the two cards selected by the player. In this case, we will delete both cards.

First let's create a function called **checkCards**; this function will check whether the two cards selected by the player are identical; if this is the case, they will be destroyed; otherwise, they will be hidden again; the checking will happen after a slight pause, so that the player can see the cards that have been selected before they are hidden again (if this is the case).

- Please add the following function to the class **ManageCards**:

```
public void checkCards()
{
    runTimer ();
}
```

In this function we call another function called **runTimer** (that we yet have to create).

- Please add the following code at the beginning of the class.

```
bool timerHasElapsed, timerHasStarted;
float timer;
```

In the previous code:

- The new variables defined will be employed to create a timer that will be used to pause after the second card has been collected.

- **timerHasElapsed** will be used to know whether the **pause time** has elapsed.

- **timerHasStarted** is used to determine whether the timer has already been started.

- The variable **timer** will be used to count the number of seconds between when the second card has been selected and when we start to compare the two cards.

Please add the following function to the class:

```
public void runTimer()
{
    timerHasElapsed = false;
    timerHasStarted = true;
}
```

In the previous code, we just initialise the timer and the associated variables.

Next, we will create and implement the timer; it will be done in the **Update** function; the timer will increase until it reaches **2** seconds; after two seconds, we will start to compare the two cards.

- Please add the following code to the **Update** function.

```
void Update ()
{
    if (timerHasStarted)
    {
        timer += Time.deltaTime;
        print (timer);
        if (timer >= 1) {
            timerHasElapsed = true;
            timerHasStarted = false;
            if (card1.tag == card2.tag) {
                Destroy (card1);
                Destroy (card2);
            } else {
                card1.GetComponent<Tile> ().hideCard ();
                card2.GetComponent<Tile> ().hideCard ();
            }
            firstCardSelected = false;
            secondCardSelected = false;
            card1 = null;
            card2 = null;
            rowForCard1 = "";
            rowForCard2 = "";
            timer = 0;
        }
    }
}
```

In the previous code

- We check if the timer has started.

- We then check whether the timer has started and that we have reached the end of the pause.

- In this case, we reinitialize the timer (using the variables **timerHasElapsed** and **timerHasStarted**).

- We check if the cards match and destroy (or hide) them both if we have a match.

- We then initialise the variable linked to the card selection, so that the player can restart the process of selecting two cards.

- Last, please check that the function **cardSelected** includes a call to the function **checkCards**, as highlighted in the next code (in bold).

```
secondCardSelected = true;
card2 = card;
card2.GetComponent<Tile> ().revealCard ();
checkCards ();
```

- Please save the code and test the game.

You should see that as you select one card from each row: if they match, then they should be destroyed after a few seconds.

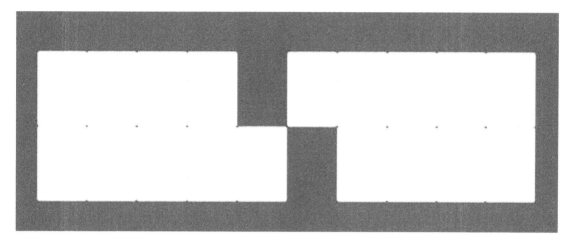

Figure 340: The game after two cards were matched

Next we will add a sound when the player has managed to match two cards:

- Please add an **AudioSource** component to the object **gameManager** (i.e., select: **Component | Audio | AudioSource**).

- Import the audio file called **ok.mp3** from the resource pack to the Unity **Project** window.

- Drag and drop this audio clip from the **Project** window to the **AudioClip** attribute of the component **Audio Source** for the object **gameManager**, as illustrated in the next figure.

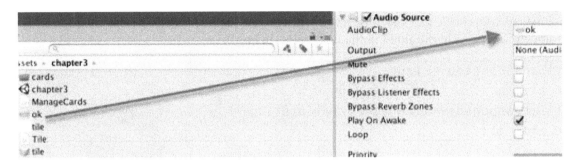

Figure 341: Adding an Audio Clip to the Audio Source

- Set the attribute **Play on Awake** to false.

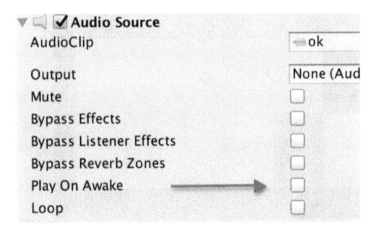

Figure 342: Setting the attribute Play on Awake

Next, we need to check how many cards the player has managed to match.

- Please, add this code at the beginning of the class **ManageCards**:

```
int nbMatch = 0;
```

- Add this code at the beginning of the script.

```
using UnityEngine.SceneManagement;
```

- Modify the function **Update** as follows (new code in bold).

```
Destroy (card1);
Destroy (card2);
nbMatch++;
if (nbMatch == 10)
    SceneManager.LoadScene (SceneManager.GetActiveScene().name);
```

In the previous code, we reload the current scene if the player has managed to find the 10 sets of identical cards.

LEVEL ROUNDUP

Summary

In this chapter, we have managed to create a challenging card game and we have learned some interesting skills too, including: hiding or revealing sprites, setting sprites or scaling images at run-time.

Checklist

You can consider moving to the next stage if you can do the following:

- Understand how to access sprites from a script.

- Understand how to create an array of integers.

- Know how to use the **substring** function.

Quiz

Now, let's check your knowledge! Please specify whether the following statements are true or false.

1. To select all the assets in a given folder, you can just press CTRL + A.

2. To be able to detect clicks on a sprite, this sprite needs to have a collider.

3. The function **OnClick** is called automatically when the player clicks on an object if this function is added to a script linked to this object.

4. To create an empty object, you can select: **GameObject | Create | Empty Object**.

5. If a sprite with a width of 200 pixels is imported in Unity, and the **Import Settings** are **100 pixels per unit**, then this sprite will be 2 units-wide in the game.

6. In Unity, it is possible to use tags that have been created in other scenes in the same project.

7. The following code will save a sprite that is stored in the folder called **Resources**.

```
Sprite s1 = (Sprite) (Resources.Load<Sprite>("mySprite"));
```

8. The following code will create an array of 10 integers.

```
int [] newArray = new int [] {0,1,2,3,4,5,6,7,8,9};
```

9. If a function is declared as **public**, it cannot be accessible from outside the class.

10. For an **Audio Source** component, the attribute **Play on Awake** is set to true by default in Unity.

Answers to the Quiz

Now, let's check your knowledge! Please answer the following questions (the answers are included in the resource pack) or specify whether they are correct or incorrect.

1. TRUE.

2. TRUE.

3. TRUE.

4. TRUE.

5. TRUE.

6. TRUE.

7. TRUE.

8. TRUE.

9. FALSE.

10. TRUE.

Challenge 1

For this chapter, your challenge will be to modify the game as follows:

- Change the color of the cards chosen for each row (i.e., hearts for first row and spades for the second row).
- Display the number of correct matches onscreen.

CHAPTER 14: CREATING A PUZZLE GAME

In this section, we will be creating a game where the player has to complete a puzzle by moving the corresponding pieces; after completing this chapter, you will be able to:

- Slice an image into several sprites (i.e., pieces).

- Shuffle the puzzle pieces.

- Make it possible for the player to move (i.e., drag and drop) these pieces.

- Make these pieces "snap" to a particular location.

- Detect when the player has dragged and dropped a piece to the correct location.

INTRODUCTION

Our complete game will look as follows:

- At the start the full puzzle is displayed to the left; the pieces are in the correct order.

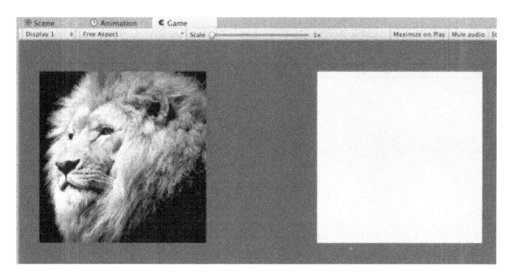

Figure 343: Overview of the game (part 1)

- After a few seconds, the pieces will be shuffled to add more challenge.

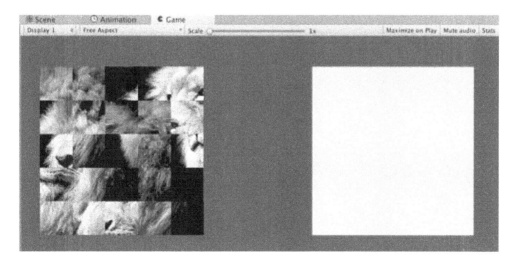

Figure 344: Overview of the game (part 2)

- The player will then need to drag and drop each of the pieces to the right location on the right panel.

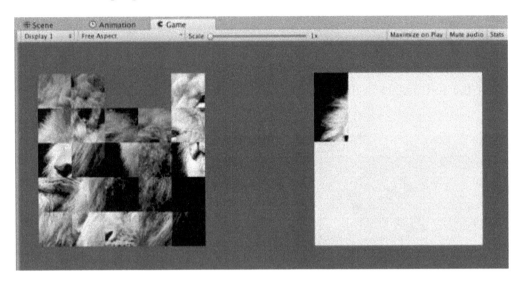

Figure 345: Overview of the game (part 3)

CREATING AND MOVING A PIECE OF THE PUZZLE

In this section, we will create a piece of the puzzle and make it possible for the player to drag and drop it:

- The player will be able to drag and drop this piece to a placeholder.

- The piece will be snapping to this placeholder, to make the game easier to use.

So let's get started.

In the next steps we will implement the **drag** function, which is the ability for the player to drag an object across the screen; for this, we will simply make sure that once the player drags the mouse over an object, that the position of the object is then the same as the position of the mouse. For this purpose, we will create a function that will be called every time an object is dragged (i.e., left click + move the mouse), and that will update the position of the object accordingly, so that it is exactly at the same as the position of the mouse, hence creating a dragging movement.

- Please save your current scene (**File | Save Scene**).

- Create a new scene (**File | New Scene**).

- Save your scene as **chapter4** (**File | Save Scene As**).

First, we can remove the sky background (if there is any in your current scene) using the menu **Window | Rendering | Lighting Settings**.

Then we can start to create a puzzle piece (i.e., an image) that we will be able to drag and drop.

- Please create a new **Image** (i.e., select **GameObject | UI | Image**) and rename it **image**.

- This will create a white square, as illustrated in the next figure.

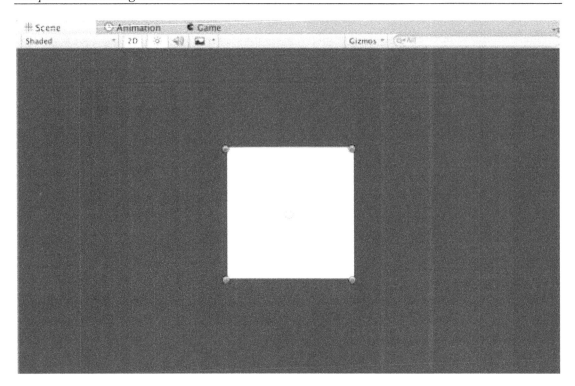

Figure 346: Creating a new image

We will now create a new script:

- Please create a new script called **DragAndDrop** (i.e., from the **Project** menu, select: **Create | C# Script**).

- Open this script (i.e., double click on the script **DragAndDrop** in the **Project** window).

- Add the following code to it (just before the end of the class).

```
public void Drag ()
{
     GameObject.Find("image").transform.position                =
Input.mousePosition;
     print("Dragging" + gameObject.name);
}
```

In the previous code, the position of the object called **image** will be the same as the position of the mouse. This function will be called when the object is dragged.

- Please save this script, and add it (i.e., drag and drop it) to the object **image**.

- Select the object called **image** from the **Hierarchy**.

- Using the **Inspector**, add a component called **Event Trigger** (**Component | Event | Event Trigger**) to the object **image**.

- The following new component should now appear in the **Inspector** for the object image.

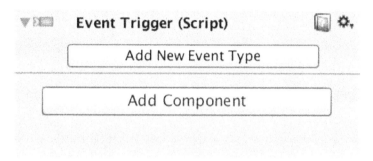

Figure 347: Adding an Event Trigger component (part 1)

- In the component **Event Trigger**, click on the button called **Add New Event Type** (as illustrated in the next figure) and then choose the option called **Drag** from the drop-down menu.

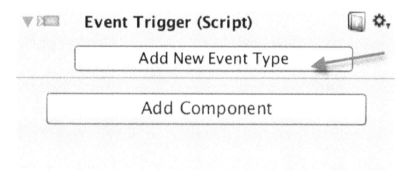

Figure 348: Adding an Event Trigger component (part 2)

- A new field called **Drag (BaseEventData)** should appear, as illustrated in the next figure.

- Please click on the + sign that is below the label **List is Empty**.

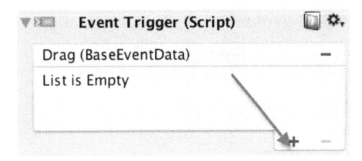

Figure 349: Configuring the new event (part1)

- This will create a new empty field with the label **None (Object)**.

Figure 350:Configuring the new event (part 2)

- Drag and drop the object called **image** from the **Hierarchy** window to this field.

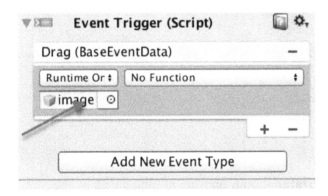

Figure 351: Configuring the new event (part 3)

- Next, you can click on the drop-down menu entitled **No Function**, and select **DragAndDrop | Drag**, as illustrated in the next figure.

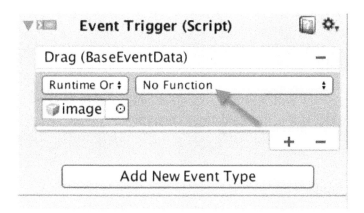

Figure 352: Configuring the new event (part 4)

Figure 353: Configuring the new event (part 5)

You can now test your scene, and you should be able to drag the white square around the screen.

545555555555555555555555555555

555

DROPPING THE TILE TO A PLACEHOLDER

Now that we can drag and drop the image, we will add a placeholder and modify our code so that the image snaps to the placeholder if it is dropped close enough.

The process will consist in:

- Creating a new image for the placeholder.
- Dropping the image near the placeholder.
- Checking the distance between the placeholder and the image.
- Placing the image atop the placeholder if the image is close enough.
- Placing the image back to its original position otherwise.

So let's proceed:

- Please create a new image (**Game Object | UI | Image**).
- Rename this image **PH1** (as in **P**lace**H**older **1**)
- Move this object **PH1** to the right of the object called **image**.
- Change the color of the object **PH1** to green, using the **Inspector**.

Figure 354: Adding a placeholder

Now that the placeholder (i.e., green square) has been created, we will create a new function in the script called **DragAndDrop**, that will be called when the user drops the image.

- Please open the script **DragAndDrop**.

- Add the following function at the end of the class.

```
public void Drop()
{
    GameObject ph1 = GameObject.Find("PH1");
    GameObject img = GameObject.Find("image");
    float  distance  =  Vector3.Distance(ph1.transform.position,
img.transform.position);
    if (distance <= 50)
    {
        img.transform.position = ph1.transform.position;
    }
}
```

In the previous code:

- We create two game objects that refer to the objects **image** and **PH1** that we have created earlier.

- We calculate the distance between the object called **image** and the object **PH1** (i.e., the placeholder).

- If this distance is less than 50, then the object called **image** is moved to the same position as the placeholder; this is the "snapping" effect that was mentioned earlier.

- Please save your code and check that it is error-free.

Now, we just need to add a new event to the object **image** to detect when the player drops (or stops dragging) the image; we will then link this event to the new function that we have just created (i.e., **Drop**).

- Please select the object called **image** in the **Hierarchy**.

- Using the **Inspector**, in the component called **Event Trigger**, click on the button called **Add New Event Type**.

Figure 355: Creating a new event (part 1)

- From the drop-down menu select the event called **End Drag**; this will create a new event, as illustrated on the next figure.

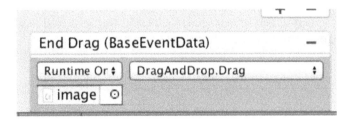

Figure 356: Creating a new event (part 2)

- Once this done, click on the drop-down menu to the right of the label **Runtime**, as illustrated in the next figure.

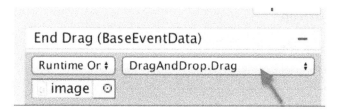

Figure 357: Creating a new event (part 2)

- From the drop-down menu, select: **DragAndDrop | Drop**, to indicate that, in case, the player stops dragging the image, then the function called **Drop** should be called.

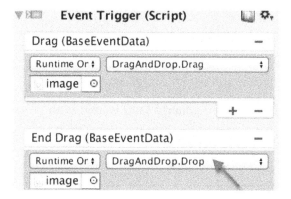

Figure 358: Creating a new event (part 3)

- Using the **Hierarchy**, you can also move (i.e., drag and drop) the object called **image** so that it is the second element listed within the object **Canvas**, as illustrated in the next figure; this is so that it is displayed atop the placeholder when dragged and dropped.

Figure 359: Moving the object image down the Hierarchy

You can now test your scene, and you should see that, as you drag and drop the image close to the placeholder, the image snaps to the placeholder.

Next, we will add code that will move the image back to its original position if it was dragged too far away from the placeholder.

- Please open the script called **DragAndDrop**.

- Add the following code at the beginning of the class.

```
Vector3 originalPosition;
```

- In the previous code, we declare a new variable that will be used to store the initial position of the image (i.e., before it was dragged).

- Modify the **Start** function as follows:

```
void Start ()
{
    originalPosition = transform.position;
}
```

- In the previous code, we record the initial position of the image and save it in the variable called **initialPosition**.

Next we will modify the function **Drag** to make our code more generic (and usable with other images later-on).

- Please, modify the function **Drag** as follows:

```
public void Drag()
{
    print ("Dragging");
    //GameObject.Find("Image").transform.position          =
Input.mousePosition;
    gameObject.transform.position = Input.mousePosition;
}
```

In the previous code we comment the previous code and we also change the position of the object linked to this script.

Note that before you modify the function **Drop**, you can copy the code within, as we will be using this code in the function **checkMatch** later-on.

- Please modify the function **Drop** as follows:

```
public void Drop()
{
    checkMatch ();
}
```

In the previous code, when the image is dropped, we call a function named **checkMatch** that we yet have to define.

- Please add the function **checkMatch** at the end of the class, as follows:

```
public void checkMatch()
{
    GameObject ph1 = GameObject.Find ("PH1");
    GameObject img = GameObject.Find ("image");
    float distance = Vector3.Distance (ph1.transform.position,
img.transform.position);
    print ("Distance" + distance);
    if (distance <= 50)
        snap (img, ph1);
    else
        moveBack ();
}
```

In the previous code:

- This code is similar to the previous code in the **Drop** function.

- The only difference now is that if the image is close enough to the placeholder, we then call the function called **snap**, that we yet need to define, and that will snap the image to the placeholder.

- Otherwise, the function **moveBack** is called; this function, that we yet have to define, will move the image back to its original position.

So we just need to define these two new functions (i.e., **moveBack** and **snap**)

- Please add the function **moveBack**, as follows:

```
public void moveBack()
{
      transform.position = originalPosition;
}
```

In the previous code, we just move the image back to its original position.

We will now define the function **snap**.

- Please, add the function **snap**, as follows:

```
public void snap(GameObject img,GameObject ph )
{
      img.transform.position = ph.transform.position;
}
```

In the previous code:

- We define the function snap.

- It takes two **GameObject** parameters.

- It then sets the position of the first **GameObject** to the position of the second; so effectively, if the first parameter is the image, and the second parameter is the placeholder, it will snap the image to this particular placeholder.

Once this is done, you can test the **Scene**; as you drag and drop the image, it should snap to the placeholder, if you drag it close enough to the placeholder; otherwise, the image should be moved back to its original position.

USING MULTIPLE PLACEHOLDERS

So now that the snapping feature works, we will create multiple placeholders and check that the image snaps to the corresponding placeholder.

We will check that we are dropping the image on the right placeholder; for this, we will create a tag for the image; the name of the corresponding placeholder should then be **PH** followed by the corresponding tag (e.g., **PH1** for the image with the tag **1**, **PH2** for the image with the tag **2**, etc.).

- Please modify the function **checkMatch** as follows:

```
//GameObject ph1 = GameObject.Find ("PH1");
//GameObject img = GameObject.Find ("image");
GameObject img = gameObject;
string tag = gameObject.tag;
GameObject ph1 = GameObject.Find("PH" + tag);
```

In the previous code:

- We comment the first two lines that define the variables **ph1** and **img**.

- Instead, the variable **img** is now referring to the object linked to this script.

- The variable **ph1** (i.e., the corresponding placeholder) is then defined based on the tag of the image linked to this script.

Please save your code. We will now create the necessary tags.

- Please create a new tag called **1** (if you don't already have a tag with this name, based on the previous chapters).

- Assign the tag **1** to the object called **image**.

Figure 360: Adding a tag to the image

- Using the **Inspector**, check that the name of the placeholder is **PH1**.

- Duplicate the object **PH1**.

- Rename the duplicate **PH2**, and change its color to **red** (i.e., using the **Inspector**).

- Move the duplicate to the right of the green placeholder. The scene view should look like the next figure.

Figure 361: Creating a second placeholder

- Using the **Hierarchy**, you can also move (i.e., drag and drop) the object called **image** so that it is the third element listed within the object **Canvas**, as illustrated in the next figure; this is so that it is displayed atop the placeholders when dragged and dropped on them.

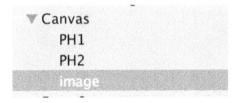

Figure 362: Moving down the image in the hierarchy

So, as the system is set-up, because the image has a tag called **1**, then its corresponding placeholder should be **PH1**, which is the green square. You can now test your scene and check that the image only snaps to the green placeholder, and that if you try to drag and drop it to the red box, that it is moved back to its original position.

Remember: because the **image** object has a tag called **1**, the corresponding placeholder is **PH1** (i.e., **PH** followed by the tag of the image).

USING AND SLICING A FULL IMAGE TO CREATE THE PUZZLE PIECES

Now that the drag and drop feature works we will start to create the visual aspect of the game, and create tiles for our puzzle, based on a main image.

- Please locate the image called **lion.png** in the resource pack.

- Import this image in **Unity** and rename it **lion**.

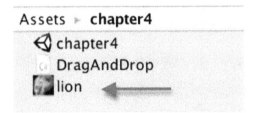

Figure 363: Importing the main image for the puzzle

- Select this asset (i.e., **lion**) in the **Project** window.

- Using the **Inspector** set its **Texture Type** to **Sprite (2D and UI)**, its **Sprite Mode** to **Multiple**, and its attribute **Pixels Per Unit** to **1000**, as per the next figure.

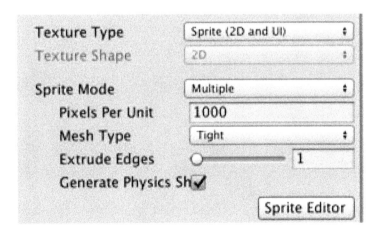

Figure 364: Setting the attributes of the image imported

- Once this is done, you can press the **Apply** button, located in the bottom-right corner of the **Inspector**.

Figure 365: Applying changes

Once this is done, we will slice this image in individual cells that will make-up the pieces of the puzzle.

- Using the **Inspector** window, click on the button called **Sprite Editor**, as illustrated in the next figure.

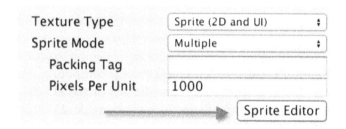

Figure 366: Modifying the image's properties

- This should open the **Sprite Editor** window.

However, if the following message appears.

Please install the 2D Sprite packacge as follows:

- Select: **Window | Package Manager**.

- Select the package 2D Sprite.

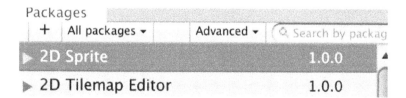

- Select the option to "**Install**".

- Once this is done, please close the **Package Manager** window, and click again on the **Sprite Editor** button;

- In the new window, click on the button called **Slice** located in the top-left corner.

Figure 367: Slicing the image

- In the new window, please select the option **Grid by Cell count** for the attribute **Type**, and then specify a value of **5** for both the attributes **C** and **R**, as illustrated in the next figure This means that we want to slice the main image and create 25 images (5 by 5) based on a grid of 5 columns and 5 rows.

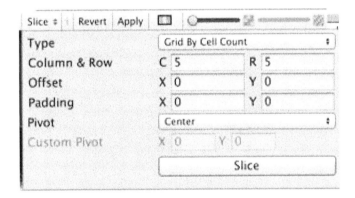

Figure 368: Specifying the slicing options

- Once this is done, you can click on the button called **Slice**.

- You should then see that the image is part of a grid, as illustrated in the next figure.

Figure 369: Creating the new grid

Now, we just need to apply these changes so that the corresponding pieces can be created.

- You can click on the button called **Apply**, located in the top-right corner of the screen.

Figure 370: Applying changes

- Once this is done, if you look at the **Project** window, you should see that the image **lion** has turned into a folder were **25 sprites** have been created (e.g., **lion_0**, **lion_1**, **lion_2**, etc.). These new sprites are effectively the cells of the grid that we have defined earlier in the **Sprite Editor**.

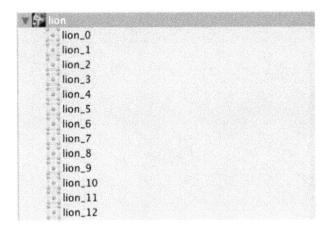

Figure 371: The 25 pieces have been created

Next, we will add the code that will create objects (i.e., puzzle pieces) based on these new sprites.

- Please close the **Sprite Editor** window.

- Using the **Hierarchy** window, please change the name of the object called **image** to **piece** (i.e., its new name should be **piece**).

- Create a prefab from it (i.e., drag and drop the object **piece** to the **Project** window).

- This prefab should automatically be named **piece**, as illustrated in the next figure.

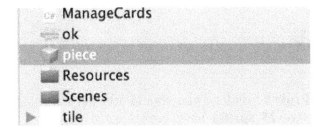

Figure 372: Creating a new prefab

- Please duplicate the object called **piece** and rename the duplicate **piece2**; change its tag to **2** (<u>you may need to create a new tag called **2** prior to that</u>).

- Using the **Hierarchy**, move the object called **piece2** slightly above the object **piece**.

- Select the object called **piece**.

- Using the **Hierarchy**, you should see that it includes a component called **Image** with an attribute called **Source Image**.

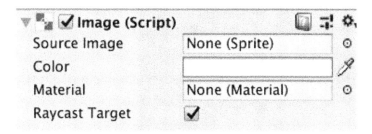

Figure 373: Checking the Image component

- Please drag and drop the image **lion_0** from the **Project** window, to the field **Source Image** for the object **piece**, as illustrated in the next figure.

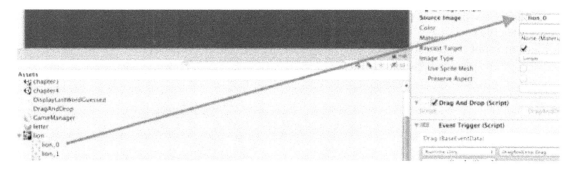

- Please repeat the last step so that the image **lion_1** is dragged from the **Project** window, to the field **Source Image** of the component called **Image**, for the object **piece2** this time.

- Once this is done, the **Scene** view may look as follows:

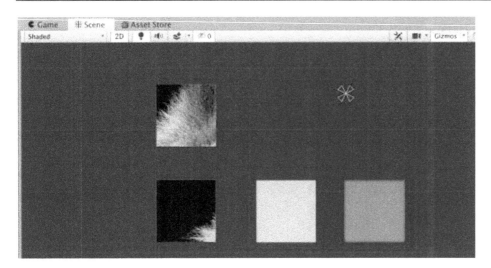

Figure 374: Adding texture to pieces

You can now play the scene and test that the first piece only snaps to the first placeholder, and that the second piece only snaps to the second placeholder.

GENERATING SPRITES AT RUN-TIME

At this stage the snapping of each image is working; so next, we will generate all the pieces of the puzzle from our code, along with the placeholders where they should be dropped to.

- Please create a new empty object (**GameObject | Create Empty**) called **managePuzzleGame**.

- From the **Project** window, create a new script called **ManagePuzzleGame** and link it (i.e., drag and drop) to the object **managePuzzleGame**.

- Create an empty text object (i.e., **GameObject | UI | Text**) called **centerOfTheScreen** located in the middle of the screen (i.e., PosX=0 and PosY=0 for the component **RectTransform**). Please make sure that its text is empty.

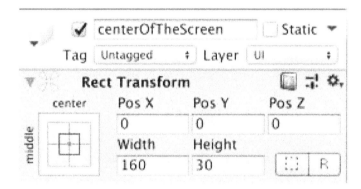

Figure 375: Centering the text object

- Duplicate this object (i.e., **centerOfTheScreen**) twice to create an object called **leftSide** located halfway between the object **centerOTheScreen** and the left edge of the white rectangle, and an object called **rightSide** located halfway between the object **centerOfTheScreen** and the right edge of the white rectangle.

- The position of these three **UI Text** object, could be as illustrated in the next figure.

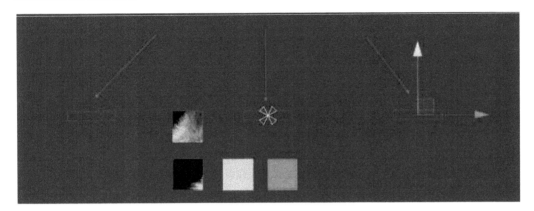

Figure 376: Adding invisible markers

- Using the **Hierarchy** window, create a prefab from the object called **PH1**, and rename this prefab **PH**.

- You can also create additional tags, as we have done before, so that your tags range from **1** to **25**; these tags will be used for the 25 pieces of the puzzle.

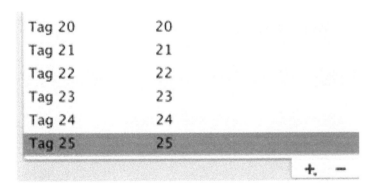

Figure 377: Creating 25 tags

Once this done, we can start to work on the script **ManagePuzzleGame**.

- Please open the script **ManagePuzzleGame**.

- Add this code at the beginning of the class.

```
using UnityEngine.UI;
public class ManagePuzzleGame : MonoBehaviour {
    public Image piece;
    public Image placeHolder;
    float phWidth, phHeight;
```

In the previous code:

- We include the **UI** library that will be used to gain access to **UI** elements from our script (i.e., text fields); we also declare three variables. Two of these variables are **public** which means that they will be accessible from outside the script, including from the **Inspector**.

- The variable **piece** will be used for an image template to be employed for each piece of the puzzle.

- The variable **placeholder** will be used for an image template to be employed for each placeholder (where the pieces have to be dragged and dropped to).

- The variables **phWidth** and **PhHeight** will refer to the width and height of the placeholder.

Please save your code.

- We can now initialize the variable **piece** and **placeholder**:

- Please select the object **ManagePuzzleGame** in the **Hierarchy**.

- You should see, using the **Inspector**, that the component called **managePuzzleGame** has now two variables accessible from the **Inspector**.

- Please drag and drop the prefab **piece** and **PH** from the **Project** window to the fields **piece** and **placeholder**, respectively, as illustrated in the next figure.

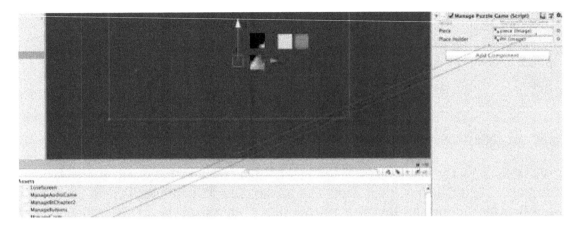

Figure 378: Initializing the variables piece and placeholder (part 1)

- The **Inspector** should then look as the next figure.

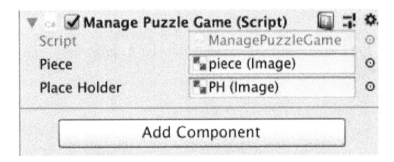

Figure 379: Initializing the variables piece and placeholder (part 2)

We will now modify the script **ManagePuzzleGame** to create the necessary placeholders for the game, based on the prefab **PH**.

- Please open the script **ManagePuzzleGame**.

- Modify the **Start** function as follows:

```
void Start ()
{
    createPlaceHolders ();
}
```

- Add the following function at the end of the class.

```
public void createPlaceHolders()
{
    phWidth = 100; phHeight = 100;
    float nbRows, nbColumns;
    nbRows = 5;
    nbColumns = 5;
    for (int i = 0; i < 25; i++)
    {
        Vector3 centerPosition = new Vector3 ();
        centerPosition           =           GameObject.Find
("rightSide").transform.position;
        float row, column;
        row = i % 5;
        column = i / 5;
        Vector3 phPosition = new Vector3 (centerPosition.x +
phWidth*(row-nbRows/2), centerPosition.y - phHeight * (column-
nbColumns/2), centerPosition.z);
        Image    ph   =   (Image)(Instantiate   (placeHolder,
phPosition, Quaternion.identity));
        ph.tag = ""+(i + 1);
        ph.name = "PH"+(i + 1);
        ph.transform.SetParent(GameObject.Find
("Canvas").transform);
    }
}
```

In the previous code:

- We set the width and height of all placeholders.

- We then define that the placeholders (i.e., where the puzzle pieces should be dropped to) consist of a grid of 5 rows by 5 columns.

- We then go through this grid, row by row.

- The row and column numbers are defined by dividing **i** (which ranges from **1 to 25**) by **5** or by saving the remainder of this division.

- For example if **i=12** , the row will be **2** (i.e., the **quotient** of **12/5**) and the column will be 2 (the **remainder of 12/10,** noted as **12%2**).

- The position of each placeholder is based on these calculations

- We set the tag of the placeholder.

- We also specify that the parent of each placeholder is the object called **Canvas**; this is necessary so that the placeholder can be displayed through our canvas.

- All the new objects are centred around the object **rightSide**.

Please save your code and play the scene; you should see that 25 placeholders have been created.

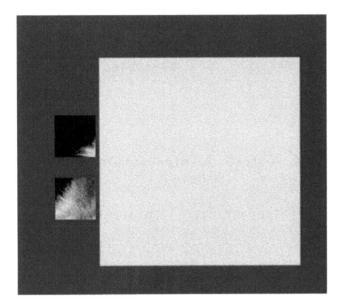

Figure 380: The new placeholders in the game view

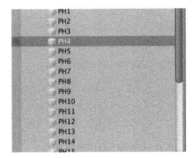

Figure 381: The new placeholders in the Hierarchy view

Next, we need to create the pieces of the puzzle; to do so, we will use the sprites created from the **lion** image; however, while these sprites are now in the folder called **lion**, we will move these to the **Resources** folder, so that they can be accessed from our script.

- Using the **Inspector**, select all the images under the folder **lion** (i.e., the sprites generated after we sliced the **lion** image)

- Drag and drop them to the folder called **Resources** (if you don't have this folder yet in your project, you can create it using **Create | Folder**).

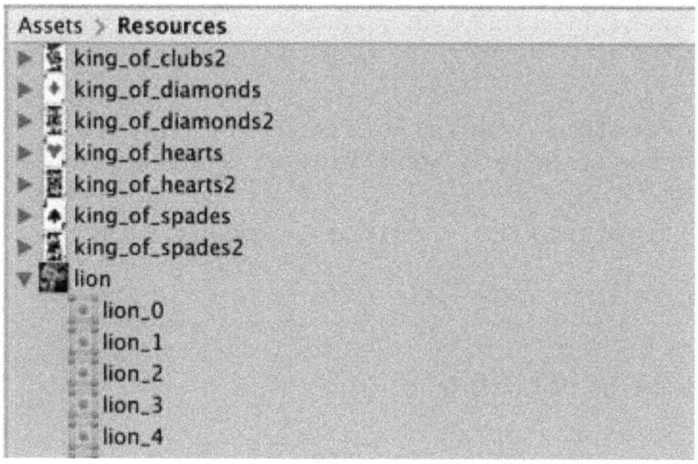

Figure 382: Moving the images to the Resources folder

Next, we will create the code to generate the puzzle pieces from our script.

- Please add the following code to the class **ManagePuzzleGame**.

```
public void createPieces()
{
    phWidth = 100;
    phHeight = 100;
    float nbRows, nbColumns;
    nbRows = 5;
    nbColumns = 5;

}
```

In the previous code, we use the same code as we have done earlier for the placeholders to define the size of each image (i.e., **phWidth** and **phHeight**), along with the size of the grid used to display these images (i.e., **nbRows** and **nbColumns**).

- Please, add the following code at the end of the function **createPieces**.

```
for (int i = 0; i < 25; i++)
{
    Vector3 centerPosition = new Vector3 ();
    centerPosition                    =            GameObject.Find
("leftSide").transform.position;
    float row, column;
    row = i % 5;
    column = i / 5;
    Vector3 phPosition = new Vector3 (centerPosition.x + phWidth
* (row - nbRows / 2), centerPosition.y - phHeight * (column -
nbColumns / 2), centerPosition.z);
    Image ph = (Image)(Instantiate (piece, phPosition,
Quaternion.identity));
    ph.tag = "" + (i + 1);
    ph.name = "Piece" + (i + 1);
    ph.transform.SetParent(GameObject.Find
("Canvas").transform);
    Sprite[] allSprites = Resources.LoadAll<Sprite> ("lion");
    Sprite s1 = allSprites [i];
    ph.GetComponent<Image> ().sprite = s1;

}
```

In the previous code:

- The previous code is very similar to the code that we have created in the function **createPlaceholders**; the only difference being that...

- The images are centered around the object called **leftSide**.

- The images used for each piece are from the folder called **Resources**.

Please save your code.

- You can now deactivate the objects **PH1**, **PH2**, **piece**, and **piece2** in the **Hierarchy**.

- We can also add the following code to the **Start** function (new code in bold) in the script **ManagePuzzleGame**.

```
void Start ()
{
    createPlaceHolders ();
    createPieces ();
}
```

- Please save your code, and play the scene; it should look as follows:

Figure 383: Displaying the start of the game

- You can also try to drag and drop pieces from the left to their correct location on the board to the right.

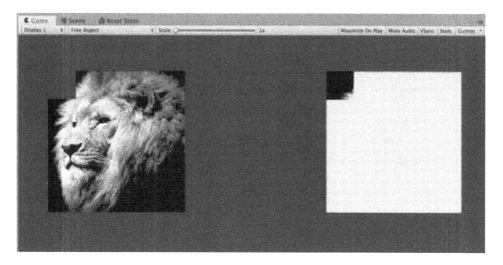

Figure 384: Testing the game

Next, we need to shuffle the cards; their values (i.e., tags or images) will remain the same; however, their position will be changed, in order to challenge the player.

- Please add the following function to the script **ManagePuzzleGame**.

```
void shufflePieces()
{
    int[] newArray = new int [25];
    for (int i = 0; i < 25; i++)
    newArray [i] = i;
    int tmp;
    for (int t = 0; t < 25; t++ )
    {
        tmp = newArray[t];
        int r = Random.Range(t, 10);
        newArray[t] = newArray[r];
        newArray[r] = tmp;
    }
    for (int i = 0; i < 25; i++)
    {
        float row, nbRows, nbColumns, column;
        nbRows = 5;
        nbColumns = 5;
        row = (newArray[i]) % 5;
        column = (newArray[i]) / 5;
        Vector3 centerPosition = new Vector3 ();
        centerPosition           =         GameObject.Find
("leftSide").transform.position;
        var g = GameObject.Find("Piece"+(i + 1));
        Vector3 newPosition = new Vector3 (centerPosition.x +
phWidth*(row-nbRows/2), centerPosition.y - phHeight * (column-
nbColumns/2), centerPosition.z);
        g.transform.position = newPosition;
    }
}
```

In the previous code:

- We create an array of 25 integers.

- We then initialize this array so that its values are ranked from 0 to 24.

- We then use a loop to shuffle the values in this array.

- The random numbers are saved in the array called **newArray**.

- Once this is done, we use another loop where we modify the position of each of the pieces onscreen, using the random numbers generated earlier (the array **newArray**).

Once this is done, we can add the following code at the end of the **Start** function

```
shufflePieces();
```

- Please, save your code and test the scene; you should see that the pieces have been shuffled.

Figure 385: Displaying shuffled pieces

The last thing we could do is to make sure that the user can see the completed puzzle before the pieces are shuffled. To do so, we will include a delay just before the pieces are shuffled.

- Please add this code at the beginning of the class:

```
float timer;
bool cardsShuffled = false;
```

- Modify the **Start** function to comment the shuffle function as follows (new code in bold):

```
void Start () {
createPlaceHolders ();
createPieces ();
//shufflePieces ();
```

- Modify the **Update** function as follows:

```
void Update ()
{
    timer += Time.deltaTime;
    if (timer >= 4 && !cardsShuffled) {
        shufflePieces ();
        cardsShuffled = true;
    }
}
```

In the previous code:

- We create a timer.

- This timer's value will increase every seconds.

- 4 seconds after the game has started, the pieces are shuffled.

- We then set the variable **cardsShuffled** to true so that the card shuffling happens only once.

Last but not least, we need to set the initial position of each piece after they have been shuffled as follows:

- Please open the script **DragAndDrop** and add the following function to it:

```
public void initCardPosition()
{
    originalPosition = transform.position;
}
```

- Save your script, then open the class **ManagePuzzleGame**.

- Modify the function **shufflePieces** as follows (new code in bold):

```
g.transform.position = newPosition;
g.GetComponent<DragAndDrop> ().initCardPosition ();
```

You can now save your code and play the scene; as the game starts, the player will have 4 seconds to look at the completed puzzle before the cards are shuffled.

Note that if you see a warning message saying "**Parent of RectTransform is being set with parent property. Consider using the SetParent method instead, with the worldPositionStays argument set to false.**", you can change the following code in the class **ManagePuzzleGame**.

```
ph.transform.parent = GameObject.Find ("Canvas").transform;
```

to...

```
ph.transform.SetParent(GameObject.Find ("Canvas").transform);
```

LEVEL ROUNDUP

Summary

In this chapter, we have managed to create a challenging puzzle game where the player has to memorize an image, before trying to complete the puzzle; we have learnt some interesting skills along the way, including: dragging and dropping objects, snapping sprites to placeholders, shuffling images, creating a timer, slicing an image, and creating sprites based on a grid layout.

Checklist

You can consider moving to the next stage if you can do the following:

- Understand how to access sprites from a script.

- Understand how to create an array of integers.

- Know how to create and process drag and drop events .

Quiz

Now, let's check your knowledge! Please specify whether the following statements are true or false.

1. To select all the assets in a given folder, you can just press **CTRL + A**.

2. To be able to detect that a sprite was dragged, this sprite needs to have a collider component.

3. The component **Event Trigger** can be used to detect events such as drag or drop.

4. To create an empty object, you can select: **GameObject | Create | Empty Object**.

5. In Unity, it is possible to use tags that have been created in other scenes (but in the same project).

6. The sprite editor can be used to slice images.

7. Images can be sliced based on a grid (column and rows).

8. When an image is sliced, all the sub-images created are automatically added to the folder **Resources**.

9. The following code will save all sprites stored in the folder called **lion** to the array called **allSprites**.

```
Sprite[] allSprites = Resources.LoadAll<Sprite> ("lion");
```

10. The following code will create an array of 10 integers.

```
int [] newArray = new int [] {0,1,2,3,4,5,6,7,8,9};
```

Answers to the Quiz

Now, let's check your knowledge! Please specify whether the following statements are true or false.

1. TRUE.

2. TRUE.

3. TRUE.

4. TRUE.

5. TRUE.

6. TRUE.

7. TRUE.

8. FALSE.

9. TRUE.

10. TRUE.

Challenge 1

For this chapter, your challenge will be to modify the game as follows:

- Detect when the puzzle has been completed.
- Create a button to restart the game.

CHAPTER 15: FREQUENTLY ASKED QUESTIONS

This chapter provides answers to the most frequently asked questions about the features that we have covered in this book. Please also note that some <u>videos are also available on the companion site</u> to help you with some of the concepts covered in this book.

ACCESSING RESOURCES

Where should I store assets if I want to access them from a script?

You can create a folder called **Resources**, and then save your imported assets in this folder.

How can I access a text file that I have saved in the Resources folder?

To access this file (and the text within) you can use the following code snippet.

```
TextAsset      t1      =      (TextAsset)Resources.Load("words",
typeof(TextAsset));
string s = t1.text;
```

How can I access an image file that I have saved in the Resources folder?

To access an individual sprite from the **Resources** folder, you can use the following code snippet.

```
Sprite s1 = (Sprite) (Resources.Load<Sprite>(nameOfCard));
```

However, if you'd prefer to access and save several sprites at once, then you can use the following snippet:

```
Sprite[] allSprites = Resources.LoadAll<Sprite> ("lion");
```

DETECTING USER INPUTS

How can I detect keystrokes?

You can detect keystrokes by using the function **Input.GetKey**. For example, the following code detects when the key **E** is pressed; this code should be added to the **Update** function.

```
If (Input.GetKey(KeyCode.E)){...}
```

How can I detect a click on a button?

To detect clicks on a button, you can do the following:

- Create an empty object.

- Create a new script and link it to this object.

- Select the button in the **Hierarchy**.

- Using the **Inspector**, click on the button located below the label called **OnClick**.

- Drag and drop the empty object to the field that just appeared.

- From the **Inspector**, you should then be able to select the function that should be called in case the button is clicked.

How can I detect drag and drop events on an image?

To detect drag and drop events or actions on an image:

- Select the image from the **Hierarchy**.

- Using the **Inspector**, add a component called **Event Trigger (Component | Event | Event Trigger)** to this image.

- In the component **Event Trigger**, click on the button called **Add New Event Type** (as illustrated in the next figure) and then choose the option called **Drag or End Drag** from the drop-down menu.

CHAPTER 16: THANK YOU

I would like to thank you for completing this book; I trust that you are now comfortable with creating 2D games

While you have learnt a lot in this book, this is the first step towards learning to create games, and now, you need to learn more about 3D games development. So you may consider starting the series "Unity from Zero to Proficiency" that will teach you all you need to know about creating 3D games with Unity.

So that the book can be constantly improved, I would really appreciate your feedback. So, please leave me a helpful review on Amazon letting me know what you thought of the book and also send me an email (learntocreategames@gmail.com) with any suggestions you may have. I read and reply to every email.

Thanks so much!!